FIGHTER PILOT'S
SUMMER

FIGHTER PILOT'S SUMMER

Norman Franks and
Wg Cdr Paul Richey dfc and bar

Grub Street · London

Published by
Grub Street
The Basement
10 Chivalry Road
London SW11 1HT

Originally published in hardback in 1993

This edition first published in 1999

Copyright © 1993 Grub Street London

Text copyright © Norman Franks

British Library Cataloguing in Publication Data
Richey, Paul, B.1916
  Fighter pilot's summer
  1. Fighter pilots - Great Britain 2. World War, 1939-1945 –
  Aerial operations, British
  I. Title II. Franks, Norman L.R. (Norman Leslie Robert),
  1940-
  940.5'44'941'092

ISBN 1-902304-24-1

Typeset by BMD Graphics, Hemel Hempstead

Printed and bound in Great Britain by
Biddles Ltd, Guildford and King's Lynn

Photo Credits
Several of the photographs came from Paul Richey's archives, including some which are believed to have been taken by the late Jimmy Baraldi and given to Paul for his use.
Other credits, where known, are:

Mr Peter Richey; Sir Alec Atkinson; Gp Capt J.D. Bisdee; Central Press Ltd; Westminster Press; the late Mr R.L. Watson; the late Wg Cdr M.V. Blake; British Rail; The Associated Press; Mrs D. Barnato-Walker; Count Francesco di Robilant.

My thanks to them all.

CONTENTS

ACKNOWLEDGEMENTS

I wish to thank the following people who have given generous help with information, without which this book would have been difficult to complete.

Firstly of course, to Diana Richey, who loaned me numerous documents from Paul's archives as well as giving me the encouragement to place Paul's subsequent war career on record. She was magnificent in her approach to editing my words, putting me on the right course when I had, through ignorance, strayed from the correct path. I have much to thank her for and I appreciate my time spent with her.

Also to Teresa, now Mrs Peter Ryde, who was not only generous in her recollections of Paul but of her brother Michael Robinson. It was a conscious decision of mine to entwine Paul's and Michael's stories during 1941-42, so I was happy to get 'two for the price of one', spending a couple of delightful afternoons with her, at her London home.

I was also pleased to receive help from some of the fighter pilots who flew with Paul during the war. My thanks therefore extend to Sir Alec 'Joe' Atkinson KCB DFC, Group Captain T A F Elsdon DFC, Group Captain J D Bisdee OBE DFC, Wing Commander Roland Beamont CBE DSO and bar, DFC and bar, DL FRAeS, Colonel Raymond Lallemant DFC CdeG (Belge), CdeG (Francais), and Roger Malengreau CBE CdeG. Thanks too go to Group Captain Frank Carey CBE DFC and 2 bars, AFC DFM, for talking about Paul during a few days spent together at a mutual friend's home on Majorca. Also to General Adolf Galland, former Kommodore of JG26 and General der Jagdflieger der Luftwaffe, and Oblt Adolf Glunz, II/JG26.

Also to John Davies of Grub Street, for his help and encouragement, not only with this book but others we have done and are doing together.

And I must not forget my best friend, who gives me constant encouragement — my wife Heather.

NORMAN FRANKS
Surrey, England 1993

INTRODUCTION

I FIRST met Paul Richey on 10 September, 1982. I was researching in the Public Records Office at Kew, when I noticed him. I didn't know it was him then but his face looked familiar, although I knew we had never met. Even at this time of his life — he was now 66 — he was a fine looking man; tall, upright, broad-shouldered, a full head of hair, even if it was now silver-white. So it was not difficult for me to notice this still strikingly handsome man.

Some time after first seeing him sitting at a desk, files and papers in front of him, I saw him stand up and walk across to the document counter. Now interested, and anxious to know who this man was, I followed, and casually looking across the counter while standing next to him, could easily see the name printed on the document request form as the lady behind the counter sorted out his next file.

It has often surprised me how things happen. Here I was, taking a day off work to do some research on my next book and quite by chance I catch sight of a man, become interested in his features only to discover that he is Paul Richey. I knew the name, of course; and now that I had a name for the face, understood why I had thought I'd seen him before.

I had first seen that face, much younger, in a paperback book I had bought from my local 'newsagents' shop back in 1955, when I was still at school. It was an Arrow Book edition (which then came under the Hutchinson Company), priced 2/6d.

Two things had caught my eye as the book lay on the counter. Firstly the title *Fighter Pilot* (in bright red), chosen by the publishers in 1941, to be catchy and instantly recognisable, and which fourteen years later, achieved with me exactly what was expected. The second was the superbly illustrated cover design of the book. A camouflaged Hawker Hurricane fighter curving across the sky, a burning Messerschmitt 110 heading earthwards, while more Hurricanes and Me110s were becoming engaged in a dog-fight around them. As I now know, the picture was far more accurate than I knew at the time. The markings on that Hurricane were correct, even down to the individual aircraft letter "G" which I was later to discover was the one Paul used. So many book cover or dust jacket designs prove inaccurate if the author lets them, that it is refreshing to see such a good true picture. I was to learn that nobody would get an inaccurate picture past this man.

These were the days when many of the well known fighter pilots of World War Two were bringing out their autobiographies, or others having biographies written about them. In those years, Douglas Bader's story *Reach for the Sky* had been written by Paul Brickhill, Larry Forrester had written Bob Stanford Tuck's story in *Fly for your Life*. Al Deere would be writing his famous *Nine Lives*, Pierre Clostermann his *The Big Show*, Neville Duke *Test Pilot*, while Johnnie Johnson would bring out his *Wing Leader*.

In 1955 I thought I knew a great deal about the RAF, World War Two, Hurricanes and Spitfires, and so on. I could reel off the names of all the top fighter aces and instantly recognise a good 75% of all WW2 aeroplane pictures. I had read Guy Gibson's *Enemy Coast Ahead* (as I recall the first book about the RAF I ever read, also out in paperback in 1955), took the monthly RAF Flying Review magazine regularly and watched avidly the War in the Air series on black and white television.

Being an 'expert' I devoured Paul Richey's book avidly. Although I noted that the book had been published first in 1941, (when I obviously had no knowledge of it), I saw that printed on the third page was "250th Thousand". Being young and inexperienced it meant little to me; it is only now that one can hardly imagine any aviation book selling in such quantities. When I had read it I realised I knew 100% more about the air Battle of France than I had beforehand.

I used to give my books a 'star rating' in those days. I see that I gave both *Enemy Coast Ahead* and *Fighter Pilot* four stars — the maximum! I have kept both editions of these two books, for nostalgia really, but also because both books had a profound effect on me. Both helped to fire my enthusiasm for military aviation history, a pastime and now a second career, which has given me immense pleasure for some forty years. I no longer class myself an expert — but I know and understand a lot more now than I did in 1955!

Having now realised who this man (who had now returned to his seat in the PRO) was, I returned to mine. There were no two ways about it, I had to introduce myself. However, I was faced with the dilemma of what to say. I didn't like to admit that I had sneaked a look at his name on the document request form; but equally I felt awkward about going up to a complete 'stranger' and saying — "Hello, who are you?"

It took some thought, but finally I sauntered across to where he was sitting, and the conversation (whispered of course) went something like:

"Excuse me, Sir, your face seems familiar to me, but I can't place where I have seen you."

"My name's Paul Richey."

"Paul Richey!" I exclaimed in mock surprise, "Of course, One Squadron in France!" It was almost rehearsed but I hoped that Mr Richey would not see through my instant ploy of putting the name next to the squadron with whom he had served in France in 1940.

"Yes, that's right," said Paul, "How do you know that?"

"Well, my name is Norman Franks, and I'm a bit of an aviation nut, so it goes without saying that I've read your book."

"I'm pleased to meet you Norman," we shook hands, "are you researching something now?"

"Yes, I'm working on a book about Typhoons," I replied.

"Really? I flew Typhoons."

"Did you? Perhaps I could talk to you about them?"

"Certainly," and giving me his address, "if you're ever in town, give me a call."

We then had to curtail our chat, as other Readers become agitated when people talk in the Reading Rooms at the PRO. So shaking hands again, I returned to my seat, determined to do two things. Find out more about Paul Richey and Typhoons, and to visit him and have a chat.

Well, I did both. I knew, of course, that Paul Richey had flown with 609 Squadron and the Biggin Hill Wing in 1941, having already noted that fact in my book on Sailor Malan, *Sky Tiger*, which I had published in 1980. But checking further, I found that he also commanded 609 Squadron later in the war, when it was first equipped with Typhoons. Armed with a number of questions, I telephoned him and in due course, visited his mews house in London.

We had a pleasant talk about Typhoons. I went through his log book and chatted about other people and about his RAF career in general. I remember feeling quite at ease with Paul, although I was to learn

that some people found him a little difficult to get on with. He
certainly had his own ideas on many subjects, and while I wouldn't
suggest his ideas were fixed, I can imagine people who were unable
to persuade him to a different point of view, thinking him too
pedantic. But to me he was easy and a pleasure to listen to; full of
interest, and a Master on his subject.

It was then I asked him a question which had occurred to me some
days before and one in which I thought might stimulate many anec-
dotes. Why had he never written a sequel to *Fighter Pilot*?

> "Do you think a sequel would be of interest?" he merely asked.
> I said I thought it would. "After all," I continued, "that summer
> of 1941 is full of action and interest. The RAF had survived the
> Battle of Britain and were now looking to go onto the offensive
> over Northern France. You were a flight commander in a success-
> ful fighter squadron, flying from Biggin Hill under one of the first
> Wing Leaders — Sailor Malan — and your squadron commander
> was your brother-in-law, Michael Robinson. And you received a
> bar to your DFC that summer."

Paul looked amused, wondering why this near stranger was trying to
encourage him to write a book about events so long ago.

> "It would be worth thinking about," said Paul finally. "Although
> at the moment I am totally immersed in the French campaign and
> the causes and events which led to Europe once again being
> plunged into a world war. That and the relationship between the
> British and French."

He now saw the French Campaign of 1939-40 on a very broad canvas.
Fighter Pilot had merely been a personal record of No. 1 (Fighter)
Squadron from September 1939 and June 1940, through the eyes of a
young RAF fighter pilot. The intervening years had matured his
thoughts and whilst living in both France and England, he had inten-
sively researched the causes of the war and Anglo-French relations
throughout their history, working in the archives at Freiburg,
Vincennes and London. Paul was a Francophile. He'd known France
as a boy. He had fought in France and he had lived in France for
several years post-war. In 1982 he was made a Chevalier of the Legion
d'Honneur for services to that country.

Some months later I met Paul again, at his little house in Mayfair,
with his delightful wife Diana. The occasion for that meeting was for
Paul to help me with another book and we spent several hours talking
about it and about his flying war.

What I liked about Paul was that while he could recall so clearly the detailed events of the war, the air battles, the people, the minutiae, and so on, he could also put them into a balanced context; to encompass a much wider scope of understanding. I have met and interviewed scores of former fighter pilots, but very few have been able to talk so naturally about the wider political and historical implications, and with such authority.

Diana prepared a small meal for us, and as we changed subjects, I asked him again if he'd given any more thought to the sequel. Whether he had or not I could not tell, although he was once more interested in my view that the story should be told. Yet even then I had the feeling that if he lived to be a hundred he would probably never get around to doing it.

I only met Paul on a few more occasions, and he helped me with another book I was writing concerning the RAF in India and Burma, as he had also seen service in that theatre of operations. Again I badgered him about a sequel although now it was more or less a formality rather than a serious question. We exchanged a number of letters and telephone calls. He was always interested in what I was doing. His active mind always seemed to see things that I had missed. He often asked me for photo-copies of documents I had found which aroused his interest.

One of our last telephone conversations, concerned the book and the TV series A Piece of Cake. I could tell Paul was outraged by the whole issue. In his last letters to me, it was this subject which was now filling his mind, his life's work, the history about the French campaign and Anglo-French relations being forced aside as he tried to defend the memory of former comrades, many who had died during the war, whose achievements seemed to be put into question.

Then came the fateful day — 23 February 1989 — when Paul died. I knew he had not enjoyed good health for some while, but his death was still a great shock. I am not claiming that he and I were bosom pals — far from it — but I knew, liked and respected him and was happy to think I could pick up the telephone at any time and talk to him. And to know he would be pleased to chat while taking an interest in what I was doing, or writing.

I wrote to Diana, offering my condolences. I told her of my several attempts to get Paul to write a sequel to Fighter Pilot, knowing now that it would never be written. Or would it?

I said "Or Would it?" in my letter, and in her reply she referred to this and, knowing I was a writer, had read between the lines. If Paul couldn't write it, then someone else qualified could — perhaps should.

Some time later, Diana asked me if I would advise her concerning some of Paul's papers. I was pleased to think I could help and a visit was planned.

Diana was enthusiastic about the sequel idea. And why not? I could see that Diana missed Paul very much and that they must have been very much in love. She had prepared a bundle of material from 1941, including a hand written journal and some typed-out manuscript that Paul had begun writing around 1942, clearly the start of a *Fighter Pilot* follow-on. Why hadn't he continued with it, I wondered? And why had he not mentioned that he had in fact begun to write a sequel, when I first broached the subject?

Anyway, carrying away his written words, and several other documents covering his period with the Biggin Hill Wing, plus material from his time in the India-Burma theatre of operations, and still having most of the tape recordings I had made when talking to him over the years, the sequel, even if written — or finished — by someone else, could now begin.

Fighter Pilot — A Personal Record of the Battle of France — had been published in September 1941 by B T Batsford Ltd, of London. It was dedicated 'To my Comrades killed in action in the Battle of France.' There was no author named, for Paul not only wanted to remain anonymous, as he was by then back in action, it was better that he remain so. Also, as a serving RAF officer, it was the correct thing to do, and it lent itself to the traditional way of doing things; to remain anonymous in a time of war.

In my copy of the original book, it records that the edition is a first reprint, but also dated September 1941. Thus the initial print run must have been virtually already pre-sold on publication, forcing Batsford to reprint almost immediately. So successful was it that it was reprinted three times in 1942, and again in 1944. By that date the book was firmly established among the classics of air warfare alongside such books as *The Last Enemy* by Richard Hillary, *Arise to Conquer* by Ian Gleed and *Spitfire* by Brian Lane. With its distinctive royal blue cover, RAF wings picked out in white, its 122 pages are packed with interest.

These various editions retained the anonymity of the author and the pilots, although most of Paul's comrades and acquaintances knew all about it. An edition which was published in the United States in 1942, did, however, record the name Squadron Leader Paul Richey DFC on the cover.

It was 11 years before the next edition came out. The paperback that had first aroused my interest, published by Hutchinson/Arrow in both 1955 (Hutchinson also producing a hardback edition) and again in 1956. These versions had been revised to include not only the author's name (although by this time, aviation enthusiasts knew the author's identity) but also the full names of the men mentioned within the pages, names which until now had been only known by certain nick-names — 'Bull' or 'Pussy', or just first names, or merely as Sgt S--.

A further revised edition came out in 1969 by Pan Books Ltd, again in soft covers (priced 4/– or 20p, as it was the time of decimalisation), this edition being edited by Diana Richey. Another reprint saw the light of day in 1977. Jane's Publishing Company printed a further revised edition in 1980, this time with over 100 additional photographs and profiles of a number of Paul's French pilot friends. The dust jacket of this version had a photograph of Paul's medal ribbons as they would appear on his uniform jacket. The DFC and bar, the 1939-45 Star, Air Crew Europe Star and Rosette, Burma Star, Defence Medal, War Service Medal, Air Efficiency Medal, Belgian Order of the Crown, and the French and Belgian Croix de Guerre avec Palmes.

That was the final version during Paul's lifetime. Another was in the works at the time of his death, and indeed was published the following year, 1990, by Leo Cooper, edited by Diana (which was also published through Guild Publishing Ltd that same year), then by Arrow in paperback in 1991.

To write (complete) another man's sequel is not easy, and *Fighter Pilot* is an acclaimed classic. I have done it for two reasons. One is simply that I think it should be done; Paul's subsequent story should be told. Secondly as a mark of respect for this fine fighter pilot, whose gifted writing gave the world such a wonderful book which undoubtedly inspired so many other fighter pilots who followed in his footsteps.

The reader will find here four chapters of this book as written by Paul Richey, untouched (or virtually untouched) by me. I am happy that his words will at last be read by many who have already enjoyed his own classic over the last fifty years.

CHAPTER I

REPRISE

I SUPPOSE it is just possible that some people may never have heard the name of Paul Richey, or read at least one version of his famous book. I say this with due honesty and not condescendingly. But if you, the reader, haven't done so, I recommend you read both the original and certainly one of the later revised editions.

Paul (Paul Henry Mills) was born in Chelsea, London, on 7th May 1916, son of an Irish father and an Australian mother. His father in fact was fighting in France when he was born. Lieutenant Colonel George Henry Mills Richey CMG DSO & Bar, had been born in May 1867, so was nearing his 49th birthday (and his mother was 35), when Paul came along. Indeed, his father had already seen considerable military service even before WW1 began.

Educated at Colchester Grammer School and then Winchester, the elder Richey served in Methuen's Horse, 12th Royal Lancers and the 2nd Dragoon Guards before serving with the BSA Police and Cape Colonial Forces. He had seen service in the Bechuanaland Expedition between 1884-5, action in the Matabele War of 1896, the Mashona Rebellion in 1897-8 and then the Boer War of 1899-1902.

In that conflict he had been Adjutant to Kitchener's Horse as well as a Staff Officer with Doran's Column. He was twice wounded in 1900, firstly at Waterval Drift and then at Houtnek. He was recommended for the Victoria Cross, for bringing in a number of wounded men while under fire, but received the Distinguished Service Order (because the paper-work got lost and with due modesty, his father didn't bother to re-submit a report when asked) and was also mentioned in despatches three times.

The Colonel had been married before, he and his first wife having four children. His second wife, Paul's mother, Adelaide, had been an Australian heiress, but any money she may have had had long gone by the time Paul was a young man.

During World War One Colonel Richey commanded the 1st Sportsman's Battalion of the Royal Fusiliers, then the 4th East Lancashire Regiment and the 4th South Lancs Regiment before being commandant of the VI Corps School at Woolwich. A year after Paul was born, he was wounded at Ypres and received a bar to his DSO. Before the war ended, he commanded the 1st Battalion of the Royal Fusiliers, the 25th Regiment of The King's Regiment in Palestine and Egypt and temporarily commanded Brigades in both Palestine and France.

It was not surprising that he had commanded the 1st Sportsman's Battalion, for he was a keen and expert horseman, an excellent shot and had won many prizes for skill-at-arms.

Paul therefore had been born into a military family, in fact, his grandfather had been a Captain in the Royal Artillery, and later City Marshal of London, although Paul didn't initially show any real signs of following his father into the Army. Some of his formative years were spent on the Continent, with his parents and younger brother Michael, in France, and in Albania, where his father assisted in the organisation of the Albanian Gendarmerie between 1925-29. Paul received his education at the Institut Fisher, in Switzerland, and later at Downside School, near Bath, England. It was at Downside that he met Michael Robinson.

Michael, or Micky as his family more usually called him, was the son of Sir Roy Robinson, an Australian (later Lord Robinson), and brother to Teresa. At Downside he became Head Boy and some good humoured rivalry started up between them, as Teresa, Micky's sister, and Paul's future wife recalls:

> "There was a certain rivalry between Micky and Paul, always. At school Micky was head boy and Paul wasn't; then Paul would be head of something else and Micky wasn't, and so it went on.
>
> "Micky was always mad on flying. Whenever we were on holidays we'd have to go and sit on an aerodrome and watch the damn things; he rarely ever thought of anything else — never!
>
> "My father minded very much because he wanted him to go to university. He himself had had a very good career, having been a triple blue, etc; But Micky didn't think much of that and wanted to fly. So he joined the RAF about eighteen months before Paul which made him that much more senior all through their flying careers."

At this stage in their young lives, neither were particular friends of each other. Both went their separate ways, although both were to gain the desire to fly and join the Royal Air Force. Paul was one of the finest all-round athletes of his generation. Captain of Boxing for three years, variously captain of the First Rugger XV, gymnast, swimmer, a keen hockey player and superb in athletics. He was a school Prefect, Captain of his House and Senior Cadet in the School's Cadet Corps. As drum major he led the Corps on a ceremonial march through London on one occasion. His mace twirling and throwing were memorable by all accounts.

Michael, meantime, was Head of the School in their final year and a tremendously keen flyer. Both had now firm ideas on joining the RAF and from the outset went on to achieve this in different ways.

In 1935, Paul sat the Cranwell entrance examination. The intake for the Sandhurst entrance exam was something like 200, and 80 for Woolwich, but was a meagre 20-25 for the RAF. Paul "passed the exam easily" but came out 27th. He was advised to re-sit the exam in six months' time and went to a crammer to swot for the next round. His next attempt resulted in another pass, but this time he was four places away from a coveted vacancy, so he gave up.

Micky did not sit the Cranwell exam. Instead, in 1935 he went straight into the RAF by way of a Short Service Commission, the scheme whereby young hopefuls signed on for a trial period of four years. He, therefore, progressed ahead of Paul by some eighteen months.

Paul left Downside in the mid-1930s and as Teresa recalls "...sort of messed about for a couple of years, not doing anything much, before finally going into the airforce." He did have one or two jobs — he was gloriously and uproariously sacked from one job at the stock exchange (see later) — but he never stuck to anything for very long. His mother had tended to spoil him so undoubtedly his father, who due to his age had very little real influence on Paul, may well have thought the discipline of the Service would do him good.

From all reports and photographs, Paul was stunning to look at, perfectly mannered, a superb dancer, and outrageous. Certainly the sort of young gentleman considered a dire threat by naturally protective, ambitious, wealthy and aristocratic matrons. He was in great demand and wildly popular with the 'Debs' of the period. Uninhibited, unemployed, and original, from a notable military family, he lived graciously with his father and mother, and brother Michael, at Cadogan Square. But there was no serious money to reward that great old warrior, his father, so his courageous and resourceful mother Adelaide did everything she could, from taking in friends as lodgers to renovating and selling properties.

Perhaps because his parents were older than is usual, Paul had a touchingly deep love for them which never wavered throughout his life. Paul's letters to his parents spanning some forty years amply demonstrate a rare and profound relationship and consistently express gratitude, admiration, love and respect.

During this period Paul became what was termed a 'Deb's Delight'. This was really a list of the suitable and eligible dancing partners and prospective husbands for the debutants each season. Once a chap was on this list, kept by the mothers, then he would be asked to every dance during the season, the names being passed from one mother to another. Paul, however, managed to put up some sort of 'black' and was crossed off the list.

One of the Debutants of 1936 was Miss Diana Barnato, the daughter of millionaire Wolf Barnato of Bentley fame, who remembers him vividly. She recalls him as very good looking, with fair hair and blue eyes. She also remembers that he seemed to have been struck off virtually every mother's suitability list, the name having been quickly passed on to other mothers with debutante daughters. Paul would, however, appear at the various parties once he knew where they were being held, which Diana Barnato thought very brave, so that she was not in the least surprised to learn that his 'bravery' continued when war came.

Another thing she recalls is that on these evenings, Paul, who like all the eligible batchelors naturally always wore full evening dress, white tie and tails, did not wear the customary top hat — although he had one. Instead he would turn up wearing an opera hat, generally perched rakishly on the back of his head. (For the uninitiated, the opera hat was the type of 'top hat' which folded down so that it could be placed under the seat while in the opera house or theatre, as opposed to the 'proper topper'!) This combination was frowned on by all the 'toffs' of the period, and only went to emphasise to the mothers that they had been quite right to strike him from 'the list'! Being a very practical person, Paul probably felt an opera hat more convenient, and was probably right. Apparently he did have access to a proper top hat but obviously he enjoyed the role of non-conformist. The girls of course, thought him tremendous fun — and he was certainly much in evidence at parties. If anything, being struck from the list tended to make him a bit of a hero. Diana Barnato was always delighted to find him every evening in the bar, of those dances that he deigned to attend, for even if the mothers might not invite him, someone usually would, sometimes to two in one night.

The opera hat, in fact, belonged to his father and survived until relatively recently. In fact the box still survives. One friend recalled seeing Paul, while still wearing this hat, in 1938, doing a hand-stand on the roof of a taxi-cab as it motored down Park Lane!

Paul enjoyed every minute of his two uproarious 'Seasons', and it is clear his parents had much to put up with and no doubt went through more than the usual anxieties of similarly placed parents, with both their sons. The charming, gifted, spectacular Paul, a "force de La Nature", and his much-loved brother, the intellectual, artistic, fine-looking Michael.

For the cosmopolitan, elegant and supremely confident Paul, the, in his view, 'Bourgeois' preoccupation of the upper-classes with money, was nothing but an English eccentricity; in his eyes there was no man, whether Duke or millionaire, better than his splendid father, and no woman the equal of his adored mother. Such was the security and confidence these two extraordinary people gave him, that the conviction was never shaken.

With the 1936 'season' in full swing, to the great relief of his parents, Paul went to work in the stock broking offices of Sir George Henderson, in the City. The idea was for him to start at the bottom as a "Blue Button" — carting "Script" round the various City offices, and progress through the firm. He enjoyed it enormously because he could explore the City from end to end, visit the many superb Wren churches and immerse himself in recitals and concerts held in the churches throughout London. Music was one of his great loves and here he had the good fortune to be able to enjoy the very best, literally, "on the job". This "City idyll" came to an abrupt end when there was a dramatic conflict of his professional and social interests. As Paul told it:

"I was asked to a particularly lavish lunch in the City by some friends. As I was leaving, the Office Manager, a very decent, hard-working man called Rogers, handed me a cheque for £50,000 and asked me to bank it. Foolishly I decided to do so after lunch, which turned out to be a gastronomic masterpiece, liberally juiced with the finest wines and rounded off with copious quantities of superb vintage port and stilton cheese. I staggered back to the office to find the place in uproar. It was about 4 pm and the Banks were now closed.

"Rogers grabbed me and all but shrieked, 'What have you done with the cheque?' 'Oh, the cheque...' and I very sheepishly fumbled it from my pocket. Poor little Rogers swooned with rage and relief. I was sent for by Sir George Henderson himself — the first and last time we met. I sidled into his office to find him in a state of cold shock and fury.

"'This has never happened to me before, Richey! You're sacked!'

"I waited a minute, then said, 'I do apologise, Sir. Are you sure of that?'

"'You're sacked! Go at once!'

"'You're sure you won't re-consider, Sir?'

"'Go now! Now!'

"I returned to the office thoroughly chastened, to be greeted by a now recovered Rogers, who was very sporting about the whole thing and said how sorry he was I'd been sacked, but who added, 'After all, I know you want to join the Air Force, so I think it might be better if you just go and do that.' We both laughed and shook hands. So off I went and took a short service commission."

By this time, Micky had gained his "wings" and was with a squadron, — 111 Squadron. Several things kept Paul and Micky together. One was that their parents lived close to each other in Chelsea, and another was that he and Michael had been born just one day apart, Paul being one day older! A third event was when Micky introduced Paul to his elder sister Teresa (there was a younger sister, Magdelen, who was to die when she was 50). Paul and Teresa became friends and then fell in love.

"I had first met Paul when he and my brother were at Downside," recalls Teresa. "They were about 16 although I was a little older than them. After Paul left school, he was often in Micky's company before Micky joined the RAF, so Paul and I became close.

"Paul asked me to marry him in the organ loft of the Albert Hall, which was rather romantic really. I told him not to be so ridiculous and to come back and ask me in a year — which he did — which also sounds romantic."

Paul was eventually accepted into the RAF in 1937, and commissioned as an acting pilot officer in May. His training started with two months of Civilian Flying Training, from March of that year, run by ex-RAF Officers, to assess the flying potential of the intake. He flew 60 hours on Tiger Moths, followed in May by a month at RAF Uxbridge, for concentrated drill by ex-Guardsmen, whose job it was to get everyone to a first rate standard.

While all this was going on, for the second year running, Paul was invited to do the 'Season' and used to turn up on parade still in full evening dress under his regulation greatcoat, having just returned from dances.

His reports at Civilian Flying Training School were the best; he was posted to No.2 Flying Training School at Digby and after being interviewed by the Group Captain, who commanded the Station, was told by him he would be Senior Pupil there. Paul was uncomfortable about this, particularly to start with, as there were many older and more experienced men on the course and he felt it would lead to resentment. He was right — it did. Apart from that, he and the Group Captain did not get on well together and soon he was — extraordinarily — being reported to the Groupie for every minor misdemeanour he committed, on the Group Captain's express instructions.

For the Junior Course at Digby, they flew two-seater Hawker Harts. The Senior Course divided the pilots into the two categories of bomber and fighter pilots — the fighter pilots going onto Hawker Furies. Paul loved them. The Group Captain's displeasure with Paul continued and he called him in one day and announced he was breaking him as Senior Pupil. Paul had already been warned that this sort of thing had happened before and was advised just to concentrate on his training. At this point he was confined to the camp for six weeks after coming back late from a leave. After a month of this the other trainee pilots insisted he join them at a dance at Oxford; they thought it unfair he should have such a long punishment.

Paul agreed. First he dined in Oxford, then made his way independently to the Dance Hall. The doors were closed and two local police constables were guarding the door. When Paul asked to go in they refused to allow him access. He persisted and the policemen gave him a good shove. When he remonstrated with them they took him along to the local police station. Next morning he was paraded before the Group Captain, who put him under close arrest on a charge of disorderly conduct.

Paul's father came poste-haste from London to see the Air Officer Commanding (AOC), Air Vice Marshal L A Pattinson, who commanded the Group. Father saw the AVM first. Paul was then sent for. Pattinson asked what the trouble was. Paul explained the incident with the Police and the AVM brushed this aside, saying he was not concerned about Police but wanted to know, 'What about your other trouble?'

The Group Captain was present during the interview and at this point leaned over the AVM, who was seated at a table, and pointed ponderously to something in the file. Paul had no idea what it was, but the AVM then said he was going to call for all his reports and would see him again in an hour. When Paul returned, the AVM was more cordial and told Paul that all his flying and training reports were top drawer, and that he was recommending that Paul should transfer to No.7 FTS at Peterborough straight away.

Paul's chief flying instructor told him how sorry he was to lose him; he had an "exceptional" pilot classification — which was extremely rare in those days. Paul was very disappointed to leave these instructors and friends but tried to be philosophical about it.

Arriving at Peterborough, his new Group Captain sent for him on arrival. Paul thought him a very nice fellow; a champion archer of England. The Group Captain told him to forget about the past — there would be no adverse reports. He was to start with a clean slate, which Paul was relieved to hear, but it was short lived, when the CFI — known not for nothing as 'The Black Buddah', curtly announced, "You've come here with a bad conduct report. Watch your step or you'll be out on your ear!"

He was indeed watched constantly and felt the atmosphere to be unfriendly and discouraging. The CFI made no secret of his dislike of Paul and when he asked permission to leave the camp from the Duty Officer, he heard the CFI say quite loudly, "Give him enough rope and he'll hang himself." That was the attitude and it did not change. Paul hoped that if he persevered, a posting to a squadron would come through at the end of the Course.

Since they had left school, Paul and Micky Robinson had become very good friends and there is no doubt that he was encouraged to hang on and get through this difficult phase by Micky; for they both hoped to be able to serve together in the same squadron. Micky took great interest in Paul's flying and was very pleased with his excellent progress.

At the end of the Course, no postings came through. They were all sent on drogue-towing duties, which was uniquely demoralising and boring. Then came a posting signal for Paul — just in time. He was posted to 111 Squadron — Micky's squadron! As quickly as he received it, a cancellation was announced by AVM Pattinson, who objected because he said he would not have pilots "fixing" their own postings. The posting was as much a surprise to Paul as to the AVM, but one wonders if Micky had had anything to do with it! So it was back to the dreaded drogues in North Wales, then flying air observers and gunnery trainees about in twin-engined Boulton Paul Overstrand bombers, which were no longer front-line aircraft. Paul was miserable.

The AOC of 13 Group wanted a PA, so Paul was selected to go to Montrose for an interview. At the same time a posting to No.1 (Fighter) Squadron at Tangmere came through. The AOC offered him the PA job, so what to do? Squadron Leader H J L Hawkins, Paul's CO (according to Paul, a very decent New Zealander), advised him to choose the 1 Squadron posting. Paul was jubilant.

During his training Paul had gone to the annual Hendon Air Display, and seen a flight of four silver and red Hawker Fury biplane fighters belonging to No.1 Squadron, RAF. He had thrilled to witness their immaculate flying and aerobatic display. Little did he know then that he would become a member of that elite squadron although the aircraft had changed. Neither could he guess that two of the quartet of pilots he had been watching would become firm friends and comrades in arms — Johnny Walker and Prosser Hanks.

The chances of a pilot becoming a fighter pilot were no more than even in the late 1930s. Bomber Command and Army Co-Operation Command had just as much call on new pilots as had Fighter Command. Although Air Marshal Dowding was rapidly building and expanding his Command as fast as he was allowed, much of the military thinking at this time was about bombing, and there would always be a need for aircraft to co-operate with the army, either in ground attack, artillery direction or in just finding out where an enemy was on the ground. That Paul not only succeeded in becoming a fighter pilot, but also managed to be posted to No.1 Squadron, was luck indeed. Not that he didn't deserve it. He had been Senior Cadet at RAF Digby, also being rated as 'Exceptional' by his flying instructor. He was also an outstanding athlete and gymnast and later was 'Victor Ludorum' at the combined Athletic championship, No's 1 and 43 Squadrons at Tangmere.

No.1 Squadron base at RAF Tangmere was near the south coast of England, not far from Southampton and within easy reach of London. Here he found that P R 'Johnny' Walker was one of the flight commanders (in fact Paul's flight commander — A Flight) while Peter Prosser Hanks was a Flying Officer and section leader.

The Squadron was commanded by Squadron Leader I A Bertram but just a month later, Squadron Leader Patrick J H Halahan — a huge, square-set Dubliner who was known to everyone as the 'Bull', took command. The Squadron was equipped with the Hawker Hurricane single-seat day fighter, which Michael Robinson had been flying with 111 Squadron for well over a year. It had eight guns, retractable undercarriage, a sliding cockpit hood and a powerful Rolls-Royce Merlin engine. Quite a big jump from the light silvery biplanes Paul had seen 1 Squadron flying just 18 months earlier.

The Munich Crisis of 1938 had passed, but nobody was in any doubt that a war with Germany was fast approaching. It was not so much if as when it would begin. For now, the RAF, including Paul's squadron, was fast trying to become efficient with its two new day fighters, the superb Supermarine Spitfire, and the robust Hawker Hurricane.

Micky meantime, was still a fighter pilot with Treble One Squadron (111) at RAF Northolt, just north of London. Treble One was famous for having been the first RAF fighter squadron to receive the new Hawker Hurricane monoplane fighter. 111 Squadron had done all the service testing and endurance work with the Hurricane, Michael having taken his share, thereby becoming an expert modern-day fighter pilot in the last two years of peace.

Paul was undoubtedly pleased to have 'caught up' slightly, having been posted to what was accepted as the RAF's premier fighter squadron — Number One — which also had Hurricanes. At this stage, the Spitfire too was a new fighter within Fighter Command, and most fighter pilots of 1938-39 were equally happy to be assigned to a Hurricane or Spitfire unit, so long as the unit had one of the new monoplanes.

These fighter squadrons of the 1930s tended to remain in close association with their parent Fighter Station for years. Most squadrons which had moved or been reformed at a certain Station in either the late 1920s or in the 1930s, usually remained there. So it was that 1 Squadron, along with 43 — The Fighting Cocks — had both been at RAF Tangmere since 1926/7, and both had shed their shiny biplanes for the sturdy camouflaged Hurricanes in late 1938. Therefore both squadrons were really still working-up on Hurricanes when Paul arrived in March 1939.

Paul was to have little more than six months in the peacetime RAF but it gave him time to be more proficient in his chosen career. They practised constantly, but only the true test of combat would prove how well they had trained or how efficient their tactics were. As Paul related years later:

> "We'd learnt to fly for fun before the war and the RAF is said to have been the best flying club in the world. When war came, for which we had been prepared and trained, we felt very privileged to be able to fight it in the air and not be slogging it out on the ground like the poor infantrymen had to do."

CHAPTER II

OFF TO THE WAR

WHEN war was declared on 3rd September 1939, Paul, because of his recent intense training, was as operational as most of the other pilots. There was no reason to believe that World War Two would not be similar to World War One, that is, fought out on the Continent, with British and Commonwealth armies fighting once more on the old battlefields of France. The only difference this time would be that both sides had a more advanced airforce which could inflict more damage than had the Zeppelins, Gothas, Handley Pages and De Havillands in the Great War, against civilian targets in both Germany and Britain.

What was also of note was that both sides thought that they could defend against the bomber, while at the same time, both sides firmly believed their own bombers would be able to fight their way through defending fighters! Both sides were proved equally right — and wrong!

Other than a false alarm within minutes of war being declared, when the air-raid sirens wailed over Southern England, the war failed to 'start'. Only at sea did any real action take place and that was desultory, although items such as the *Graf Spee* action off Montevideo, or German submarines sinking the occasional ship, made the headlines.

Paul wrote home regularly, and his first letter after the declaration of war is of interest. It is dated, Monday, 4th September, 1939.

> Darling Mum & Dad & Mike,
>
> Sorry I haven't been able to write sooner. Have been on duty continuously for last 48 hours.
>
> Well, the war's started, and we're waiting to deal with any Germans who cross our coasts. As a matter of fact, we thought

we'd be attacked and bombed just before dawn this morning. At 12.30 some of us lay down to rest, but at 3.15 am we took off — in heavy ground-mist but a very clear moon-lit night. However, nothing happened, and we were soon down again. We then awaited the landing of some of our bombers who had been to Germany — five, we were told. At 6.30, one appeared. We were somewhat shaken at the thought of what had happened to the rest! Then came another through the mist. No more. We all turned out to greet the poor blighters — they'd been in the air eight hours. To my surprise I saw a whole lot of paper stuck around the tail-wheel of one — and guessed the answer: pamphlets! Flying largely through heavy cloud, and thickly covered with ice, they had bombarded the Ruhr Valley with — paper! It took three men in each aircraft one hour to chuck it out. They could see the great blast furnaces below, otherwise nothing. Very few search lights or AA fire. Only one fighter — and he vanished after a burst from the bomber. A really fine effort, I think, and I believe those concerned will be decorated. I'm not sure whether the others got back, but I fancy they did. I enclose a couple of copies of the stuff I pulled off the tail. It is headed "Warning. From Great Britain to the German people." Get someone to translate it if you can — but be discreet.

The sequel to our dawn flip was this: our intelligence learned that a large concentration of bombers was massing in Germany on the Dutch frontier at about 3, followed by an even larger mass, bound for England. However, at about 3.30 they unaccountably turned back. I can't tell you how we knew they turned, but it is quite interesting. So here we still are, having not yet received our baptism of fire, feeling rather nervy as a result, and finding it quite hard to believe the incredible fact that we are at war.

One must not dwell on the tragedy that we all know this war to be. One's mental condition is far from stable, and varies alarmingly between elation and depression, courage and honest-to-goodness fear. We are all jumpy, and care must be taken not to tread on any one's "corns". I suppose its the inaction and suspense. It will be better when we start.

I've sent you my will, and my luggage has just left. The latter won't reach you for a day or two. I am informing the Bank to let you know the state of my account on your request at any time. Naturally I can't say or hint at anything about our future plans, but you will hear from me again soon.

In the meantime, much love to you all and the best of luck. We'll all need it!   Paul.

What was Paul hinting at in the last sentence of his penultimate paragraph? In accordance with alliances made with Britain's Allies on the Continent, troops and supporting aircraft were already being prepared for France and among them were the Hurricanes of No.1 Squadron.

Paul mentions Micky only once in his book, and there was probably good reason, especially in the original, for Micky was not part of his squadron and the book was really about *his* squadron. But undoubtedly Micky must have been a little envious of his friend heading off for France — and possibly the war — while he, the senior of the two, remained in England with 111 Squadron in case the German Luftwaffe decided to attack London and other British towns.

Not that Paul didn't share in that bit of excitement on that evening of the first night of the war. Many people expected the Luftwaffe to bomb at night and without any real or effective night fighter aircraft or squadrons, it was expected that the Spitfires and Hurricanes would take on the role of night interceptors. So the Squadron was not surprised when they were called to Readiness, followed some time later by a call to get three aircraft into the air as hostile bombers were crossing the frontier of Holland.

Led by Johnny Walker, Paul and Sergeant Soper 'Scrambled' to patrol up and down above the line Brighton to Portsmouth, on what was, fortunately, a wonderful moonlit night. As Paul wrote, they saw nothing, which was not surprising, for enemy raiders were not in the air. In all probability, the radar boys and girls were picking up either some French or Dutch aircraft, or some of those British aircraft from England, throwing out 'hostile' leaflets over western Germany! In point of fact, ten RAF Whitley bombers had flown over the Ruhr, Hamburg and Bremen, turfing out 5.4 million leaflets. There had been no losses although three aircraft had had to make landings in France.

This sort of thing was about to happen with all too frequent regularity, giving rise to the period known as the 'Phoney War' — a war that appeared not to be happening. Both sides, of course, were reluctant to start a hot war. Britain was ill-prepared and Germany was still hoping that the British and French Governments would see the futility of a full scale European war and lay off, letting Hitler continue to expand his empire without too much hindrance or bloodshed. Germany and Hitler were to be disappointed.

Bull Halahan's squadron became part of the Air Component of the British Expeditionary Force (BEF) during that first week of September. They had known for some time that in the event of a war beginning, they would be among the first handful of squadrons to fly to France, but the days passed tensely at Tangmere, with everyone standing-by, or racing to their fighters at the slightest provocation.

British radar — or more correctly, radio-location — while more advanced than that of the Germans, was still in its infancy. The 'boffins' were still experimenting while the 'users' were still trying both to understand it and use it properly. No one wanted to be so unsure of a radar plot and do nothing, only to discover enemy aircraft had bombed some town or factory with huge loss of life. The spectre of H G Wells' predictions in the recent film 'The Shape of Things to Come' was all too real in many minds.

But finally, on the 7th, came the movement order. At 9.30 am the next morning — Friday the 8th — they were off. As recorded in *Fighter Pilot*, Paul's father, Colonel Richey came down to Tangmere to see his son away. Paul was going to a war fought on soil he had fought on just over twenty years earlier and the old soldier must have had many thoughts as he watched his eldest son off. Would he ever see him again? Who could tell? Later in the war, he would say good-bye to his other son Michael Richey, when he went off to serve in the Navy, like his half brother George, in the RNVR.

At this time airmen still flew in white (generally off-white!) overalls on which they proudly displayed their squadron cloth badges. Now they had orders to rip the badges off, so if they were brought down inside enemy lines their unit could not be identified. As Paul noted in his book, he handed his to his aircraft fitter to give to his father, who Paul could see leaning against the airfield fence, watching the squadron prepare to fly off. Moments later the Hurricanes were moving forward, Paul giving a last wave to the man by the fence, then in four sections of three aircraft, 1 Squadron took off and went to war.

For the record, the 16 pilots and Hurricanes which flew to France that day were:

L1905 S/L P J H Halahan	L1685 P/O W H Stratton
L1676 F/L P R Walker	L1960 F/L G H F Plinston
L1681 Sgt F J Soper	L1686 Sgt G F Berry
L1943 F/O S W Baldie	L1697 F/O B Drake
L1944 Sgt New	L1689 Sgt A V Clowes
L1989 F/O P P Hanks	L1927 Sgt Albonico
L1925 F/O M H Brown	L1693 F/O L R Clisby
L1971 F/O P H M Richey	L1842 P/O P W O Mould

Having taken off at 1130 am, they landed at Octeville, an airfield near Le Havre and as befitting their squadron number, they were the first

RAF fighter unit to land in France. After a night of youthful cele-brations in the local hostelries, the next day found them digging slit trenches and then flying to Cherbourg where they gave a demonstra-tion of strength by flying along the coast for the benefit of the French civilians. In the afternoon the Hurricanes of 73 Squadron flew in from RAF Digby, to make up the two-squadron Wing of the Air Com-ponent — No.67 Wing, BEF. This would be followed by the arrival of 85 and 87 Squadrons, making the total Hurricane strength in France four squadrons. This, together with ten light Battle squadrons of the Advanced Air Striking Force, and some reconnaissance Blenheims and Lysanders, would comprise the RAF's presence in France to support and protect the BEF troops. Then on the 30th, the Squadron moved to Norrent-Fontes, to the west of Lille.

Shortly after this the Squadron moved to a new base — Vassincourt, near Bar-le-Duc, which was 40 miles east of Nancy and bang in the centre of where some of WW1 had been fought. In 1918 it had been part of the American front, so daily the pilots of 1 Squadron were flying over such famous places as St Mihiel, Toul, Vaucouleurs, Pont-a-Mousson, and so on, which had meant so much to the US Air Service in WW1.

Not long after this, Paul had his first combat, but as he was attacked by two 'friendly' French Morane 406 fighters while carrying out a lone patrol, he was unimpressed by the whole affair. In fact, he got him-self lost, due to the rapid manoeuvres he had to make to escape the French pilots' attentions, and without maps, this was easy to do. Sighting an airfield he landed, to find it was Joinville — the French base which had been called up by the jubilant French Morane pilot and instructed to capture the German pilot that he had just forced down in the area!

Paul was, quite rightly, treated royally by his French hosts. They invited the 'victorious' pilot over to meet his recent victim, Paul having been persuaded to have imaginary wounds bound while he himself acted out the part of the wronged and wounded airman. One look at the mournful face of the Sergeant-Chef (Flight Sergeant) as he came to apologise and record his concern for his wounded ally, made Paul stop the charade and greet the Frenchman with a smile and a hand-shake, followed by a 'few' drinks!

There is another letter written by Paul to his parents, dated 16th November 1939, which is well worth reproducing. It shows the boy starting to become a man, and how much he thought of his Mother and Father.

Darling Folks,

Thank you so much for your grand letters of congratulations. I appreciate all you say very much, and what you are doing for me too. As a matter of fact I often think about what an extraordinarily lucky person I am to have such marvellous parents, relations and friends — and how extremely unworthy I am of any of you. The letters I receive from home are a source of constant joy and encouragement to me.

I told you I had been to Paris, didn't I? We had a very good time. Four of us went — 'Johnny' Walker (my Flight Commander), Kilmartin (who's just joined us from 43 at Tangmere — do you remember my bringing him in my first day at Tangmere?), 'Boy' Mould (who got his Hun the other day — he's the fellow who used to drive me up in his little green two-seater and sleep the night at 68), and myself. We stayed at the Gibbon, who give special terms for 1 Squadron. We had a somewhat expensive time, but it was worth it really, for it was our first break since the war began and the strain tells after a while. The strain of doing nothing, as any soldier knows, is the worst of all, and one would not last and remain an asset to a unit if one didn't get an occasional relief. Perhaps that's why leave is granted!

The weather here was quite nice and dry for a few days, but now it is right back to normal and raining like hell. This has been quite one of the filthiest days I can remember, and it's still going strong tonight. We are all very bored with it, and this war too. We heard with envy of the French victory over the German 27. Unfortunately that sort of thing is not for us, or you should long since have heard daily of the British fighters. The task assigned to us is not to go and find it as we should like, but rather to wait for it — and we're all heartily sick of waiting. Incidentally, the French victory tends to confirm certain notions of mine on tactics; but time will tell whether I am right or not — and anyway, I'm still only a very junior officer!

As you say, Dad, when you fought in the mud and filth of the last war you didn't think your son would have to follow you and do it all over again. Neither did he! It is perhaps an interesting comment on the selfish post-war generation to say that probably none of us were truly grateful for the sacrifices made in 1914-18. The reason — I hope — was that none of us could quite realise what they were. Now there must be very few of us, if any, who are not truly and humbly grateful. We young men of today are not as you were in 1914. We have been brought up differently — some would say softly. We have grown up in an atmosphere of peace, and have believed all our young lives that no such catastrophe as a Second Great War was possible. Most of us, unlike you in 1914, realize what a filthy and useless business modern war is. In 1914, you went laughing and cheering to war. In 1939, we go solemnly, sadly almost: we are under no delusions. But what enables us to face death bravely and unfalteringly now are two things: first, the knowledge that you had in 1914, that our cause is just; and secondly, the magnificent and undying example you gave us. We feel that your great effort was not in vain; and our effort now is a continuation of a fulfilment of it.

Much love to you all,

Paul.

One assumes the congratulations was for his forthcoming marriage to Teresa.

There was some evidence now of how other young men were fairing in this war and how friends and acqaintances were starting to disappear from Paul's life. In another letter home during that terrible winter of 1939-40, Paul wrote:

The weather here is much warmer — above freezing at times, as opposed to the 25 degrees below of a few days ago. There is fog and drizzle now, but I expect it will clear and freeze again soon. It does everything thoroughly here — rains buckets, blows a gale, or freezes the — well, you know the expression, Dad!

I'll write again soon. Drop me a line some time. By the way, don't be alarmed by gaps or irregularities in the arrival of my correspondence: the weather sometimes makes communications in these parts very difficult — snow and ice particularly.

Cheerio for the present,

All love, Paul.

PS. The latest casualty-list informs me that several acquaintances have been killed in action. Firstly, F/O B., who was with me at FTS. Secondly, Lines, also with me. Thirdly, Sgt Pearce, one of the best instructors at my FTS and a very nice follow. Fourthly, my instructor, Hue-Williams — 'Hue-Bill' to everyone who knew him. Do you remember him at Brize Norton, Dad? He was one of the best pilots in the Service, and I owe to him what knowledge I possess of flying generally and fighting tactics in particular. I suppose he must have got something into my head, for I was told before I left B.N. that the instructors there considered me the best pupil, and he himself said I was the best he'd had — which was a compliment considering he'd been instructing five or six years. Anyway, I always think of old Hue-Bill with affection and gratitude. I'll have a Mass said for him.[1]

Following Paul's earlier rebuff from Teresa Robinson, he asked her again if she would marry him, and this time she said yes. They were married shortly before Christmas, 1939, Paul having two weeks leave from France. His best man was Bobby, the Earl of Craven, who had been his best friend at Downside School. They were married in St Mary's Catholic Church, in Cadogan Street, the Richey's living in nearby Cadogan Square, behind Sloane Street. Of the honeymoon, Teresa recalls an amusing story:

"Bobby Craven loaned us his car which had a huge family crest mounted on it. We went down to stay at a hotel somewhere in Sussex and immediately Paul went down with 'flu. He stayed in our room the entire time, although I continued to have my meals downstairs in the hotel dining room, by myself.

"We were only there about four days and when we left, Paul was presented with a huge bill, which he reluctantly paid. When we got home we repeated the story and someone said, of course, they must have thought Paul was the Earl, and had taken a girlfriend to the country for a naughty weekend, especially as Paul had stayed out of sight in our room!"

The Phoney War continued and what made it worse was the terrible winter weather that year. But occasionally there was a brush with the enemy, as both sides gently probed each other's defences. A few German reconnaissance aircraft were engaged, some shot down, but it proved a long winter.

Undoubtedly Paul enjoyed his time in France, after all he spoke the language fluently, having lived there for periods in his youth, and if he wasn't then, he was probably well on his way to becoming a Francophile. Even if the exhilaration of action against the enemy was missing from the war at this stage, there were moments of excitement when sections were sent off on a 'Scramble' with always the chance of engaging one of the elusive German recce Dorniers. But the mere feeling of 'being there' and being a part of the war must have been very real to a man like Paul, who was interested in all aspects of living and revelled in the knowledge that he was doing what he wanted to do.

---

[1] Flight Lieutenant I V Hue-Williams RAF.

His first real chance of action came in the early spring of 1940. Until then, little had been seen of the German fighters — the much vaunted Messerschmitt 109E single-engined, single-seat fighter, and the twin-engined, two-seat Messerschmitt 110. Both fighters had received a good deal of 'press' and propaganda, the early version of the Me109 having had some success in Spain during the Spanish Civil War. That only a relative few had been available for action in the conflict was usually ignored, although due to the lack of numbers, the Me109 pilots had fallen on their feet and been able to develop a superior tactic to any used by the RAF — the two-plane element.

Men like Werner Molders, who had achieved 14 aerial victories in Spain, had found this leader and wingman section easy to operate. They called this a Rote, the idea being that while the leader searched and made the initial attacks, the wingman — or Rottenfleiger — would keep his leader's tail clear of enemy aircraft, thereby allowing the leader to give his full attention to the business of shooting down hostile aircraft. Prior to combat the two fighters would usually fly in line abreast, say 200 yards apart. This enabled each pilot to search the sky and cover each other's blind spots. When combat was joined, the wingman took up a covering position above, behind but to one side. When flying in Staffel formations, the German pairs would double up in sections of four, called the Schwarm. Three such Schwarm would constitute a full Staffel.

Meanwhile the RAF fighters had developed and maintained sections of three, usually flying in a 'vic' formation — leader and two wingmen. The role of the two wingmen was to stay close to the leader — generally tucked right in. The problem with this was that the two wingmen had to concentrate so much on keeping station, they had little real chance of checking the sky about them, leaving only one pair of eyes of the three free to search. And if the leader had a couple of novices in his section, he most probably kept one nervous eye on them to see that (a) they didn't wander off, and (b) they didn't ram him! The wartime RAF, flying peacetime formations, were soon to have a very rude awakening.

This was the scene then, when on 29 March 1940, 1 Squadron came into contact with Luftwaffe fighters for the first time. As will be seen later, Paul was always very meticulous in his reporting, and his ability to observe and write what he had observed, often proved very useful. On this occasion, after he had landed from this, his first combat, he submitted the following letter, dutifully addressed to his CO. (Combat Reports — RAF Form 1151 were not as yet in general use.)

From: F/O P H M Richey
To: Officer Commanding, No.1 Squadron
Date: 29th March, 1940
Subject:

Combat with Me109, 29-3-40

Sir.

I have the honour to report the following in connection with a patrol on 29-3-40.

2. My section was led by F/O Palmer, I was No.2, and P/O Matthews No.3. At approximately 1910 hours we were over Metz, at 20,000 feet, and I drew the Section Leader's attention to AA fire to the north and north-east. Flying north-east the Section Leader picked up an aircraft which we chased. We were unable to close and lost it.

3. Flying north-east in the hope of finding this aircraft again at about 0930 hours, when we were at 25,000 feet, I drew the Section Leader's attention to two Me109s. They were quite close on our left about 1,000 feet above us and flying in the opposite direction.

4. Climbing to attack, we turned towards their tails and they circled opposite us, keeping their height and position relative to us. P/O Matthews then called up and said, "They are under our tail." Thinking he said "under your tail," I called to my Section Leader, "It is me." My Section Leader, however, dived down steeply to the left and I let him go. I continued to climb towards the two Me109s keeping a look out behind. I saw a fighter approach me from astern, but at that angle was unable to determine whether it was a Hurricane or Me109. I watched for him to open fire if he were the latter and when he did so, I did a twisting dive to the left, watching him take a deflection shot at me and shaking him off by twisting more violently and pulling out very hard. As I flattened out an Me109 passed very close just above my head coming from the port quarter. He pulled up, turned left, and dived down again under my nose. I followed him down some 3,000 feet at high speed, but was not able to close and open fire until he pulled out very hard and climbed again. I opened fire at about 300 yards when we were climbing at about 45 and doing about 250 mph. Because my gun button was sticking in, my bursts were far too long and I wasted many shots. After three or four long bursts his starboard wing started to smoke about a quarter of the way out from the fuselage. He did not take immediate evasive action but fell slowly to the right into a steep vertical spiral, whilst I kept on his tail and continued to fire into him. My ammunition

gave out and I pulled out. I was unable to watch him further as another Me109 was coming towards me at about 2,000 feet above. I turned towards him in a climb but then he turned away and I dived to ground level, flying south for some ten minutes. I then found myself at Nancy and returned to the aerodrome.

5. On thinking the incident over, I would suggest that the Me109 which passed over me was the one that first attacked me. I was pulling out very hard and it is probable that he was able to catch up on the dive but was unable to pull out so sharply and over-shot me. Alternatively, he started pulling out earlier, lost me beneath him and did not know where I was when he crossed over me. The manoeuvre in itself seems to be without sense, for I was not fired at, as far as I know, as I was pulling out. If it were the second Me109 attacking, his bullets must have passed behind me. I was travelling very fast, but he was doing about 50 mph more.

I have the honour to be,

  Sir,

Your obedient servant,

  P H M Richey

    Flying Officer.

Paul also had to complete a combat and gun behaviour report, Part 1 of which had to be completed immediately on landing, then given to the armourer of his machine who had to complete Part 2, and then had to hand in the form to the Orderly Room. That is how it was done in 1 Squadron, in the early stages of the war. All very formal, of course; only when things got a bit more hectic did the system alter somewhat!

There were various questions on the form which the successful pilot needed to answer. Looking at the form today, and bearing in mind this was early 1940, when the war was still in its infancy, the impression seems to be of an intelligence officer making up the questions as he went along. There may well have been good reasons for them at the time but few of them seemed to elicit war-winning information.

Part 2 is interesting. Gun harmonisation was noted as being 250 yards — 150 yards less than Fighter Command's dictates, so obviously 1 Squadron — 'in the field' — had already decided that the closer the better — which was proved correct. Paul had used all his ammunition — due in part to the sticking gun button, but the loading of the guns is of interest. The port No.4 gun and starboard No.4 gun (the outers) had incendiary ammunition while the 1 to 6 guns all had ball type ammo. Thus only the two outer guns carried incendiaries, in the hope of helping the pilot to check where his fire was going. Later ammunition loading took on various methods, each gun having a mixture of ball, incendiary or high explosive bullets. The problem with the early incendiary ammunition was that it tended to drop quicker than ball or HE, so that a pilot who concentrated on where his incendiary bullets were going, might undershoot his target with his damaging bullets. The later De Wilde ammunition proved much better than incendiary, in that it 'sparkled' (exploded) when it hit the enemy aircraft, giving the attacking pilot instant knowledge that he was on target.

The three pilots involved in this action had taken off at 0830 to fly a standing patrol near to the front. Flying Officer C D Palmer — 'Pussy' to everyone — had been leading, in Hurricane N2380, Paul had been flying N2382 and Pilot Officer P G H Matthews had been in N2326. Palmer was in fact one of the few Americans in the RAF, coming from Cleveland, Ohio. He had already helped to knock down a Dornier 17 the previous November, although his fighter had been hit in the action and he had had to make a forced landing in a field. When Paul had called him up during this action and he had made a rapid manoeuvre, he had in fact got himself into a spin which took him several thousand feet to recover from.

The Messerschmitt had fallen inside Germany, so there was no immediate knowledge of a confirmed victory for Paul. Everyone was keen to know how he had fared in a fight with a 109 and were pleased that the 109 didn't seem so invincible as some commentators would have led them to believe. Paul later discovered that the Me109 had indeed come down. As the pilot had taken no evasive action, Paul believed he had been wounded, and so it proved. The pilot was Leutnant Joseph Volk of the 9th Staffel of III/JG53, who crash landed his crippled and badly damaged 109 near Saarbrucken within the German lines.

Later that same day, 1 Squadron engaged and shot down their first Me110 — scored by Johnny Walker — which was also the first 110 to be brought down by any Allied pilot, so the day ended with a double celebration.

Experience had indeed told 1 Squadron to change its gun harmonization from the normal Fighter Command spread to something a bit more realistic. Paul was to tell me in 1985:

"The substitution of spot harmonization of our Hurricanes' guns at 250 yards for the Dowding spread of 400 yards was one of our contributions. I believe Harry Broadhurst, one of the RAF's pre-war champion shots claims to have started spot harmonization in 1940, but we had already done it secretly at our annual squadron armament exercises at Sutton Bridge as early as April 1939 and had secretly kept it. It undoubtedly accounted for our marksmanship in France and was later the subject of a special investigation of the Air Ministry in the spring of 1940 and subsequent adoption by all RAF fighters.

"We also fitted armour plating to the Hurricane behind the pilot, later adopted on all fighters. We did it on our own initiative, after Pussy Palmer had been shot down by the front gun of a Dornier, using armour from a crashed Battle and demonstrated it at Farnborough in December 1939.

"Something else 1 Squadron changed was the painting of our Hurricane undersides in duck-egg blue rather than the one black, one white under wings that Fighter Command used at this time. This also was unilaterally adopted for all RAF fighters."

But now the skirmishing with the enemy was all but over. No.1 Squadron had encountered the Luftwaffe's bombers and now fighters and had not been found wanting. Yet the real war, the real test, was only now about to begin.

CHAPTER III

THE BATTLE OF FRANCE

MICHAEL was, by this time, also in France. Leaving 'Treble One' he had flown out to join 87 Squadron in January, based at Lille, Seclin. 87, together with 85 Squadron, were the two units of 60 Wing of the Air Component, although, by and large, they saw less action during the Phoney War than 1 and 73 Squadrons. If Michael was chaffing at the bit, especially after Paul got his Me109, then he was to be doubly disappointed.

Both Paul and Michael managed to see each other from time to time and naturally they had planned to get together for their birthdays, on 7th and 8th May. The 8th was the agreed date and Michael flew over to 1 Squadron for the celebrations. It is not recorded why he crashed on the 9th, but he did, his Hurricane ending upside down and badly bent; Michael scrambled out of the wreck but he had broken a thumb which ended his flying career for the time being. More galling for him was that the war was about to begin — in fact it started the very day after he was injured!

When finally the Blitzkrieg happened, at dawn on 10th May, 1940, Paul and the others were to be in the thick of it for the next couple of weeks. Here Paul's book gives us a graphic account of his and 1 Squadron's desperate fight against overwhelming odds during the rest of May.

On the first day, Paul, Hilly Brown and Sergeant Soper shot down a Dornier 215 (in reality a Dornier 17z, one of several lost by KG2 this day) which crashed at Longwy. Paul flew three more patrols on the 10th, to be followed by two more on the 11th. On the first of these Paul, after a general engagement, chased after a lone Dornier 17, which promptly dived for the trees and then began to head for

Germany. Paul followed, finding it difficult to keep up as the Dornier was really travelling. Burst after burst hit the bomber. First the rear gunner stopped firing, then glycol began to spew back from one engine. Oil splashed on Paul's canopy, so not only was the German losing his coolant but also his oil. Then he ran out of ammunition. When the German pilot became aware that the Hurricane was no longer firing at him, he stopped his evasive manoeuvres and turned due east for Germany. Paul made a last defiant half-roll over him to wish him luck then headed back to base.

Having lost his way in this fight, he found an airfield and landed, finding it was Mezieres — a French Potez base. In landing, Paul hit a bomb crater, and bent the tip of one propeller. The French CO got one of his pilots to fly Paul back to Berry. It was the end of his 'G' — L1679 — for it was badly damaged in a bomb attack on the 14th, while still at Mezieres, before it could be repaired.

Of these hectic days, Paul was to record for me the following recollections for a book I was writing about the Hurricane.

"We and 73 Squadron took it in turns for dawn readiness and B Flight of No.1 Squadron were on duty that morning of 10 May, while 73 were having a morning in bed. The Germans attacked 73 Squadron's base at first light — four Heinkels bombed their airfield while they were still horizontal. As a result of that, our B Flight was sent off and A Flight, who were supposed to be in bed, was sent for and we had to dash up to the airfield straight away. We were sent off ourselves, had a fight and chased and shot down a lone Dornier — and it took a lot of shooting down so must have been full of armour — then the battle was on. We had no idea it would start that day, of course. In fact most of A Flight had been out in Metz the night before and got back late, so we weren't really battle-worthy that morning.

"The battle went on at a very hot pace for ten days then it eased off, but the tenth day happened to be the day I was shot down for the third time, and wounded. In those ten days the Germans established complete air superiority.

"We had soon got used to being out-numbered. The first fight with the lone Dornier, with five Hurricanes, we felt, well this isn't so bad, but very soon the tables were turned and we then used to run into 40 or 50 enemy aircraft at a time, sometimes over a 100 — a flight of five Hurricanes wasn't really a match for them! We operated in flights of five always until the 19th and that was the first time we operated as a squadron. We asked to fly as a squadron earlier but they just used us in penny numbers. They also said our job was to protect the Battles, and we were not to be used for interception; the French were supposed to make interceptions. However, we used to take off and have a go without orders, but our HQ stopped that. We were supposed to sit around and wait to be sent off on escort jobs.

"The squadron, I think, were agreed that the best battle that ever took place in France, or perhaps in any other battle, was on 11 May. Five of us of A Flight intercepted 15 Me110s which were covering 30 Dorniers. The 110s put up a very good fight but we shot down ten for the loss of one — which was me! I never quite knew if I was shot down or whether I collided with a 110. I hadn't used much ammunition and I'd shot down two, but I was then stuck with five 110s and had a 15-minute battle with them, which was a very long time to dog-fight. The average dog-fight lasted at most, a couple of minutes. This battle was watched on the ground and timed.

"The 110s were firing at me from all angles, front as well as rear guns, the other Hurricanes having all gone home, out of ammunition etc. I knew at the time that the 110 was faster than a Hurricane in a dive and faster on the level too, so thought there wasn't much future in diving away from this fight. So I decided to carry on with it; knowing too that the Hurricane was more manoeuvrable than the 110, I thought I might get away with it. Anyway, I fought these five for 15 minutes without result from either side and all I could do was to fly at them head-on. They'd make a diving attack below me, pull up and fire, but at the receiving end I'd do as tight a turn as possible and dive under their noses so they couldn't follow without bunting. I did this dozens of times in that dog-fight but at the end I was getting very exhausted and then I was flying head-on at a 110 when suddenly there was a terrific bang in front of me and my aircraft was on fire. I thought at the time I'd been hit by a cannon shell in the front tank or in the engine. With the aircraft on fire I bailed out but afterwards, I often wondered whether I didn't collide with the damned thing.

"Some French gendarmes and villagers on the ground who took me in tow after I landed had watched the whole thing. A farmer said whilst it lasted he'd walked from one nearby village to another, which normally took him about 20 minutes, but he said he'd been walking particularly fast on this occasion. It was the French who said they saw ten Messerschmitts come down, which corresponded exactly to our claims of two each. It was a very tight dog-fight at 5,000 feet over a very small area and the gendarmes later counted ten German wrecks on the ground. Anyway, it was a very successful fight and encouraged us a lot for the rest of the battle."

The fight was recorded in Paul's log book as being fought over Brune-hamel, and that he had come down in his parachute near Rumigny, both towns to the west of Charleville-Mezieres. It had not been a text-book bale out. After the supposed collision, Paul had felt stunned and his mind went blank. Smoke in the cockpit and then a flicker of flame brought him to his senses and concentrated the mind. He pulled out the pin of the harness, slid back the cockpit hood (grateful it was not jammed!) and hauled himself out of the falling fighter.

At first the slipstream held him tightly against the side of the fuse-lage, his legs still draped over the rim of the cockpit. Catching hold of the trailing edge of the wing he pulled himself free and suddenly he was clear and falling in space. Fumbling for the rip-cord, he yanked the handle and thankfully the parachute cracked open above him, but then he saw he was heading for a wood and a village. Reckoning it would be the trees before roofs, he also watched two French gendarmes running along a road trying to judge where he would land. They probably thought he was a German.

Closing his eyes, he felt the swish of branches and then he was on the ground. He had fortunately come down between the trees and not in one. No sooner had he got his breath back than the two policemen rushed up, guns in hand, but Paul was quickly able to establish his nationality and soon the two men were embracing him warmly.

Paul got back to the Squadron at tea-time on the 12th, bringing with him the tail-fin of one of the 110s shot down which the French gendarmes had presented him with. The following day he did not feel well — possibly suffering from a mild concussion — and so the Doc put him to bed for 24 hours. Because of this he missed the escort mission to the Battles of 12 Squadron, whose near suicide attack on the bridges just to the west of Maastricht was to lead to the first two air VCs of the war. Bull Halahan, who had led the escort was missing, but he would turn up later.

Feeling a little more himself late on the 13th, Paul caught up with the news of several air fights on both the 12th and 13th, but Paul did not fly on the 14th — when the Squadron claimed 16 — being available again on the 15th.

The Squadron base at Berry-au-Buc had been bombed several times already and was bombed again on the morning of the 15th. At 1130 am A Flight were Scrambled to meet an incoming raid over Vouziers. They found 40 Dorniers in close formation with masses of Me110s flying above them — Paul estimating about 80! What was more disturbing though, was that the whole lot was coming straight at them!

Johnny Walker led the six Hurricanes into the fighter escort, which were typical odds during the Battle of France, odds which did not improve overmuch later in the Battle of Britain. In that fight, Paul claimed two 110s, during an attack on a 110 defensive circle, at which the 110 pilots were fast becoming adept in flying. Not that they liked it, but it was the best way for them to stay alive when up against single-seat opposition. Goring's much vaunted 110 fighter was generally no match for the Hurricane, nor later, the Spitfire.

However, moments after despatching his second 110, another got him. After feeling his Hurricane hit, he glanced back as he side-slipped, to see a Messerschmitt right behind him, its guns blazing. Holes appeared in his wing and then a thin trail of whitish smoke began to trail back from his engine cowling. Paul half-rolled rapidly and fell away in a dive, aileron turning as he did so. Pulling out at lower level, smoke still spewed out and he quickly guessed that he'd been hit in the glycol (coolant) tank, which usually meant an over-heating engine, then silence or fire — or both.

Throttling right back he tried to head for home, hoping to save his fighter — which was a new Rotol prop machine — but then the smoke increased and changed to a grey colour. The engine was getting hot and was about to burst into flames. For the second time in two combats he was faced with a parachute descent, and again did not hesitate. Dangling beneath the white silky parachute he watched his Hurricane hit the ground after a long curving dive which left a trail of smoke behind it, and heard the explosion as it went in.

Landing safely — except that he had ripped two fingernails in his hurry to pull the rip-cord — he saw French troops approaching and for the second time called that he was British. Not that it stopped one trigger-happy soldier from firing a pot-shot at him, which thankfully missed! He had landed near St Hilaire, not far from Amifontaine, and the nearby airfield of St Hilaire-le-Grand was being bombed. Members of 75 Wing HQ, led by Lord Bill Waleran, the Intelligence Officer, came to his rescue, taking him to the Wing Mess. He telephoned the Squadron confirming he was alright.

Once more he had to return by road, but he arrived back safely, claiming one Messerschmitt for certain and one probable. It appeared, however, that six crashed 110s were located in the area of the fight and only four had been claimed, so his second one must have gone in too. He was also admonished by the CO for trying to fly back rather than bale out right away. The Bull couldn't afford to lose a fighter but was even more anxious not to lose an experienced pilot.

Paul flew two patrols on the 18th, the first between Vraux and Pleurs and later another to St Quentin. Then on the 19th came his last flight and combat in France. The end in France was not far off now. The Germans were making steady progress towards the Channel coast, their Blitzkrieg tactics working effectively, and almost without hindrance. RAF Battle and Blenheim bombers tried their best to stem the tanks but they were too few to be effective. The air seemed filled with enemy fighter planes and the ground troops brought with them their very effective anti-aircraft guns which tended to cut the poor Battles to pieces in low-attack sorties.

On Paul's last day, the Squadron was at Readiness by daybreak. All were tired after nine days of intense action. Some had not even shaved for two or three days. It was a Sunday, but few would have known what day it was if asked. The pilots had been briefed the previous evening that there was to be an all-out effort the next morning. Every available bomber was to be hurled at the on-coming Panzers and the Hurricane squadrons would provide what protection they could. No support would be forthcoming from the French — it was the RAF's baby!

The pilots took off at 10 am, Johnny Walker leading ten towards the north-east. On the way they saw formations of unescorted bombers but had to ignore them in order to carry out their escort duty. Over their assigned patrol area the skies remained empty of either bombers or fighters, and after a frustrating fifteen minutes had to turn back. Only then did they see some Blenheims, or so they thought, heading back too. As it happened, there were no bomber Blenheims operating this day — 2 Group in England had taken heavy casualties in previous days, which was why the Battles had been called up yet again. Walker took a closer look. They were not Blenheims — they were German Heinkel bombers.

Paul was flying Number Three on Johnny Walker's left, as the leader (Johnny) turned for the bombers. Paul slid under the No.2 man in the section — the Canadian Hilly Brown — in order to get into echelon starboard. What everyone could now see, was that the bombers had no fighter escort — lovely grub!!

The Hurricanes went in, Johnny taking one left-hand aircraft, Hilly the second and Paul the third, while the other section took the right side Heinkels. In the subequent fight, eight Heinkels were claimed shot down — three by Paul above Chateau-Thierry — the old WW1 battlefield area. One went down vertically after receiving a long burst of fire in the cockpit area, the second fell away with its wheels down and both engines on fire, while the third went down with smoke and flame streaming from both engines and wing roots. It was just as he'd finished off this bomber, and was rolling jubilantly — but too slowly — to the left, that a last defiant burst from the doomed bomber's rear gunner, hit Paul's fighter. He had felt other hits during the combat, but this time there was a terrific bang by his right ear. A spurt of blood stained his right sleeve and glove. Then he noticed, as his Hurricane began to fall away, that his right arm seemed to be floating in mid-air, the hand hooked like a dead claw, but there was no feeling. The realisation that he had been wounded — he assumed in the right arm or shoulder, possibly a hit which might have almost severed his arm, which was why it seemed to float before him — was followed by another shock. His left arm didn't appear to work either!

As his Hurricane plummeted down, Paul tried desperately to get the hood open and bale out, but his arms didn't respond. When finally his left arm did move, he grabbed the hood handle only to find the canopy jammed. Feeling certain he was about to die, to his surprise his injured right arm flopped down and his hand caught the stick and pulled it back. As he was now only about 2,000 feet from the ground, this happened none too soon.

As he took a moment to glance about, he noticed some of his instruments were not working, bullet holes peppered his wings and a bullet hole in the right hand side of the windscreen was causing a hell of a breeze. As he wondered vaguely where the bullet might have gone, he started feeling pain from his injury. The right side of his neck and face were now troubling him. He guessed correctly that an exploding cannon shell had taken a chunk out of his neck. As the hood remained stubbornly shut, Paul had now to decide to crash land somewhere.

Paul looked down, spotting a likely looking field near a village, selected so that he could quickly get some medical attention. Pumping down his flaps but leaving his wheels up, he brought the battered fighter down onto the field, bracing himself with his left hand on the gunsight. As the Hurricane bounced and careered across the earth, Paul noticed blood spurt onto the instrument panel and windscreen.

Coming to a halt, he tried frantically to get the hood open but it was still jammed. With his every thought believing that any moment the fighter would burn and then explode, he finally managed to jerk the hood half open, and then he was out and free. French soldiers arrived with rifles pointed but Paul was almost too weak and shocked to raise his hands. Finally an officer arrived, who had seen Paul shoot down the third Heinkel, pointing to a nearby column of smoke as he did so. When Paul mumbled about having shot down two before that, the Frenchmen seemed to look at him as some kind of superman.

However, the look may have been something else, for what they could see but Paul could not, was his gaping wound. As he was later to learn, what was assumed to have been an armour-piercing bullet had hit him in the neck. It had nicked the angle of his jaw as it entered, exposed the carotid artery, before lodging against the front of his spine at the base of his neck. It was this shock to the spine which had caused the temporary paralysis to his arms. Now he realised where the bullet which had come through the side front perspex section of the windscreen had ended up. He had been extremely lucky. A fraction of an inch to one side and the artery would have been severed and he would have bled to death before reaching the ground. Or had the bullet lodged a little harder against the spinal cord, the paralysis would have been permanent and he would have had to sit unmoving while he watched himself and his fighter dive into the ground.

The soldiers took him to a nearby French hospital at La Ferte-sous-Jouarre, a short distance to the south west of Chateau-Thierry. As this hospital was about to evacuate, they merely put on a quick dressing, gave him an anti-tetinus jab and then drove him off to another medical centre, which, in the event, the driver couldn't find. Finally Paul ordered the man to drive to an American hospital in Paris. In the event the driver found the American hospital at Neuilly, who took him in.

Within two hours of his admission, the celebrated neurosurgeon, Professor de Martel, removed the bullet and sewed him up. By the following Sunday — the 26th — he was sitting up in bed, sore but cheerful. Some of the Squadron pilots visited him, but only to say they were about to depart for England. It took another week before he managed to haul himself out of bed. He couldn't turn his head and the trapezius muscle in his right shoulder wasn't working as the nerve had been destroyed.

By this time, the British forces were evacuating from Dunkirk to the north, but Paris was still free — for the time being. In Paris, walking down the Champs Elysees, he spotted the ace New Zealand pilot of 73 Squadron, Edgar 'Cobber' Kain DFC. He was chatting to the war correspondent, Noel Monks at a pavement cafe. Kain said that the main part of his unit had gone back to England and he was about to join them. Kain, Paul knew, had shot down about 17 German aircraft to date. The very next day, Kain took off for home, but couldn't resist a beat-up of the airfield. He misjudged it, crashed and was killed instantly.

By Monday the 9th of June, Paul, anxious to get back to the Squadron, had managed to organise permission to travel by train from Paris to Blois, where the AASF HQ was now located. However, he found that route impossible so headed out of the city in a small RAF convoy on the 11th, which deposited him at Chateaudun, where 1 Squadron had reformed, prior to going home. Three days later, Paul left Chateaudun in a de Havilland Rapide eight-seat mail plane, heading out over Normandy, and the Channel Islands, then crossing the English coast over Dorset. Shortly afterwards the Rapide landed at RAF Hendon.

It was a very different Paul Richey who arrived back that June day, to the one who had headed out to France so eager the previous September, or even the happy Paul who had returned to France after his marriage in December.

War had taken on its usual serious face after the slow period of the Phoney War. It had shaken the British, the RAF, and Paul, to realise that the Germans had smashed their way through to the Channel coast in just ten days, and within twenty were forcing the BEF to evacuate from Dunkirk. In just over a month France capitulated. Hitler and his armed forces had achieved in that short a time, something the Kaiser's men had failed to do in four years between 1914 and 1918.

No.1 Squadron had acquitted itself well in France, not only before the *Blitzkrieg* but during it. By the 10th of May 1940, its pilots had claimed some 26 German aircraft shot down, and according to Paul's diary notes, a further 114 had been claimed during the period 10 to 19 May. In all it had lost three pilots, one pre-Blitz, two afterwards. Two more had been wounded and one was a prisoner of war.

Squadron Leader Bull Halahan wanted his pilots rewarded for their splendid efforts and their devotion to duty. He and Johnny Walker had already received the DFC. He wrote up award recommendations for eight of them, all dated 21 May. Those type-written sheets still survive, the Bull's blue ink handwriting filling in the achievements of each man.

For four of the pilots he recommended the "non-immediate" award of the Distinguished Service Order — Killy Kilmartin, Boy Mould, Prosser Hanks — and Paul. For three others, the DFC — Pussy Palmer, Stratton and R G Lewis, with a DFM for Sergeant F J Soper. These eight went forward to the Officer Commanding No.67 Wing, Wing Commander Cyril Walter who approved them over two days, 31 May and 1 June, but downgraded the four DSOs to DFCs!!, and

disapproved one! Having passed through thus far, they were then for-
warded to the AOC-in-C, AASF, Air Vice Marshal Philip Playfair CB
CVO MC, at HQ BAF in France, who approved the six DFCs and
one DFM. The forms now proceeded through channels to the Under
Secretary of State for Air at the Air Ministry in London, on 15 June.
Being agreed by him, they were then submitted to His Majesty King
George VI in July. This final stage was little more than a formality; a
courtesy to the King of England.

Once approved, the pilots could be informed, but only Halahan
knew that his four DSO recommendations had been reduced to DFCs.
It would have been especially appropriate if Paul had been awarded
the DSO, because his Father had won two DSOs himself. But it was
not to be. As anyone in military service will agree, awards for gallantry
often create a good deal of discussion. Undoubtedly Halahan had
aimed too high for Paul and the others, especially at this early stage
of the war. Very few squadron pilots managed a DSO, squadron
commanders sometimes did, but for the more junior officers, a DSO,
if awarded at all, usually came after at least an earlier award of the
DFC. Then again, although pilots of several squadrons in France had
achieved extraordinary results during the Blitz, the French campaign
and the subsequent Dunkirk episode, it was nevertheless, a period of
defeat!

In the event, 1 Squadron received an almost unique number of
awards during the French campaign. In all ten Distinguished Flying
Crosses (DFC) and three Distinguished Flying Medals (DFM). The
recipients were:

Squadron Leader P J H Halahan	Flight Lieutenant P R Walker
Flight Lieutenant P P Hanks	Flight Lieutenant M H Brown
Flying Officer J I Kilmartin	Flying Officer L J Clisby (Dec'd)
Flying Officer P H M Richey	Flying Officer P W O Mould
Flying Officer C D Palmer	Pilot Officer W H Stratton
Flight Sergeant F J Soper	Sergeant A V Clowes
Sergeant G F Berry	

The one who 'lucked out' was Pilot Officer R G Lewis, the Canadian,
whose recommendation had not been approved by 'higher authority'.
Dick Lewis was to fly again with 1 Squadron during the latter stages
of the Battle of Britain, but was lost when he baled out into the
freezing waters of the Channel on 5 February, 1941 after a fight with
some Me109s.

The ink-written recommendation by Halahan, for Paul's first decoration read:

> "On 29 March, near Metz, Flying Officer Richey attacked two 109s and shot down one. Since 10 May he has been concerned in seven combats, has shot down six EA (approx), has parachuted twice and was finally shot down and wounded. In all these engagements he displayed courage of the highest order when faced with overwhelming odds."

This is almost the same as the official citation which appeared in the London Gazette on 5 November 1940 (see appendix A).

Although released from his Paris hospital, Paul was still not fit and certainly was not able to resume his role as an operational fighter pilot. For the next part of his story, we can turn to Paul Richey's own words, which he wrote in 1941, when he began to think of a sequel to his first book. As we can see, his attitudes had changed since the Battle of France, but he knew he *had* to return to operational flying, even if others did not agree with him.

CHAPTER IV

A MAN IN A DREAM

FOR some time after my return to England I felt like a man in a dream. The unhurried efficiency of London, with its tubes and buses, restaurants and theatres, ATS and WAAFs and WRENs, made me wonder as much as did the quiet, unruffled peace of the June countryside.

These things could not be real. They were imaginary, dreams soon to be blasted to nothing by the real things, by the roaring planes and the whistling bombs and the clattering tanks and guns. And yet these people I saw were everywhere going about their business and pleasure, sublimely ignorant of what had just been going on, on the other side of the Channel. I was amazed and infuriated to find how little it seemed to mean to them. However, I thought, the awakening would not be long now.

For my part, I felt beaten down, numbed, utterly exhausted. The sight of an aeroplane, instead of exciting my alert interest, as previously, now made me turn away feeling physically sick. However, the Medical Board at RAF Halton, having depressed me by telling me my right arm and shoulder would never again be strong enough for, say a game of tennis, nevertheless condescended to grant me a month's sick leave. I spent it with Teresa in Devon where I could lie in the sun and, in spite of the continual nightmares, sleep and sleep and sleep.

In my conscious moments I would try and thrust all thoughts of the war out of my head. I never wanted to see an aeroplane again! Gradually, of course, and inevitably, I recovered. An aeroplane once more became for me an object of interest and beauty. The will to fight on came up again, the sense of responsibility returned and with both came a hint of shame. I packed my bags with alacrity, went back to Halton for another Board, refused more sick leave and heard the sentence with a sinking heart:— "Three months' ground duty; then we'll see."

In the Royal Air Force a Central Medical Board is probably the most powerful body in the Service. What it says definitely goes, and no one, not even the Chief of the Air Staff, can over-ride or sway it. I knew there was nothing for it but to lump it. So, with regret perhaps not altogether untinged with a fatalistic relief, I resigned myself to 'sitting on my bottom' for the rest of the summer.

But there was one job, if I could do it properly, in which my flying experience would be of the utmost value — controlling. Accordingly I pulled a few strings that happened to be available, did a short course to put myself in touch with recent developments in the English fighter defence system, and was shortly posted to RAF Middle Wallop, in Hampshire, as a Fighter Controller.

There have been one or two descriptions published, either in print or on the cinema screen, of the organisation of Fighter Command. However, a brief resume may not come amiss here and may serve to make more clear what comes later.

Fighter Command embraces the whole of the fighter force of the Royal Air Force in the United Kingdom. It is subdivided into a number of Groups, which are merely geographical areas quite arbitrarily delimited, whose strength varies with the number of squadrons in the area. Each Group is further subdivided into Sectors, which again are geographical areas under the protection of their particular Sector Stations, which are aerodromes, under the command of a Group Captain, one Sector Station per Sector.

Satellite aerodromes are smaller aerodromes near the Sector ones and provide for dispersal of the squadron should the Sector Stations be attacked or become overcrowded or unserviceable. There may also be Forward aerodromes, which are used by the Sector Stations when they want to distribute their squadrons to better strategic advantage.

The Squadrons of each Group are distributed among the various Sectors. In a busy Group such as No.11 Group (which covers London, Essex, Kent and Surrey) there may be four or even more Squadrons per Sector, whereas in a quiet Group such as No.81 (which covers Northern Ireland) there may only be one or two Squadrons per Sector. Each Group, however, is ready to reinforce another should the need arise, and the whole of Fighter Command's operational strength could be concentrated in any Group at very short notice.

A Squadron normally consists of 23 pilots and 18 aircraft. As a rule only 12 aircraft fly at once in a Squadron formation, the other six providing a margin to allow for maintenance, losses, etc. The Squadron is commanded by a Squadron Leader and is divided into two Flights, A Flight and B Flight, each of which is commanded by a Flight Lieutenant. Although a Flight consists of nine aircraft on the ground it does not normally fly more than six together. Thus the two six-man Flights make up the 12 in a Squadron formation.

The pilots are about half officers and half NCOs — Flight Sergeant Pilots and Sergeant Pilots. In addition, a Squadron has its own Adjutant ('Adj'), Intelligence Officer ('Spy'), Medical Officer ('Doc') and Engineer Officer ('Plumber').

The airmen of a Squadron normally number about 150. They have various trades, such as Fitter, Rigger, Wireless Operator, Armourer, Clerk, and so on, though there are some aircraft-hands without a trade (ACHGD) — aircraft-hand general duties — who do miscellaneous and unskilled work. All these airmen under the general supervision of their NCOs and the Engineer Officer, have one main object in life: to keep the Squadron's aircraft serviceable and in first class order. No inefficiency is tolerated, for the pilots' lives and success in battle depend on the airmen's work.

Nevertheless, a good indication of the general morale and discipline of a Squadron is provided by its 'serviceability state' — ie: the number of aircraft it manages to have serviceable and on the line, each day. Morale, which is primarily dependent on the pilots, is inevitably reflected in the airmen's work.

Fighter Command was formed primarily as a defensive force. Thus its whole fighting organisation was worked out on defensive lines and a very elaborate and very efficient machine was set up with its one object — the interception and destruction of every enemy raid by our fighters, both by day and by night.

One of the most important links in this defensive system is the chain of raid-detecting stations round the coasts of the United Kingdom, known to the general public as Radio Location Stations.[1] These remarkable stations, and the people who man them, are capable of detecting hostile aircraft at a considerable distance from our shores (which varies with the height of the raid, being greater at high altitude), thus giving our fighters, when Scrambled, sufficient time to

---

[1] Known in the early days as RDF — Radio Direction Finding — but more familiarly known later as Radar. *(Ed)*

gain height to position themselves to attack the raid as it crosses our coast or even before.

Once a raiding force has crossed our coast, information concerning it is supplied (provided the country is not totally covered by low cloud) by the Observer Corps [later Royal Observer Corps. Ed], whose visual observation posts cover the whole country.

All information concerning a raid is passed simultaneously through various channels, to the Operations Room at Headquarters, Fighter Command, at Bentley Priory, Middlesex, then down to each Operations Room at each Group Headquarters, and then the Operations Room at each Sector Station that may be concerned. In these operations rooms, the raids (and friendly aircraft as well) are plotted on a large table map of the country or general Group area.

Headquarters Fighter Command normally play no part in the interception of raids, their job being merely to keep an eye on the whole country, make decisions with regard to reinforcing a particular Group, issue instructions to meet special circumstances, and so on. The interception of the raid is normally left to the Group HQ concerned. The Group Controller decides which Sector or Sectors will be affected and issues orders to them regarding how many of their aircraft are to take off. Once the fighters of a Sector are in the air, the interception is left to the Sector Controller who is in communication by radio telephone with his pilots. The Sector Controller is thereafter responsible for his aircraft. A pilot can soon tell a good controller from a bad one, and will know how far to obey his instructions and how far to trust him to get him safely home again in bad weather or in darkness.

At the Sector Stations, the Squadrons, of course, have to maintain certain 'states'. These are laid down as 'Readiness', 'Available' and '30 minutes available', and are taken in turns by the squadrons based there. Pilots at Readiness must be dressed in their flying kit and must hold themselves ready to be in the air within, at the most, five minutes of receiving the order to 'Scramble' — take off immediately. Those at Available must be prepared to be in the air within fifteen minutes, while those at 30 minutes must be ready to be in the air within that time. States are sometimes relaxed to one hour's notice in unflyable weather.

This is a simplified account of the somewhat elaborate machinery of Fighter Command. Elaborate as it is, however, it is surprisingly efficient. For instance, the time-lag between a raid being detected by the Radio Location or Observer Corps and the pilots receiving the information in the air is never more than two minutes. In two minutes a bomber flying at 240 mph travels eight miles. A trained controller will make allowance for the small time-lag to direct his fighters accordingly while an experienced pilot will also make allowance for the limitations of the controller's sources of information.

When I arrived at Middle Wallop at the end of July 1940, the Germans had already started to send what they described in their Communiques as "armed reconnaissances" over the 11 Group area and the English Channel. These consisted of large bomber-formations which, generally speaking, attacked convoys, coastal ports and some aerodromes. These were timed so that several of them coming from different directions would arrive over our coasts simultaneously or in quick succession; as a result, the 11 Group fighter squadrons were having a good deal of work to do and little respite. Accordingly, 10 Group in which Middle Wallop was situated, were required to reinforce 11 Group from time to time. Meantime, 10 Group had to maintain sufficient squadrons to deal with any attacks that might materialise against Southampton, Portsmouth, Portland, Plymouth, Bristol, Yeovil, etc. All these places had important docks, shipyards, aircraft works and factories which had to be protected.

As August began, the German Luftwaffe started its assault on Fighter Command airfields with the object of destroying its aircraft, thereby gaining air superiority over the possible areas of invasion. The German bombers suffered severe casualties at the hands of our fighters and very often their formations were broken up and dispersed into small formations or even individual aircraft before they could reach their objectives. Accordingly the Germans started using large numbers of fighters simultaneously with their bombers, some escorting, others sweeping through the areas concerned to engage our fighters. The onslaught was intensified and was directed principally at our fighter aerodromes.

In spite of the very large number of fighters and bombers the Germans were sending over, our own fighters, for reasons that will be discussed later, continued to exact a heavy toll. Only one aerodrome was made totally unusable — Biggin Hill, which had a very large number of bombs dropped on it — but it was only out of action for six hours.

My arrival at RAF Middle Wallop, situated near Andover, coincided with yet another switch of German tactics. The cessation of large-scale attacks on fighter aerodromes and the commencement of a series of attacks on the docks and warehouses at Portsmouth,

Southampton, Portland, Bristol, Newcastle — in other words, on naval installations and food supply depots.

[RAF Middle Wallop when Paul arrived, was commanded by Wing Commander D N Roberts, who was both Station Commander and Sector Controller. Its resident squadrons were 238, 604 and 609, later joined by 234. No.238, which flew Hurricanes, was commanded by Squadron Leader H A Fenton. 604 and 609 were both Auxiliary Air Force units. 604, commanded by Squadron Leader M F Anderson, was one of the RAF's few night-fighter units, equipped with Blenheim IFs and later with Beaufighters. Among its pilots was John Cunningham, soon to become one of Britain's top-scoring night-fighter experts. No.609 Squadron was commanded by Squadron Leader H S Darley, and flew Spitfires. 234 Squadron, which flew Spitfires, was commanded by Squadron Leader J S O'Brien DFC. As things were to turn out, by the following spring he would be an operational flight commander with this famous 'West Riding' Squadron. Ed]

Arriving at Wallop I was just in time for one of the last aerodrome attacks. Ju88 dive bombers attacked all the new aeroplane hangars in very pretty style and formation. They got away with it comparatively lightly, as most of the available fighters were otherwise engaged.[1]

After this bit of excitement our main pre-occupation became the defence of Portsmouth, Southampton, Portland and Bristol both by day and by night, and then London by night.

Almost every day we would have to call all our four day squadrons to Readiness as a "100 plus" or "150 plus" raid was suddenly plotted off Le Havre, heading north. At this time our four squadrons were 234, 238 and 609, with 152 at our satellite base at Warmwell. In fact all the squadrons used Warmwell as an advanced base, only coming back to Wallop each evening when flying was finished. Little did I know then how close I should be associated with 609 later in the war.

On these occasions we needed every minute to get our squadrons to their operating height: usually the raids came in at 20,000 feet or so. Accordingly we usually didn't wait until the Group Controller had thought it out, and by the time the order to Scramble had come through we had a couple of the squadrons in the air. Sometimes we

---

[1] [Middle Wallop was raided on 13th, 14th, 15th and 21st August. A large formation of He111s headed for the aerodrome on the 14th, but in fact only one lone Ju88 bombed with any success. One of its bombs hit 609's hangar and several Spitfires and three Blenheims were destroyed and six people killed. Sergeant A N Feary, of 609, shot down the Junkers shortly afterwards. On the 15th two hangars were hit but only one aircraft was destroyed although five were damaged. Ed.]

had to land them almost immediately as the raid turned off north-easterly towards 11 Group's area, which was annoying for our pilots; but it was much more annoying for them if we waited too long and then got them underneath the enemy fighters as a result.

The business of controlling four squadrons operating independently at once calls for coolness, quick thinking and prompt and speedy action on the part of the Controller. Each squadron has to be con-tinually contacted by R/T, each on a different frequency or wave length, and all necessary information passed to it regarding move-ments, heights and positions of both friendly and enemy aircraft. In addition, the Controller has frequently to answer their questions or ask some himself. All the time he is endeavouring to intercept the raid with his squadrons, to the latter's maximum advantage, before the objectives can be bombed. In the midst of the whirl, the Group Controller is apt to come through and ask questions himself. Small wonder that some controllers have actully broken down under the strain.

When I was on duty during these big raids, or 'flaps' — which usually came in the afternoon, I would be hopping about like a mad-man in the Ops Room, jumping from telephone to telephone, giving orders, asking brief questions, watching the map board, keeping a tag on my squadrons' positions while endeavouring to talk to them clearly, calmly and with confidence.

After the fighters had seen the enemy, things would quieten down to a tense listening and the passing of any necessary information. Pilots don't want a controller babbling at them when they are carefully watching the enemy while climbing into the sun, or whirling round in a dog-fight. During those moments when we knew the fight was on, I was able to use my imagination as a pilot to try and picture the thing from the snatches of R/T talk and the look of the plotting on the board. Then, as the enemy plots receded towards the coast and across the Channel, there would come calls from pilots in trouble — perhaps short of petrol, or with their aircraft full of holes, or even wounded — who required urgent 'homings'.

At last, when everything possible had been done to help them back to the aerodromes and the enemy plots had disappeared, and if there seemed no likelihood of an immediate follow-up raid, I would wipe the sweat from my brow and run from the stuffy, artificially lighted Ops Room, into the clear cool air outside. I would anxiously wait for the distant drone of our returning fighters and count them in one by one as they circled the airfield in the golden evening sunlight and come gracefully into land. I would then think rather wistfully of the days not so long ago, when I too could fly and fight. I would wonder, with a trembling in the pit of my stomach, if I could ever again bring myself to do what those boys were doing now....

But my job wasn't over yet. There would be the eager reports from the pilots, the counting of heads, the search, by telephone, of other aerodromes for the missing ones, the reports from the Home Guard, Observer Corps and the Police of crashed aircraft to sift and confirm. Sometimes there would be the relief and joy of finding that a missing pilot had forced-landed elsewhere or been fished out of the sea by the Navy: at others there would be the sorrow, never dulled by repetition of learning that they had found Tommy's body or that Jimmy must have been in the Spitfire seen going down in flames into the sea off Portland Bill.

Controlling at night was a very different matter. We had one night-fighter squadron which was equipped with Blenheims. Night after night in the Ops Room we used to watch the plots of the German raiders streaming up in steady procession towards London. They would be outside our area on most occasions and although we always had pilots and crews standing-by, they would not be used unless some Huns came our way. One was filled with a sense of angry impotence, realising the death and destruction that was being wrought, and knowing how little we could do to stop it. My own personal anger was tinged with a good deal of anxiety, for my wife Teresa, and my Mother and Father were all in London. However, when the Germans came our way we were then able to get busy.

In those days, night interception was by no means the scientific and efficient business which came later. It was very much in the experimental stage. Moreover, the machines we had to use were admitted to be too slow. The combination of the skill of the Controller, the skill of the night-fighter pilot not to mention a great deal of luck, did allow us to effect an occasional interception. But time and again the enemy bomber, because of its superior speed, would draw away from our fighter. It was a game of infinite patience and infinite perseverance for all concerned; and eight times out of ten it was rewarded with failure.

This night-fighter squadron of ours was No.604, an Auxiliary Air Force Squadron. They had an exceptionally experienced lot of pilots and gunners, later better known as radar operators, and later on they became the first squadron equipped with Beaufighters. With these machines, which were fast and specially designed for the job, they quickly took the leading score in night victories and have held it ever since. As a squadron they were one of the nicest bunch of chaps I've ever met. One of the best, in both senses, is John Cunningham, known in the popular press — much to his annoyance — as 'Cat's-Eyes'. In those days he was a quiet, fair-haired boy with very blue eyes and a very charming manner. Despite the success to which his DSO, DFC and bar testify, he has not changed one bit. Before the war he was a test pilot with De Havilland's. As a matter of fact he does seem to possess exceptional night vision, but his long list of victories is principally due to perfect flying, faultless airmanship, and his equally brilliant radar operators — usually Jimmy Rawnsley, who has himself received the DFC, DFM and bar.

No. 609 Squadron was our crack day-fighter Squadron. They are also an Auxiliary Air Force unit, though some regular pilots now grace their ranks. By September 1940, they had claimed to have shot down 100 enemy aircraft, being the first Spitfire squadron to reach this figure. They too were a damned good bunch of chaps. One of them, David Crook DFC, has given a detailed account of their 1940 activities in his book *Spitfire Pilot*.

Another of its personalities in 1940 was Flight Lieutenant John Dundas DFC and bar, who was to shoot down the German 'ace' Major Helmut Wick, one of the Luftwaffe's leading fighter pilots. Unfortunately John was himself shot down immediately afterwards by Wick's wingman, and is presumed killed. Yet another personality is Michael Robinson.

CHAPTER V

WITH 609 SQUADRON RAuxAF

Michael Robinson and I were born within a few hours of each other in 1916 and also within a few yards of each other in Chelsea. Neither of us was aware of the other's existence, however, until we met at Downside School. Here, though contemporaries, our interests lay in different directions and we were not particularly friendly. However, having both failed the examination for the Royal Air Force College, Cranwell — I for the second time — and having both refused to go into the Army instead, we left school together and thereafter formed a very strong and close attachment.

I can still vividly remember the day when we left Downside. It was June and very hot. The depressing train journey to London, during which we contemplated the vague and uncertain future and thought sadly of a happy period in our lives that we knew was now gone forever. Then the open taxi across London, when I sat on a front seat and thought what a fine pair he made with his beautiful sister Teresa beside him. There was the parting hand-shake, the "Good luck, Paul!" and "Good luck, Micky!", that marked the beginning of our friendship. Little did I dream then that within five years I would be married to Teresa and that both Micky and I would be among those fighting in the air for the survival of Britain.

Although we both took Short Service Commissions, he in September 1935 and I in March 1937 — being determined to get into the Royal Air Force by the back door if we weren't allowed in by the front, it was not until 1941 that we were able to fulfill our ambition of serving in the same squadron and flying together. By that time we had both been well blooded in war. I literally in the Battle of France, and he, after recovering from an accident in France, in the Battle of Britain.

At Middle Wallop, meantime, I had one ambition; to get back into the fighting. It was not that I wanted to, or that I thought I could take it, for after all, I had undergone a good deal of physical and nervous strain in France. As a matter of fact, I had grave doubts as to whether I would be able to do it! In addition, people ranging from a Harley Street neurologist to my own and my wife's family, as well as my Service friends, seriously advised me not to try. I had done my bit, they said, why risk death or further injury? This did not make things any easier. Nor did the knowledge that I would be made an Acting Squadron Leader if I stayed in my present job. However, apart from these red-herrings, the question was really absolutely clear to me. With my experience I would be useful fighting in the air, therefore, whether I could manage it or not, I should undoubtedly try. Perhaps I even thought I had to prove it to myself. What had happened to me before, I tried to put behind me. If I was going to fail, I had to know. In the final analysis, I didn't think I could face the future not knowing.[1]

Accordingly, with the words, "Damn fool!" still ringing in my ears, I turned my back on Middle Wallop and the lovely autumn in Hampshire, to go to No.55 Operational Training Unit, Aston Down, in Gloucestershire. Symbolically, perhaps, winter seemed already to have come to that beautiful county when I arrived and life looked grimmer. However, I was passed fit for non-operational flying and so began my duties as an instructor and set my foot on the bottom step of the ladder I firmly intended to climb.

I was lucky to find that my old commanding officer, 'Bull' Halahan, was the Unit's Chief Flying Instructor. Indeed, several of the old No. 1 Squadron boys were still there too, all of which helped. Five months later, again in the face of protests from a good many people — friends and family, I managed to get a posting to an operational squadron. What is more, it was to No.609 (West Riding) Squadron, Royal Auxiliary Air Force. It was now at the RAF's premier fighter station, Biggin Hill, in Kent.

---

[1] To emphasise this point concerning his injury in France, many years later, Paul had to make a Statement of Appeal in order to try to secure a disability pension from the RAF. Doctor I C Perry MB MFOM DAv Med, a Consultant in Aviation Medicine and one of this country's foremost Aviation Medicine Specialists, examined Paul and his records, in order to be able to support Paul's appeal. One very relevant paragraph in his letter, dated 12 March 1986, reads: "He was allowed to go on flying because it was wartime, with injuries and conditions which now would command instant compensation etc. He should never have been allowed to continue and whosoever permitted him to continue was at fault." Ed.]

Should I admit its commanding officer pulled some strings to get me there? If I denied it no one would believe me. Micky Robinson was still the CO and I was to be his senior Flight Commander in command of A Flight. I was back on the job.

I arrived in London by train on the evening of 5th April 1941. I was not due at Biggin Hill until the following day so I dallied in Town and had an excellent dinner, where and with whom I now forget, but I always make a point of having an excellent meal when in Town. Accordingly it was late when the service car that had picked me up at Bromley Station was halted by the challenge of the sentry at the barrier on the road that ran through the camp.

In peace-time, this road had been a public thoroughfare, but since the war it of course had been closed, and the public detoured by another route. We drove rapidly through the camp, then passed through the barrier at the southern end.

"Where are we going?" I asked the driver, who was a small, compact little Cockney whom I was to get to know very well in the course of the next few months. "The Squadron lives at Southwood, Sir," he replied somewhat cryptically. Obviously he expected me to know this, so I relapsed into silence and wondered briefly what sort of a place Southwood was.

I was not to wonder long. Some two or three miles beyond the camp, Newmarch (that was the driver's name) swung the Ford V8 sharply off the main road, proceeded down a narrow lane for some four hundred yards, and then swung sharply to the right. To my surprise we didn't go straight through the hedge as I expected, but entered a well-concealed drive that led down a hill, up to the left, turned right and finished by circling a piece of lawn in front of a medium-sized Victorian country house. As we bumped along the drive I noticed several large dents and gaps in the iron railings that lined it. This looked encouraging, I thought, and I smiled to myself at the pleasant anticipation of being back with the boys again and a self-respecting member of a front-line fighter squadron.

I was to smile to myself again several times before going to bed. The hour was late and the house wrapped in silence. I knew how to find my room from a telephonic description. As I entered the small hall, however, I saw a light in a room on the right. Pushing the door open rather cautiously, I was confronted with a reassuring scene of desolation. The room was a sitting-room, and the solitary standard-lamp left on in a corner lit up a scene somewhat similar to that which must have greeted the discoverers of the *Marie Celeste*. The room was comfortably furnished with arm-chairs and two sofas and the lighting scheme, which I switched on fully, attractive and diffused.

The pleasantness of the room, however, was somewhat marred by a litter of beer bottles, some on the floor, some on tables, some upright and others lying on their sides, but all empty. A variety of mugs and glasses distributed on sofas, chairs and the mantel-piece helped to complete the scene. One table in one corner was evidently what had been the bar — now merely an odd assortment of two or three bottles of unopened ginger ale, a half empty bottle of rye whisky and a full syphon. As I wondered why the syphon hadn't been let off and emptied, I switched off the lights and mounted the stairs. Evidently the squadron had retired.

Upon entering my room, which was near the head of the stairs, I fumbled for and switched on the light, to be greeted with another sight that made me smile. Opposite the door was a window and against it a chest-of-drawers surmounted by a mirror. Or rather it had been a mirror! Now it was merely a mass of splintered glass relieved only by four bullet-holes! Two more bullet-holes decorated the closed window. On the right hand side of the room were two beds, side by side. In the one nearest the window lay a young man of about 22 years, apparently dead, but with a look of benign peace on his youthful, upturned and very unconscious face. Obviously I had arrived on a party night and couldn't make up my mind immediately if I was sad or glad to have missed it!

After slipping into bed and turning out the light, I lay for a moment and smiled again. Yes, it was good to be back in harness again. The sense of well-being was qualified, however, by the sense of responsibility that taking over the command of even a Flight must and should engender. Could I run the thing properly? Yes, I thought there was little doubt of that. Could I lead it well in the air? Yes, I thought I could. Could I fight again properly? That was what I was afraid of. Yes, afraid. I shivered as that cold hand of fate once more laid its fingers on me. Afraid. I had no difficulty in recalling vividly that rattle and clatter as bullets has slashed into my Hurricane. The loud 'Bang!' in my right ear. The numbing pain in my right shoulder; blood on my neck. I remembered the horror as I realised that I could move neither of my arms as my fighter began to head towards the earth out of control. The desperate struggle to move and to get the cockpit hood open... to bale out... bale out... bale out!

I clenched my eyes shut, bringing myself back to the reality of the darkened bedroom with my slumbering un-named pal just feet away. I was going to have to live with this fear. No one must ever know of it, I must tell no one and show it to no one. It was something I must fight out and beat alone, and with God's help I thought I could do it.

I woke to find the bright April sunlight flooding through the windows and no doubt would have heard the twittering of birds in the trees outside had it not been for a discordant crooning that emanated from a chap in blue pyjama trousers who was shaving by the basin in the corner and peering into a small piece of unbroken mirror. He turned as I sat up and stretched, then suspended his shaving operations to say, "Morning. You're Richey, aren't you? Come to take over A Flight. I'm Johnnie Curchin — B Flight." He held out a large wet paw.

"Good morning," I answered. "Have a good party last night?" My brother Flight Commander grinned and then fell to muttering something about "some bloody fool with a revolver," and resumed his shave.

I liked the look of Johnnie. He was of medium height, broad, with a head set low on rather hunched shoulders. His hair was brown, his eyes hazel, his skin tanned. He spoke deeply and slowly, often with narrowed eyes and with his big square jaw pushed forward. He moved slowly too, but powerfully. He was born in Australia I discovered later.

The general impression was one of strength, determination, stubborness and honesty. I was to learn he was one of the best pilots the squadron ever had. It never ceases to surprise me how different people can be in the air to what they are on the ground, and Johnnie was a good example. On the ground, almost ponderous in his slow deliberation; in the air, quick and bold, dashing, graceful and with a beautiful touch.

While I was shaving and Johnnie dressing, in walked Micky, fully dressed — that is to say, with his tunic collar turned up, his shirt collar open, and a blue silk scarf with white spots, round his neck.

> "Hullo, old boy, how are you?" he said pleasantly.
>
> "Hullo, Micky — I mean, Sir!" I said. We both laughed.
>
> "We were expecting you yesterday actually," he said, "What happened?"
>
> "Well, my posting is actually with effect from today," I answered. "But I'm sorry I missed the party."
>
> "Yes," he said, eyeing the mirror somewhat gravely. Then, "You'd better see me later about that, Johnnie. And get a move on — we're having a Squadron Formation at nine! See you later on Paul."

He then went out and clattered downstairs and we heard his car scrunching on the gravel as he drove off.

"Sydney!", suddenly yelled Johnnie, very nearly causing me to cut off my ear — I use a cut-throat. "Sydney, you bugger! Come here!" and Johnnie lumbered outside. I heard a door flying open with a crash and then sounds as of foul murder being done. Shortly afterwards the thuds and curses and cries for mercy drew nearer and Johnnie entered, dragging a half-clad body by the foot. He let go of the foot and kicked the body in the ribs until it got up. This, presumably, was Sydney; Pilot Officer Sydney Hill.

I beheld a shortish fellow with long lank, untidy black hair, small brown eyes, a mouth that I found later was permanently set in a mischievous leer and a short square face terminating in a puckish chin. At the moment, the hair was dishevelled, the eyes bleary, and the chin covered with thick black stubble!

"Good morning," said Sydney politely. Then, "Ouch!" as Johnnie kicked him on the behind and pointed dramatically to the mirror.

"Do you see that, Sydney?" he demanded, in the manner of one correcting a puppy for a misdeed.

"Yes," said Sydney with his leer.

"Well?" asked Johnnie menacingly.

"You're shooting's pretty lousy," said Sydney. "Got a cigarette?"

This led to a further assault by Johnnie on Sydney and finally the latter, with his arm twisted behind his back, yelled, "I didn't do it — I promise I didn't! Ouch!"

Johnnie let go and stood back with his hands on his hips. "You're a bloody liar, Sydney," he said, eyes narrowed and chin jutting.

"Well, I don't remember doing it. I do remember trying to shoot you when you were asleep," Sydney chuckled at the memory.

"You'd better go and tell the CO, then. He thinks I did it!"

"Does he? Good show!" said Sydney, and fled.

"Which Flight is he in?" I asked Johnnie somewhat apprehensively.

"Mine, the bugger," answered Johnnie. "You'd better step on it if you want any breakfast. We don't have it here—we have it in the Mess."

Obviously only the best of friends could behave so outrageously to each other. My first impression of Johnnie Curchin and Sydney Hill proved correct. They were bosom friends. The slow, deliberate Johnnie was the perfect foil for the gripes and gibes of the irrepressible Sydney; the mercurial and somewhat erratic Sydney depended to an almost pathetic degree on the solid, immoveable Johnnie. They were absolutely inseparable in life despite their different rank and position, and, as it was to turn out, in death. Both were lost within two weeks of each other.

Sydney's greatest claim to fame was that he and Frankie Howell, a former Flight Commander in the Squadron, had shot down 609's 100th enemy aircraft — a Ju88 — back in October 1940. The swastika marking from the tail fin, suitably inscribed, hung, I soon discovered, in the Squadron crew room.

After breakfast I walked across the road — the same one as I had been driven along on the previous night — from the Officers' Mess, through the gates of the main camp, past the office buildings known as Station Headquarters and onto the aerodrome perimeter.

Biggin Hill, as its name suggests, is built on a hill. For this reason the aerodrome had a peculiar kidney-shaped outline. Or perhaps it might be described as roughly L-shaped. There were two tarmac runways, a short and a long, hangars, most of which were destroyed in the Battle of Britain, the aircraft being dispersed at certain points on the aerodrome perimeter.

Conforming to this pattern, 609 Squadron's Dispersal Point was at the southern, or right hand end of the base of the L. No.92 Squadron, the other Squadron at Biggin, was dispersed at the eastern, or top end of the upright of the L.

The main camp buildings (airmen's barrack-blocks, messing halls and so on) were clustered on the left-hand side of the L's upright, while Station HQ, the Watch Office (which controls aerodrome activity), and the Intelligence Section, were grouped near the inter-section of the L's upright and its base. Below, or west of the L's base and parallel with it, ran the road. On the other side of this lay the Officers' Mess, built on the side of the hill and looking across a steep, wooded valley.

Biggin Hill had been probably the most bombed RAF Station in England — perhaps because its squadrons accounted for more enemy aircraft than any other Sector base. During the Battle of Britain, the Station personnel had been dispersed round the Station to avoid casualties — a measure that accounted for 609's occupation of South-wood, for the dispersion was still in force. Most of the camp's buildings had been bombed and the aerodrome's surface smothered in craters. The craters were, of course, filled in promptly to enable the squadrons to continue operating, but the less urgent business of repairing buildings and sweeping away the debris that was not in the way, was left, for time was scarce and the airmen had more urgent work on hand keeping the aircraft serviceable. Accordingly, there was now a certain air of dilapidation about the Station. However, it bore its honourable scars imperturbably.

Demolition and tidying-up was proceeding unhurriedly but steadily. The working of the squadrons from the aerodrome was in no way impaired. And the Mess, which had been evacuated with the rest of the buildings and had been itself considerably damaged, had recently been re-opened. The only signs of the bombing here were the different colour of some of the roof slates and brickwork of the building and some new flag-stones on the two terraces on the west side. Otherwise it stood solid and comfortable as ever it had been. It struck me that the whole Station was symbolic of the efficiency and practical determination of the Royal Air Force.

Once in the Station that first morning, I walked past where the hangars had been, to the aerodrome perimeter. Turning right, I started to walk along the perimeter-track (the strip of taxi-ing tarmac that runs around an aerodrome) towards 609's Dispersal. As I did so, I saw the Squadron taxi-ing out to take-off. One by one they followed Micky out, eventually forming a long snake as they moved slowly over to the far side of 92's Dispersal. I watched Micky turn into wind and stop, his propeller flicking slowly round and round. The others took up their positions carefully on either side of him. Finally, when they were all in position and stationery, each prop flicking slowly round, I saw Micky's prop stop flickering and increase speed until it was almost invisible. In a moment the others had all followed suit, but it was still a few seconds before one realised that the whole squadron was moving forward. By this time they were already covering the ground fast; in another moment one could see that their tails were up.

As they came nearer they seemed suddenly to accelerate. Micky's wheels started to go up almost before one realised he was off the ground and then so did all the others and one could see daylight underneath the whole Squadron. Then in a tearing thunder of twelve thousand-horsepower engines at maximum revs and boost, they flashed overhead. As they climbed away and the noise died, one could hear the rise and fall caused by the pilots using their throttles to formate and I watched the formation close up tight and swing away gently to the left.

There is only one thing more exciting than watching a good squadron formation, I reflected as I resumed my way, and that is being a member of it.

The Squadron's Dispersal area consisted of the usual collection of huts and string of anti-bomb blast aircraft-bays. Petrol and oil bowsers, tractors, starter-batteries, tail-trollies and miscellaneous transport stood about in their allotted places. In one of the bays an aircraft was jacked-up and having a new wheel fitted. Airmen were

Top: Paul's first CO, SL P J H 'Bull' Halahan (right), of 1 Squadron. To his right is Paul's flight commander, FL P R Johnny Walker, and FL G H Plinston. At the extreme left is FO P W O 'Boy' Mould, who brought down the RAF's first enemy aircraft in France.

Middle: Paul in France 1940 (right), with FO I G 'Killy' Kilmartin. The French officer is Capitaine Pierre Scordel, CO of a Potez bomber squadron, who became a friend.

Bottom: The leaders of 609 Squadron in April 1941. Michael Robinson (centre) the CO, and his two flight commanders, Johnnie Curchin (B Flt) and Paul Richey (A Flt).

Top left: Micky Robinson DFC in front of his Spitfire, Biggin Hill, 1941.

Top right: Paul in his well worn white flying overalls, a relic of pre-war flying days. They would see him through the summer of 1941.

Bottom: Spitfire P8271 PR-K of 609 Squadron - 'running up'.

Top: At Readiness in the crew room. (l to r): Keith Ogilvie, Syd Hill, Zbigniew 'Oleo' Olenski, Sgt ?, Joe Atkinson, -?- rear, Robert Boyd, G P Hickman, Bob Mercer (front); far right is 'Goldie' Palmer, -?-, and Sgt W H Walker.

Middle: Pilots of 609 at Biggin Hill April 1941. (l to r on Spitfire): Titley, Jimmy Baraldi, Hughes-Rees, Peter Mackenzie, Francois de Spirlet, Micky Robinson, Tidswell (adj), John Bisdee, Johnnie Curchin, Syd Hill and Keith Ogilvie. Standing and on wing: Tommy Rigler, Paul, Roger Malengreau, G C Bennett, Green, A G Palmer and S T Rouse. Front: Bob Wilmet.

Bottom: Spitfire II PR-J taxies out. Note gun patches on the eight .303 machine guns in the wings.

Top: Johnnie Curchin seated in the 'Enfield Spitfire' - P8098 (PR-Z), one of those bought with money raised by the people of Enfield. Paul's 'G' is in the left background.

Middle: John Bisdee taxies in his PR-H. Note Bisdee family crest by cockpit - a 'fleur de lys'.

Bottom: John Bisdee climbing out of his Spitfire, while the petrol bowser is already topping up the fuel tanks and the gun panels are open.

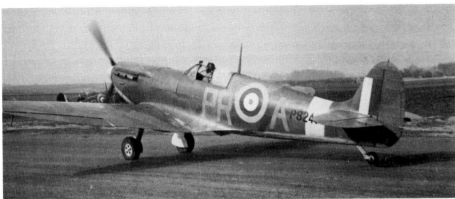

Top: The universal language of the fighter pilot! De Grunne explains the manoeuvre, while the others take it all in; (l to r): Ogilvie, Bisdee, Willi van Lierde, Robinson, Wilmet.

Middle: Spitfire II PR-A, P8241, Biggin Hill 1941.

Bottom: Keith Ogilvie, Johnnie Curchin and E G A 'Gin' Seghers.

Top: Micky resting in the summer sun.

Middle: Wing Leader Biggin Hill, WC A G 'Sailor' Malan DSO DFC (right) with WC Pat Jameson DFC, leader of the Wittering Wing.

Bottom: Sailor Malan and Micky Robinson. Micky would eventually take over the Wing from Malan in August.

Top: A serious John Bisdee, after returning from operations. 609's famous Intelligence Officer, Frank Ziegler, hopes for a good report. Note the whistle hanging from John's Mae West - to attract a rescuer if a pilot ever came down in the sea.

Above left: More 'language' - this time Micky demonstrates how he got another 109 confirmed.

Above right: Paul on the cowling of his Spitfire.

Top: Micky with some of his boys; (l to r): Tommy Rigler, Goldie Palmer, Hughes-Rees, Bob Boyd, and MLR.

Middle: Relaxing outside the Officers Mess at Biggin; (l to r): Jean Offenberg, US colonel, Keith Ogilvie, John Bisdee, Jamie Rankin (CO 92 Sqdn), Pete Mackenzie, Sailor Malan, Micky Robinson, -?-.

Bottom: Press day at Biggin, 24 June 1941, (l to r): Sgt Ken Laing, Joe Atkinson, Sgt Bob Boyd, Boudouin de Hemptinne, Pete Mackenzie, Paul, Jean Offenberg, Jimmy Baraldi; (front):Vicki Ortmans, Tommy Rigler, Keith Ogilvie, John Bisdee, Bob Wilmet. The pets are,'William B Goat' 609's mascot, 'Mack' - sergeant pilot's mascot, and 'Spit' (Malan's dog).

lounging about waiting for the squadron aircraft to return, all that is, except for those working on the new wheel. One or two others were working under the hood of one of the squadron trucks while another was making some adjustment to a petrol cock on one of the bowsers. Otherwise, with most of the pilots airborne, the place seemed deserted, except for a small group sitting outside talking.

The main dispersal-hut consisted of a large wooden bungalow just off the perimeter track. It was divided internally into a number of rooms that were allocated to the various sections that go to make up a Squadron: A and B Flight crew-rooms, for instance, where the men can sit and rest in what is officially described as "inclement weather"; the armoury, where guns are serviced and repaired and ammunition is belted; the electrician's shop, where all things electrical are tinkered with; the R/T room, where the radio men get down to it and the two Flight offices where the respective Flight Sergeants of A and B Flights see that the various forms relating to the engines and airframes of all the aircraft are kept up-to-date. From these two rooms the two 'Chiefies' are constantly emerging to dispense swift justice, to examine with an experienced eye an unserviceable aircraft, to solve a knotty problem, to spur the men to greater effort, to answer the questions of the Flight Commanders or the CO, or all too infrequently to receive the commendation for a job well done!

The front two rooms of this hut were for the use of the pilots. The first was filled with flying-kit hanging on one wall and tiers of bunks lining the other. The second was a sort of living-room, furnished with a stove in the centre, wicker arm-chairs, a number of tables, and decorated with a somewhat bewildering assortment of notices, intelligence-extracts, injunctions to pilots, maps, aircraft-silhouettes and far more detailed representations of uncamouflaged specimens of the fair sex culled from the pages of *Esquire* and *The Sketch*.

In front of the hut was a square of grass roped off with whitewashed rope and green-painted posts and in the centre of the square stood a green flag-pole from which fluttered the pennant of the Squadron Leader of No.609 Squadron RAuxAF.

I joined the group of two or three pilots and Hal Tidswell, the Adjutant, who were lounging outside in the April sunshine, awaiting the return of the Squadron. The groups of airmen were sitting about on steps or on boxes a little way off, likewise awaiting the returning Spitfires. Hal, whom I had met at breakfast, introduced me to a couple of Belgian pilots who had just arrived. Then he showed me my office, a little room in a small hut behind the main one. He then pointed out various things to me and answered my questions.

He was a tall, dark-haired chap with the somewhat leathery complexion and smoke blue eyes that came from living in the tropics (he had been a planter in India). I liked him and found him very amusing. I was later to know him as the mainstay of the Squadron and one of my best friends.

As we stood talking, our conversation was suddenly drowned in the roar and whistle peculiar to Spitfires, of the returning Squadron passing over-head. All eyes were turned up to them as they broke into sections, then formed aircraft-echelon-starboard, and came in to land by sections. Micky broke the leading section up and for a few minutes we watched them relieving the energy pent-up by the restraint of formation flying. Micky allowed himself the liberty of beating up the Dispersal Point, diving at high speed and pulling out so as just to miss the roof of the hut, then going into a couple of upward barrel-rolls, rolling out and dropping his wheels preparatory to landing.

As the machines taxied in, the pilots looking first out of one side of their cockpits and then out the other, in order to see as much as possible of what was ahead (the long nose of a Spitfire is an obstruction to vision in the air but much more so on the ground) all was bustle at Dispersal. The airmen ran out and waved the aircraft into their parking places, some assisting the pilots to turn by heaving on the wing-tip, others ducking under the wings and putting chocks under the wheels. As soon as the props of the aircraft stopped turning, airmen would swarm over it, one helping the pilot out of his straps and gear, another unscrewing the filler-cap of the petrol tank, a third opening the oil-tank, a fourth checking the R/T, a fifth turning off the oxygen and checking round the cockpit.

Sometimes a pilot would pause to explain to his rigger how he wanted an adjustment made to a control surface, or to his fitter that he wanted the slow running altered. The petrol bowsers, towed by their tractors, chugged from machine to machine, oil bowsers were hauled round by hand at the double, starter-batteries were plugged in, windscreens wiped down and polished, and the Squadron made ready for any operation again in as short a time as possible.

Although it had only been on a practise flight, and would not be at Readiness until the afternoon, the Squadron was at war and must be continually ready for anything. Besides the sooner the work was done the better, for the YMCA tea-waggon would be along in ten minutes!!

CHAPTER VI

LIFE ON THE SQUADRON

MICKY jumped from his aircraft and strolled towards the bunch of pilots discussing the practise flight by the flag pole. His face was a bit red and bore the marks of helmet and oxygen mask.

"Gather round and pipe down for a moment!" he called. "That was all right — accept for one thing: Johnnie, who was your Number Three?"

"Sergeant Chestnut, Sir," replied Johnnie Curchin.

"Sergeant Chestnut, you were much too far behind in the battle formation. That's the way people get bumped off. All right?" Chestnut nodded. The group dispersed and Johnnie beckoned to the already disconsolate Chestnut and started showing him something with the aid of his hands, each hand representing an aircraft. Micky caught sight of me and came over.

"Ah, Mon Capitaine!" he said, "have you met the boys. Hal, bring the boys in to meet Paul."

We entered the Dispersal Hut and solemnly, one by one, 'the boys' were presented to me, each with a little handshake while on my part I tried to memorise the name. After that, we fell to chatting and I tried to size up the members of my Flight as far as their character and experience were concerned. Judgement of their ability in the air would have to be deferred for the moment.

'The Bishop' — Flying Officer John Bisdee, had been running the Flight pending my arrival and showed me around. He was a big, tall, heavily-built man with straight blond hair, big blue eyes that slanted slightly downwards, a full mouth, rather a heavy jaw and the general air of a benevolent bloodhound. His slow, somewhat ponderous way of speaking sometimes caused his youngers to refer to him as

'The Pompous Bish'. Bish was young himself but he had an old and wise manner. He was, in fact, level-headed, steady and shrewd.

The rest of the morning was filled with the discussion and adjustment of various administrative details with Micky, Hal and Johnnie. Those settled, I went off to tell the storeman to draw me some flying-clothing and equipment, my own being out of date — and a parachute. It was as I was waiting for these articles, gazing at a map of France and wondering what operations the year would bring, that I heard a voice at my elbow say, "Do you know all about the IAZ?"

I looked round and beheld a tall, fair-haired man of about 30, with a lean face, square jaw and deep-set blue eyes.

"Well I know what it is — the Inner Artillery Zone," I answered.

"Good," he said in rather a sad, tired voice, "Unusually good. By the way, I'm Flying Officer Ziegler and I have the misfortune to be the Squadron Intelligence Officer. How d'you do?"

We shook hands; he smiled a trifle sadly but with an odd humour behind those eyes. I liked him. He, too, was to become one of my best friends.

A loud honking outside drew our attention to Micky waiting outside in his Service V8. Ziegler and I ran out and jumped in behind Micky and Hal. We shot off, Johnnie following in the Flight 'barouche' (Humber shooting-brake) with the rest of the officer-pilots aboard, while a Commer van with the Sergeant-pilots brought up the rear.

"I haven't reported to the Station Commander yet," I remarked to Micky.

"That's alright," he said, "I'll introduce you in the bar."

Civilians and members of the other Services have held it against the Air Force that they are given to talking an inordinate amount of 'shop'. It is true that whenever pilots foregather they invariably, sooner or later, fall to discussing flying. But when this talk is merely calculated to impress lay bystanders, which I think is rare, this being considered bad form and pilots being rather shy about their work — or unless it threatens to scatter military secrets to the multitude, which I am afraid is less rare, it should not be held against them. Flying is a cult, a religion, a disease if you like, which abounds the attention of the whole mind in execution and which also seems to claim it when at rest. The fact that most pilots constantly dream about flying is an indication of its impact on their minds. The trouble is that flying — the act, the thought, the subject of flying — tends to oust all else from the pilot's mind.

It is curious that a business that has to do with air and wind and cloud and storm, things ethereal and transitory, should be to the pilot the one concrete standard. In relation to this standard he looks at life. According to it, his perspective is proportioned. To him, it is the rest of life that is transitory and flying the one constant factor. Perhaps it is because, in flying, he is in closer contact and sometimes in mortal combat, with the elementals of life — that same air, and wind and cloud and storm — and is accustomed to look on death and eternity as a matter of course. The sailor has the same kind of thing to a rather less marked degree. But I am not competent to delve into the intricacies of the human subconscious for reasons. There it is.

There must be many a wife or sweetheart of our airmen, or even his mother, who has wondered just why she does not seem able quite to get hold of him, wonders why he never seems to be quite all with her. It is as if he loved another woman. It is true that he has another love.

In an RAF Officers' Mess, then — or at any rate in a Fighter Mess — an immense amount of 'shop' is talked. In fact the Mess is tacitly acknowledged as the common ground where different squadrons mingle and spontaneously discuss various tactical problems and theories — which is just another argument for the abolition of the sergeant-pilot and to make all of them pilot officers.

The Mess is a very excellent institution because some people, especially junior officers, tend to be shy and hesitant to put their ideas before senior and experienced officers in a formal conference. In the Mess, these same chaps, after a couple of beers, may be seen waving their arms at the Wing Commander and expounding all sorts of fantastic schemes — some of which may be good.

The hand-waving habit, by the way, to which fighter pilots are addicted, has come to be derided as the typical 'line-shoot'. This is probably a hang-over from the pre-war days of sometimes none-too-friendly rivalry between fighter and bomber pilots. In fact, it is a quick and graphic way of describing situations that would otherwise take many words and might even baffle the descriptive powers of an inarticulate pilot. It still usually calls forth a derisive chorus from the onlookers but that is good for a chap and brings him back to earth.

The bar at Biggin Hill proved to be the social centre of Mess life. The ante-room was available for those who wanted a quiet read; there was a writing-room upstairs but it was the bar that was almost universally patronised at this time of day — just before lunch. Lunch lasted from 12 noon till 2 pm, so that those going on Readiness at 1 o'clock could have it first and those coming off could eat afterwards.

As Micky pushed his way through the chattering crowd with me behind him, he answered the "Good morning, Sir," of a number of 92 Squadron pilots. They were a nice bunch, those 92 boys, and a damn good squadron too. Micky led me over to their CO, 'Jamie' Rankin, a well-built, rather thick-set Scot with black hair, a ruddy complexion, a broken nose and level grey eyes.

"Morning, Jamie. I want you to meet my brother-in-law, Paul Richey." We shook hands.

"Well, what's the order?" asked Jamie, "No spirits sold in the morning. Beer or sherry?"

"I'll have a beer, Sir, if I may."

"Sherry for me, Jamie," said Micky.

"Two beers and a sherry," requested Jamie to the WAAF behind the bar. "Nice formation this morning, Michael."

"Yaas," drawled Micky, and smiled at me. "By the way, Jamie, d'you know anything about this extraordinary patrol this afternoon?"

"No. What patrol's that?"

"We've been told to patrol Westminster. Something to do with Budget Day. Ziegler's been told to find a path through the balloons!" A deep voice behind us cut through our laughter.

"Good morning, Sir!"

We turned and I was introduced to 'Stevie' Stevenson, the Permanent Duty Pilot, who was responsible for aerodrome discipline. He was an ex-RFC pilot and wore an Air Force Cross ribbon below his wings plus his WW1 campaign ribbons. Now he was a Flying Officer on the Reserve and also, incidentally, husband of Jeanne de Casalis the actress.

"I'm afraid I have rather a serious matter to report, Sir," said Steve slowly and looking sideways at Micky.

"Go on, Stevie," said Micky with a grin.

"A pilot was flying your aeroplane this morning and he beat up the aerodrome, carrying out low aerobatics within the circuit in direct contravention of King's Regulations and Air Council Instructions, not to mention various Air Ministry Orders on the subject."

"Good show, Stevie! Have a drink?"

"Thank you, Sir, a sherry. Of course, I didn't report the matter to the Station Commander without seeing you first, Sir — seeing that your aeroplane was involved."

"Cheerio, Stevie."

"Cheers, Sir." He sipped his sherry. "I can leave the matter safely in your hands then? I know the culprit will be well punished."

"You know, Stevie, I don't think you've got such a thing as a conscience," said Jamie.

"Well, with all the years of service, I think I've got the thing pretty well in hand," replied Stevie. "Michael, here, is the one without a conscience."

"OK, Stevie, it won't happen again." Micky grinned. "Have another drink!"

"Yeah," said Stevie, and moved off.

"Poor old Stevie!" said Jamie, shaking his head. "What a job with buggers like you around."

Shortly afterwards there was a brief lull in the conversation as the Group Captain and Wing Commander Flying came in and those seated, stood up. The Group Captain nodded a cheery, "Good morning, chaps," to the assembly at large and went up to the bar.

"Morning Michael. Morning Jamie. Have a drink? What's yours Sailor?" He turned to the Wing Commander.

"Beer for me, Sir," said the Wing Commander.

"Beer, please, Sir," said Jamie.

"Mine's a sherry, please, Sir," said Michael.

"A beer for me, please, Sir." I added.

The WAAF behind the bar knew her job as well as being pretty and was already pouring the sherry while the barman drew off the beer.

"By the way, Michael," said the Group Captain, "I've been on to Group about that patrol. Someone made a balls of the order. You're to patrol with one Flight between Biggin and Hornchurch and the other between Biggin and Gravesend. If the clouds stay at this level the balloons will be in them, so you'd better talk to Group about it yourself and suggest both Flights patrolling the Gravesend line or something."

"Righto, Sir, I'll get on to them now if you'll excuse me," and he went out to the telephone.

Jamie burbled something to me through his beer, then, lowering his mug, said to the Group Captain, "By the way, Sir, this is Flight Lieutenant Richey, just joined 609. Group Captain Soden — Wing Commander Malan."

I shook hands with them both. Soden, known throughout the Service as 'Mongoose', was one of the old school of Group Captains, whose decorations testified to his prowess in the last war. He had shot down over a score of German aircraft in that conflict, won the DFC and then a bar while flying in Iraq in the 1920s.

He had a high colour and a jovial manner that went well with it, was popular with his subordinates, but inclined to be the reverse with his superiors because of a certain high-handedness and contempt for authority. Sailor Malan I was more interested in.

A peace-time member of No.74 Squadron, he had commanded it during the Battle of Britain. He not only did exceptionally well himself but led it to a number of victories. He then acceeded to the newly-created post of Wing Commander Flying at Biggin at the beginning of 1941, John Mungo-Park taking over 74 Squadron, which was still part of the Biggin Hill Sector, but at Manston at the moment, which was being used as our forward aerodrome. 'Sailor' — so called because he had been in the Merchant Service before joining the Royal Air Force, was a South African of French Huguenot origin. He was of medium height, very thick-set with a round head set on a rather short thick neck, brown hair, a square jaw and a firm mouth, very blue eyes set level in a weather-beaten face.

His manner was quiet, almost abrupt. When he spoke, he spoke quickly and concisely in rather a low voice, wasting no words. As I was to discover, he often appeared to ignore a remark and at other times merely grunted in reply. Here was obviously a man with no frills and no nonsense about him. The general impression was one of great strength, both physical and moral, absolute honesty, a character as straight as a die and a good deal of gentleness. These first impressions proved correct. I was to know him later on the one hand, as a lion-hearted, fearless leader in battle, a bold aggressive fighter who typified the offensive spirit; and on the other a simple, sincere, kind-hearted, loveable character, a family-man whose nature shrank from fighting and all deeds of violence.

After tea that evening, the Bishop took me up to the aerodrome in his little grey Austin to show me over the controls of a Spitfire. Having been a Hurricane pilot for two years, I knew little about the Spitfire and had seldom even seen one. I also had the Hurricane pilot's conversion: I never hoped to fly a better fighter.

This was perhaps understandable for though an older machine than the Spitfire, the Hurricane had been well-tried in peace-time, had done magnificently in the Battles of France and Britain and had shot down far more enemy aircraft than the Spitfire. Besides, what made most difference was that my own battles had been fought in it, so that I had every confidence in it and I was thoroughly at home in one and 'as one piece'.

I therefore approached my first Spitfire with a certain amount of distaste. I had seen them flying and admitted I had seen few prettier aircraft. But on the ground, to my biased eye, the Spit looked knock-kneed, flimsy and rather silly. It lacked the air of robust strength of my beloved Hurry. However, I had to admit its superior lines in flight. Then she really did look a thoroughbred.

"Here we are," said Bish, as he jumped up on the port wingroot and slid back the hood. "You'd better get in — you'll be able to see better." I clambered in. The cockpit felt too small and cramped.

"Now, let's see," said Bish. "Here's your throttle, the petrol cocks here, up for on; mixture control and airscrew control. Undercarriage here — lever right up and in the slot for up, where it is now for down. Lights over the indicators there. Emergency undercarriage release — this lever on the CO_2 bottle here. Flaps here — no intermediate position. Elevator trim here — forward for nose-heavy. Rudder bias here — forward for starboard, back for port. Radiator shutter here — back for shut. Switches: main engine switches, starter-mag, pitot-heating, camera-gun, IFF, pip-squeak, reflector-sight, generator.

"You won't want night flying stuff now so I won't bother you with it. R/T here — four buttons, one for each frequency. Call-signs and ground-stations you know. Oxygen — tap here, regulator there. Rudder adjustment — those things down there. Seat adjustment — this lever here. Windscreen de-icer here. And emergency hood release here.

"Instruments are standard; blind flying with artificial horizon, turn and bank, rate of climb and ascent, gyro-compass, sensitive altimeter and so on. Compass down there, glycol temperature-gauge, oil temperature gauge and oil pressure gauge here: boost pressure gauge and rev. counter here; air pressure gauge between your feet. I think that's the lot. If I've forgotten anything I expect you'll find it. Oh, yes — the gun button is here."

As we walked over to get my flying-helmet from the Dispersal Hut the Bish gave me one or two tips, regarding boost-pressures, speeds for lowering undercarriage and flaps, trimming for take-off, starting-up and so on. Then, once more seated in the cockpit, I buckled on my parachute harness and fighting harness, closed the small side door, started up, ran the engine up, waved the chocks and airmen away and taxied out to the downwind end of the runway in use.

I flew three circuits and landings, and some mild aerobatics, none of which I enjoyed. I found the elevators too sensitive, the ailerons too stiff, the nose too long and too high, the cockpit cramped and the vision restricted. The only thing I liked was the lay-out of the cockpit. The aeroplane flew alright but the thought of fighting in it I relished not at all! I taxied in feeling disappointed and worried, wondering whether it was the aeroplane or me that was wrong.

Micky was there to meet me. "How d'you like it?" he asked with a smile.

"Not much," I said glumly.

"Don't you worry, old boy," he said. "I felt exactly the same after I'd come off Hurricanes, but after I'd done about twenty hours I wouldn't change for anything. You'll see. Come on, we'll go and have a drink."

This was slightly reassuring, for Micky was an experienced and exceptionally fine pilot and I naturally respected his judgement. What really cheered me up, though — for such is human nature — was the following piece of flattery, thrown to me as we drove down to the Mess.

"I was bloody annoyed when I saw you do those landings," said Micky. I looked at him apprehensively and said, "Yes, I don't suppose they were too good."

"Too good!" echoed Micky. "My God, I was sitting in the car with Baraldi over near the end of the runway hoping you were going to make a complete balls of it and bounce the thing all over the aerodrome and you have to come in and do three perfect landings, blast you. Jimmie's still talking about them. I didn't let him see I was impressed, though."

"Thank you, Sir, for those few kind words!" I said and we both laughed.[1]

Down at the Mess we parked our caps in the hall, ordered a couple of rye highballs and went out on to the terrace. The grey clouds that had persisted since lunch-time were breaking in the west and a ray of red sunlight lit up the Mess and shone off the windows. Across the valley the budding trees were silhouetted in black fretwork against the sky.

The air was occasionally shaken by the faint reverberations of an engine being run-up on its Daily Inspection. There was a sudden double snarl as two aircraft took off and roared over-head on their way to do a dusk patrol. In the air was the first faint smell of spring.

"When is Teresa going to have her baby?" Micky asked.

"About the middle of the month, according to calculation," I announced.

---

[1] Long after the war Paul reflected on the Spitfire, saying: "Every aeroplane is a compromise between what the designer wants out of it and the operational needs. Some have good climb, at the expense of something else, strength probably, because they have to make it light and some have manoeuvrability at the expense of speed, because it won't manoeuver well if its a very fast aeroplane. The Spitfire was a good compromise; it had its faults, like all aeroplanes and it had very sensitive elevators. However, the ailerons were rather soggy. So in some aircraft you could whip very quickly into a turn but in the others you couldn't. But the Spitfire made up for it in many other ways." Ed.

"Well, you won't be doing any operational flying just yet. I want you first to fly your aeroplane about as much as possible and get the feel of the thing."

"I'm perfectly ready to operate whenever necessary," I countered.

"Yes, of course. But there's not much on now and you might just as well bum around and get on top of your form. How d'you like it here?"

"I like the place enormously," I said. "And its grand to be back in a decent squadron."

"It's grand to have you," Micky replied. "What do you think of the Squadron?"

"I like them very much, what I've seen of them."

"They're a wizard crowd really and we've the makings of a damn fine Squadron. But they're awfully inexperienced. That's why I'm so glad to have you. I don't know what's going to happen this year but we must crack in as much training as we can now. Micky lit a cigarette and blew a long stream of smoke into the air. "Well its a far cry from the playing fields of Downside to this," he said after a thoughtful pause.

"Yes indeed," I replied. "Funny how we used to dislike each other at school. Do you remember?"

"I thought you were a shit at school, Paul."

"I thought you were a bloody fool!" We both laughed.

"And then after we left we suddenly understood each other," Micky went on.

"Yes, I think we now have a great understanding. Ah! Here come the drinks."

"D'you remember how hard we tried to get into the same squadron in peace-time?" Micky said when the waiter had gone. "I tried to join you in France, too."

"I've always wanted to fly with you. Now that it's come about it doesn't seem real."

"I wonder if we'll get through this war, Paul. I think you probably will."

"I'm much more confident that you will," I laughed. "Anyway, here's to our partnership." I raised my glass. "A la Victoire!"

"A la Victoire!" Micky replied. We chinked glasses and drank.

CHAPTER VII

BACK ON THE JOB

SINCE the end of the Battle of Britain, when the Germans abandoned day-bombing for night-bombing, there had been a general lull in day-fighter operations on both sides. Activity was confined on our side mainly to interception of small raids, usually single aircraft, that used the plentiful winter cloud cover to attack special objectives such as aerodromes or aircraft factories. Another regular job was patrolling over the numerous convoys that pass continually along our coasts.

The German fighters, for the most part, appeared to be content to maintain small standing-patrols over the French coast, usually from Calais to Boulogne. Or they would make a sudden foray across the Channel to beat-up coastal airfields such as Manston or Lympne.

No doubt larger numbers of their fighters were maintained ready should they be required and we assumed these standing patrols had as their main object to give warnings of any large-scale British attacks. As far as we knew, the Germans had not yet got Radio Location or at least, they were not as advanced as we were, although we suspected they were working on it.

In addition, fighters of both sides were in the habit of occasionally giving vent to their feelings by shooting up enemy trains, coastal shipping and so on and in the case of the Luftwaffe pilots, the Dover balloons; an annoying practice, seeing that balloons cost in the region of £600 apiece!

With the advent of the finer weather that heralded the war's second spring, the Germans showed growing signs of aggression. Sometimes two or three, widely-separated pairs of Me109s would sweep round in a circle very high, over Dover, Maidstone or Dungeness. Occasionally about twenty of them might sweep inland behind Dover at only medium altitude. These tactics reminded me of the previous spring of 1940, just a year ago (it seemed like ten!) when the Luftwaffe was behaving in a very similar manner in France. Then, I and the other pilots of No.1 Squadron would take off eagerly from our French aerodrome, to answer the challenge as they circled over the Maginot Line, or swept round over Metz or Nancy.

Now we took off from our English aerodrome no less determined to shoot down in flames any Hun who dared to cross our coast. But there was something lacking; a certain purposefulness, perhaps, the punch and vigour of aggression and offensive action that alone can bring victory. This, I think was the result of prolonged defensive fighting. But now that the object of that fighting had been achieved — the defeat and withdrawal of the Luftwaffe — the aggressive spirit of the Royal Air Force was tending to wither away for lack of opposition.

When pilots start grumbling about the enemy always having the initiative, having aeroplanes that go higher and faster and not doing any harm anyway, there is probably something wrong. When they also start showing a dislike of crossing the boundary of enemy territory, to "Seek and Destroy", as one Fighter Squadron's motto enjoins, then there certainly is represented a drop in morale. There was a tendency to rest on one's laurels, though we did not realise it.

Had we but known, the High Chiefs of the Royal Air Force were exercising their minds even then on the problem, even working on plans for aggressive action that would make the present Luftwaffe efforts look ridiculous, and, incidently all but stop them. But there was still a temporary period of skirmishing and sporadic scrapping to pass through, an account of which may be of some interest.

My first operational trip since being shot down over France, took place practically without incident. I record it principally because it concerns Jock Shillito, who is distinctly worthy of mention.

On the morning of 11th April, 1941, I answered a call from Ops requesting two pilots to escort a Blenheim to Dunkirk at 7,000 feet. This seemed an odd request, so I consulted Johnnie Curchin, who was reading a book by the stove in the Flight Hut.

"This is a new one on me, Johnnie," I said. "What is it?"

"Oh, that's alright. It's for a callibration flight," he replied, "I'll see to it," and went to the telephone. After a moment he asked for Flight Lieutenant Shillito. "Is that you, Jock? What's all this about escorting one of your bloody silly Blenheims to Dunkirk? Why don't you make a job of it and go to Paris?"

I listened to their conversation on the duplicate receiver. "I would if they'd let me," came Shillito's reply in a Scot's accent. "When will you be off? My engines are running and I'm all ready. I'll be doing two runs, by the way."

"OK, we"ll be off in five minutes," said Johnnie. "Meet you over the aerodrome — and make it snappy!" Jock's reply was not very polite, but Johnnie hung up with a grin. "Shall we two go?" he suggested, hitting me on the chest.

"OK," I said, "You lead."

We walked quickly out to our machines and called to the ground crews to start us up. I climbed in, dropped onto the parachute pack already stowed in the Spitfire's bucket seat, and with some help, was strapped in.

Jock was already circling the aerodrome when we took off. I formated on Johnnie's wing and we both closed up on the Blenheim, before parting to fly one on each side of the bomber, as he turned away east and started climbing towards the layer of cumulous cloud at 2,000 feet. With our wings nearly touching his ailerons, we could just see Jock over the tops of the Blenheim's two big radial engines. He turned and gave us each a thumbs-up before fixing his attention on his instrument-board as we reached the cloud fringe.

A few dark wisps flashed between us and the Blenheim and then we were in it, the ground blotted out, the Blenheim grey and shadowy and sometimes almost ghostlike and invisible. A Blenheim's best climbing speed is lower than that of a fighter, consequently we were bobbing about a bit, and now and then I would catch sight of Johnnie's tenuous outline on the far side. There is something very eerie about formating in cloud, completely cut off from the outside world, without feeling, not knowing in which direction one is flying, or one's height or speed, or whether one is turning or flying straight and level or even upside-down. You can look at your instruments, of course, but one tends to distrust them with no physical contact with the ground, and then, I was so intent on formating with the shadowy aeroplane, it took a bit of courage to drop one's eyes onto the instruments.

One is completely dependent on the leader, who knows all these things, not from his senses, which are absolutely unreliable when blind-flying, but from his instruments which can be trusted. Not having to keep station himself, he can and does, look at his instruments all the time.

I noticed now, that even the Blenheim's rear gunner, who had been merrily traversing his turret from side to side and taking aim at first one of us and then the other, was now quite still, his guns sticking up rigidly at forty-five degrees aft. Jock's head was bent over his instrument panel, Johnnie and I had our eyes glued to the Blenheim. There was no sense of movement, just the all-pervading roar of the engines, which seemed slightly muffled, and an atmosphere of tension and concentration.

Then suddenly it got lighter and the outlines of the Blenheim and Johnnie's Spitfire became more definite. A few wisps, this time white, flashed past and the formation rose from a sea of blinding white cloud into a world of brilliant sunshine and a wide canopy of blue sky. The rear gunner twisted his turret gaily and turned to grin at each of us. Jock lifted his head and Johnnie and I broke away in steep climbing turns to left and right, opening out the formation.

The sudden brightness and the beauty up here made me want to sing, and so I did sing — loudly and into my microphone so that I could hear it above the engine. Most pilots sing or talk to themselves at odd moments in the air and I am no exception. Certainly all of them swear or pray aloud — the two are not far separated — in moments of stress or danger.

The Blenheim climbed to its height, pin-pointed its position through a gap in the clouds then set course for Dunkirk. For us, weaving some three thousand feet above and behind it, it was perfectly silhouetted against the flat, woolly white cloud-layer that stretched in all directions as far as we could see. It was also a perfect silhouette for enemy fighters, I reflected. However, although I expected some to pop up through the clouds each time we turned over Dunkirk, or to dive out of the sun on our return journey, for some reason none appeared.

Soon we were back over England and Jock was rocking his wings for us to close on him once more. We came into tight formation and dived gently but steadily towards the clouds. We plunged into it together and immediately fell once again to our concentrating. Though formating was easier now that we were travelling faster, we had to watch the Blenheim hard because of the sudden darkness. In a few minutes the grey mist around us enveloped us no longer and we saw the earth with fields and houses below us.

Coming down through the clouds always seems to me like arriving from another world, arriving on earth from heaven almost. In the magic world of sunshine and limitless blue sky above, the earth and humanity might be ten million miles away or might never exist at all. The senses of responsibility, of time, of all human values, fall from one like a heavy cloak. One is conscious only of a tremendous happiness in the joy of mere existence. One sings and throws oneself about the sky in an ecstasy of well-being that amounts almost to intoxication. But when one dives down the few thousand feet separating one from the earth and penetrates the thin veil hiding reality, the song dies on one's lips. The remembrance that one belongs to this darker and gloomy world below is not invigorating. The threads of one's life that have been let loose for a brief moment must be picked up again.

This is what had happened now. The sudden returned senses of responsibility and time, bring with them a depression verging on neurosis. Petrol gauges are hastily checked, maps consulted and the clock given more than one uneasy glance; these things once more mean something. The companionship of one's friends forgotten a short while ago, is suddenly longed for and a beer in the Mess with them suddenly becomes the most desirable thing in the world.

In a little while we skimmed low over the aerodrome and broke away in a Prince of Wales manoeuvre. But just as we were starting a dog-fight with the Blenheim, the Controller's voice came over the air:

"Vector two-two-zero — there's a Dornier at 2,000 feet going south from London!" We hadn't much petrol left but shot off on the course of 220 degrees given us. After five minutes the Controller's information evidently became unreliable, presumably owing to cloud so Johnnie announced that he was going back. I went up through the clouds and looked around but seeing nothing, turned and dived down again. Being unfamiliar with the district I had difficulty in finding Biggin and was getting very worried about my petrol. Fortunately I found it just in time. My engine cut just after I got my wheels down, but I usually throttle right back and make a practise forced-landing, and this time I had good reason for doing so, so I made it alright.

Down in the bar before lunch I met Jock. He was a broad, medium-height Scot with a small fair moustache and blue eyes. He asked why we shoved off just as he was about to give us a dog-fight so I explained about the suspected Dornier. I was very sorry we missed the dog-fight, for Jock certainly had his Blenheim weighed up and would give any two Spitfires a good tussle. Later he gave two Messerschmitts who intercepted him the shock of their lives and shot one down with his front gun!

The aerobatics we saw him doing from time to time in his old Blenheim would have been a credit to a single-engined fighter pilot, let alone a twin-engined bomber type. He had one of the war's dull but very important and dangerous jobs, so the DFC he earned was an indication of the way he did it.

This, unhappily, is where Paul's draft for his sequel to *Fighter Pilot* ends. As one can read, it was building up nicely with very interesting descriptions of some of the men he was in contact with at Biggin Hill and 609 Squadron in the spring of 1941.

His mentioning of Jamie Rankin, who was to share, along with 74 Squadron, many of Michael and Paul's adventures in the coming months, is of value. Rankin was 28 years old and when he was given command of 92 Squadron in February 1941, it was his first operational command. Not un-naturally this provoked some questioning comments from the Squadron pilots, many of whom had been with the unit for some time, quite a number having fought during the Battle of Britain and been decorated.

Among them at this time were the experienced Brian Kingcome DFC, whom everyone thought would get the Squadron when Johnny Kent was made a Wing Leader. Tony Bartley DFC was another veteran, who had flown over Dunkirk and in the Battle of Britain, but had just moved over to 74 Squadron; others were Allan Wright DFC, B Flight Commander, Wimpy Wade, Don Kingaby DFM (soon to be one of 92's and Fighter Command's top-scoring fighter pilots) and Titch Havercroft. Among its recent successful pilots, were Johnny Kent DFC, John 'Pancho' Villa DFC, Bob Holland DFC, Philip Sanders DFC and Bob (Stanford) Tuck DSO DFC — yet another who would end up among the RAF's top scorers.

The other Squadron in the Biggin Hill Wing was No.74 — the famous 'Tigers'. Until March 1941 it had been commanded by 'Sailor' Malan, soon to become Fighter Command's top-scoring pilot. It was now led by Johnnie Mungo-Park DFC, who had been with the squadron since the war started. He had around a dozen victories by this time. His two flight commanders were Johnnie Freeborn DFC & bar, who had been with 74 since 1938, and now had a score of around 14, and Tony Bartley DFC, until recently with 92 Squadron as mentioned above.

The Wing Leader, as already related, was the incomparable South African pilot, A G Malan DSO DFC & bar. Older than most — he was now 30 — Sailor had been in the merchant navy between 1927 and 1935, hence his nick-name, so was 25 when he entered the RAF. Thick-set, serious but dedicated, he did not immediately fit the picture of the perceived notion of the typical fighter pilot. But he was a great thinker and tactician, a tremendous shot who could also control a battle. Little wonder he was chosen to be among the first Wing Leaders in 1941. His score at this time stood at 20 destroyed, five probably destroyed and six damaged. He knew his stuff and the Biggin Hill pilots would, and did, follow him anywhere.

No.609 Squadron, of course, was the third squadron in the Wing.

CHAPTER VIII

THE WEST RIDING SQUADRON

NUMBER 609 Squadron of the Auxiliary Air Force had been created in early 1936, at Yeadon, which is now the Leeds/Bradford Airport. Known as the West Riding of Yorkshire Squadron, its emblem became the White Rose of Yorkshire on two hunting horns, the latter denoting the 'hunting' nature of the squadron — ie: fighter. The motto "Tally-Ho" appeared on the scroll under the badge, Fighter Command's code word for "enemy in sight, about to engage".

Originally, however, before the squadron's badge was approved and issued (in August 1941), 609 was supposed to have been a light bomber squadron, its first aeroplanes being the Hawker Hart and Hind day biplane bombers. Not until December 1938 did its role change, the unit joining Fighter Command, although it was not until August 1939 that it begin to equip with a fighter-type aeroplane — and what an aeroplane. The Supermarine Spitfire Mark I.

The Squadron was then moved to RAF Catterick, scoring its first victory on 29th January, 1940. This was a Heinkel 111 engaged after it had bombed a trawler at the mouth of the River Tay, the bomber being damaged sufficiently to convince its pilot to make a forced landing at Wick. Victory No.2 — another He111 — came on 27th February during a convoy patrol near St Abb's Head. When Dunkirk happened, 609, now fully operational, moved south to RAF Northolt, and saw some action over the evacuation beaches.

It continued to operate within 11 Group of Fighter Command, during the Battle of Britain, mainly from RAF Warmwell and Middle Wallop, before moving into the famous Biggin Hill Sector Station, in February 1941. By this time the Squadron was among the well known units of the Command, and one of the few to have achieved over 100 aircraft claimed as destroyed. It had reached this total on 21st October, the swastika tail marking of the Ju88 victim becoming a prized trophy.

Throughout the Battle, the Squadron had been led by Squadron Leader Horace Darley, whose reward had been the Distinguished Service Order. The Squadron had produced a number of successful fighter pilots, among whom were Flight Lieutenant John Dundas DFC & bar, victor in 13 air-fights, but who had been lost on 28th November, 1940, moments after shooting down a Me109E, flown by Major Helmut Wick, a high scoring German fighter ace with 56 victories. Other 1940 veterans were David Crook DFC, author of the famous book *Spitfire Pilot*, Noel Agazarian, whose Spitfire now hangs in the Imperial War Museum in South London, and James 'Mac' McArthur DFC, who had been a flight commander until he damaged his ears. He had his oxygen fail at 25,000 ft, and he fell unconscious until almost hitting the ground. Pulling out just in time, his ears were so affected that he lost his operational flying category, but he had destroyed at least eight German aircraft.

The Squadron had also hosted three American volunteer pilots who had come from the States to join the RAF before America was in the war. Red Tobin, Andy Mamedoff and Shorty Keough, had each fought in the Battle, and later became part of the first Eagle Squadron — No.71 RAF — in late 1940. All three were to die in 1941.

Still more veterans remained with the Squadron in the spring of 1941 when Paul arrived; some he has already mentioned. The CO, of course, was Michael, his brother-in-law, brother of his wife Teresa. The other flight commander, in charge of B Flight, was Johnnie Curchin, whom Paul had met on his first night.

Johnnie was from Australia, born in Hawthorn, Victoria, and was 23. His parents were living in Enfield, north London when the war started, John having joined the RAF in June 1939. After flying briefly with 600 Squadron, he had joined 609 at Northolt just after the Dunkirk show. He too had the purple and white striped ribbon of the DFC under his RAF wings, having shot down eight German aircraft during the Battle of Britain. He had only just been appointed flight commander that month. He flew a Spitfire marked with the name "Enfield Spitfire", a presentation machine purchased for the RAF by the people of Enfield, where his parents continued to live.

No.609 was a pretty cosmopolitan bunch. Pilot Officer Keith Ogilvie, was a 25-year-old Canadian from Ottawa, having also joined the RAF in 1939. He arrived on 609 in the middle of the Battle of Britain, but by the end of it had scored three sure and two probable kills. Then there was John Bisdee, who had shown Paul over the Spitfire's cockpit, another 25-year-old, from Weston-super-Mare. A Cambridge student, he had been in the RAFVR, being called for duty when war was declared, joining 609 in December 1939. To date he had four victories — all Me110s, plus pieces knocked off a Heinkel and a 109. He was big, solid and dependable with a shock of blond hair combed back. Later he would fly off the aircraft carrier *Wasp* and fight from the island fortress of Malta. He still has a piece of fabric from an Italian Cant Z1007 he shot down over the island on 10th May 1942.

Pilot Officer Sydney Hill, from Dorset, had just celebrated his 24th birthday. He had shared in 609's 100th kill back in October, he and another veteran, Flight Lieutenant Frankie Howell DFC, (who had left the Squadron in February), and who was fated to end up as a prisoner of the Japanese (and in 1948 be decapitated by the wing of a taxying Vampire aircraft as he took a cine-film of it). Paul had met Syd on his first evening too. Syd was a trifle overweight, with thick black hair, but always had a smile on his face. Like Noel Agazarian's Spitfire, the Spit flown by Hill when he helped 609 become a member of 'The Century Club' still survives. X4590 can be seen at the RAF Museum, Hendon.

The Squadron was well-served by a number of NCO Sergeant-Pilots, including John Hughes-Rees, from Newport, South Wales, R T D 'Bob' Mercer, from Broadstairs, in Kent, Tommy Rigler from Poole, Dorset, and A G 'Goldy' Palmer (he had blond hair!!). Then there were the Belgians.

There might be more than one story as to how or why Belgian pilots began to be associated with 609 Squadron in 1941, but the accepted one concerns Michael Robinson. Having been injured in that crash, just hours before the 'balloon went up' in France the previous May, he had been helped by some Belgian civilians when his hospital was evacuated. Reaching Pau, near the Pyrenees, a Belgian air force detachment equipped the hospital-clothed Robinson with a uniform, drove him to Bordeaux, where he managed to get onto a plane for England. After the fall of France and Belgium, the Belgian Government set up home in England. Belgian soldiers and airmen who escaped to Britain, were soon being organised into units in the UK, and shortly after Michael took command of 609, he became aware that the RAF were looking for a home for a number of Belgian fighter pilots, so applied to the Air Ministry to have them attached to his squadron. In this way he repaid Belgium for their help in getting him home.

Several Belgian pilots had seen action with various fighter units during the Battle of Britain, 32, 43, 87, 145, 229 each taking one or two. By early 1941, with time to take stock, but with too few Belgian pilots to form a Belgian squadron, it would certainly be a good idea to put a number within one unit. 609 was elected.

Among the first to arrive were Pilot Officer Willi Van Lierde, who had been with Michael's old 87 Squadron in 1940 after serving with his own Air Force, before escaping to the UK. Others were Vicki Ortmans (ex 229), another who had served with the Belgian Air Force in 1940, then escaped to England via Gibraltar. Vicki had shot down three enemy aircraft during the Battle of Britain. He had a younger brother Christian, who would join 609 later. Some had long, fanciful names, often strange and exotic to the ears of their British comrades-in-arms. Francois Xavier Egenoff de Spirlet had also come out via Gibraltar and had also flown with 87 Squadron before moving to 56 Squadron in late 1940. There were two counts — le Comte Ivan G Du Monceau de Bergendael, later known simply as the 'Duke'. He had flown Fiat CR42s in Belgium and then Fairey Fireflys before escaping to England. The other was Comte Rudolphe Ghislain Charles de Hemricourt de Grunne.

De Grunne was among the most experienced of the Belgian fighter pilots for he had flown on the Nationalist side in the Spanish Civil War. He had flown Fiat CR32 biplanes and then Messerschmitt 109Bs, in the famous 3rd Escadra, known as the Blue Group. He is reputed to have claimed 14 air victories in that conflict. When Belgium surrendered, he escaped into France but then managed to get to England by ship. By August 1940 he was already at Biggin Hill, flying with 32 Squadron. He shot down two 109s and a Dornier on three successive days but then was himself shot down by a 109 and badly burned. Recovering, he was then sent to Lisbon on a secret mission to try and discover what German intentions were towards North Africa. After his return he joined 609, back at Biggin.

The Fleming from Ghent, Eugene George Achilles Seghers — known as both 'Strop' and 'Gin' (after Seghers Gin) — had also seen action in Belgium, then escaped into France, and finally came to England by ship with some of the others. He was a little over-weight, but he too had flown with 32 Squadron but had been shot down by 109s, although he managed to bale out unhurt. Robert 'Bob' E J Wilmet, yet another who had flown over Belgium in 1940, was the piano player of the group.

Other Belgians who would join 609 during the spring and summer of 1941 were Baudouin Marie Ghislain de Hemptinne, who had seen action with 145 Squadron in the Battle of Britain. He would join in June, along with one of the most famous Belgians, Jean Henri Marie Offenberg DFC. Known to everyone as 'Pyker', Offenberg was nearing his 25th birthday when he came to 609. He had shot down a German aircraft on the day the Germans invaded his native country — 10th May — the same day Paul was in action over France. Both men had been engaged against a Dornier 17, early that morning, although their actions had been miles apart, and both had been successful, Offenberg in his CR42 biplane, Paul in his Hurricane.

Escaping to England, via a stolen plane to Corsica, then on to Algeria, and finally from Gibraltar by ship, Offenberg arrived at Liverpool docks in July. Joining 145 Squadron in August, he shot down three German aircraft before the end of the year and two more in May 1941. Shortly after arriving at Biggin to join 609, came the announcement of the award of the British DFC — the first Belgian fighter pilot so honoured in the war.

Another to join in April, when Paul arrived, was Roger Malengreau, a native of Brussels. Malengreau had joined the Belgian Royal Military Academy in 1934, was commissioned, then went into the air force. Flying old Fairey Fox two-seat biplanes in an army co-operation squadron, his unit was completely wiped out within the first two days of the *Blitzkrieg*. Getting away into France, no replacement aircraft were available, and soon they had to decide either to surrender or go to England. He too was among the handful who sailed to England on the SS *Appa*, on 24th June and by August was serving with 87 Hurricane Squadron at Exeter. After a brief stay with 56 Squadron over the winter of 1940-41, he arrived at Biggin and 609 Squadron. Roger knew Paul fairly well and he knew Michael too. Roger recalls:

"Though we got on very well, I found Paul an introvert and a dreamer. It might be due to his dreadful experience in France but I don't think his stamina was as good as he would have liked it to be as he often looked very tired. When the R/T silence was broken, the first Michael Robinson would ask is, 'Paul, everything all right?' It didn't effect his flying though; he was an excellent pilot and very good and considerate leader in the air. He was fond of us Belgians.

"Outside our social activities, I can only remember a mishap which could have been fatal to both of us. When he was temporarily controller at Middle Wallop in 1940, he initiated the new fighter formation; three sections of four in line astern instead of the old 'vic' formation. One day in 1941 we took off to France and had to go through a very thick layer of cloud. He was leading Blue Section while I was leading Yellow, when suddenly I noticed four aircraft passing across my beam. I could see his white flying overalls. I just managed to dive followed by my boys.

"We were all very shaken but in spite of the heavy turbulence we managed to rejoin the Squadron above the clouds and carry on the mission. Paul never noticed anything. I presume somebody's compass might have gone wild and I had to take it that it must have been mine rather than his, though he never blamed me when I told him what had happened. He didn't blink an eyelash and we had a drink in the bar later on. I badly needed it!

"Michael, of course, was a very different character. He was communicative and the Squadron was his first concern in life, either in the air or on the ground.

"I met Michael on 15th August, 1940, while on the train from Exeter to London to collect my new RAF uniform, having just joined 87 Squadron. He didn't know me but he suggested immediately that we meet at the Berkeley Hotel at 12.30 pm. His fiancee then, would be there; she spoke good French and would be easily recognisable as she was very beautiful — and she was.

"My worry was that with Pilot Officer pay (11/6d a day) I wouldn't go very far in this luxury hotel! Anyhow, when I arrived the charming girl was waiting for me and offered me a drink... but no Michael. I felt I had to renew the order, hoping he would soon turn up as lunch was out of the question. Well he did, nearly one hour later, having met some friends in the Buttery next door.

"I was very glad when having joined 609 in April 1941, he was our CO. He was very fond of the Belgians who had helped him escape in 1940 while in hospital in France. There is no doubt that he is the one who created what was to become the nucleus of the Belgian section of the RAF. It was he who asked the Air Ministry to send the Belgian pilots to 609 and we took a great part in the life of this Yorkshire Squadron up to the end of hostilities in Europe."

That the Belgians had close links with 609 Squadron for the rest of the war, can be attested in that it was commanded by three later on. There has occasionally been reference to "the Belgian Flight" within 609, although this was never an official term. Belgian pilots did command flights from time to time, among the first being Pyker Offenberg, but each Flight was just a Flight. From the start, Paul got on well with the Belgian pilots, liking them a lot.

One other pilot who must be mentioned, who arrived on 609 Squadron in July 1941, was not a Belgian, but a Frenchman. Maurice Philippe Cezan Choron, from Bethisay St Pierre, was 29. He had lived in Corsica before the war where he was a flying instructor with the Aero Club de Corse, so was a pretty experienced flyer. It is understood that he met Michael in one of Michael's pre-war jaunts around Europe, when he flew from the South of France to the Corsican island. Arriving in England after the fall of France, Maurice joined 64 Squadron at Biggin Hill in October 1940, prior to his posting to 609, where he renewed his friendship with the man who was now his CO. He would often fly as No.2 to Michael Robinson, with whom his life would be irrevocably linked until April 1942.

A trap so easily fallen into when writing or reading of events fifty years after they happened is that one knows how things turned out. The historian has the benefit of hindsight, not available to those whom he may be researching and writing about. If one is not careful, therefore, it becomes all too easy to forget what may then have coloured peoples' thoughts and actions then. The knack, of course, is to understand what went on, while realising the possible limitations of those involved in history. Limitations imposed on the participants by the times and events through which they lived; and in this case, in which they also fought.

In the spring of 1941, when Paul Richey joined 609 Squadron at Biggin Hill, the war was 19 months old. For the first eight of those months, the Home Command fighter pilots had merely been involved in the occasional skirmish with Luftwaffe bombers or reconnaissance aeroplanes, mainly over Scottish naval bases, or along the eastern coast of England. The handful of squadrons sent to France as part of the BEF had likewise only seen the occasional bit of action. That winter of '39-40 had proved severe, and not until the spring did the 'air war' warm up a little, as the Germans began to probe the Allied defences along the famed (or infamous) Maginot Line, or over the Belgium frontier.

Once the *Blitzkrieg* erupted on the morning of 10th May, it had taken the German Army just over three weeks to kick the BEF back to the northern French coast, forcing it then to evacuate out of Dunkirk. By 22nd June the French had accepted German armistice terms in the equally famous railway carriage in the Forest of Compiegne (the same carriage in which the Germans had accepted surrender in 1918). Germany's lightning-war tactics of massed panzer units (tanks) which over-ran all opposition which had already been blasted by Ju87 Stuka dive-bombers, was a proven success. The Luftwaffe bombers and fighters, supporting the army too, had achieved equal success in crippling lines of communication, smashing air bases and gaining air superiority over the battle fronts.

Having then turned his attentions towards Britain, Hitler had failed to dominate or destroy Fighter Command over southern England and any ideas he may have entertained about invading, had to be postponed. To continue his efforts to keep Britain on the defensive and try to limit her ability to produce war materials, not to mention the hopeful possibility of forcing the British people to surrender, he had ordered the night blitz. From the autumn of 1940 until May 1941 he subjected much of Britain to almost nightly bombing raids against towns and cities as well as factories, with Fighter Command, lacking in any real night-fighter defences, almost unable to counter the raiders.

Although few people in government or the military knew it, or suspected it, the Germans were now planning to turn their attentions to what they felt was their real enemy, the communist regime and country of the Soviet Union. The night-blitz all but came to an end after 10th May, 1941 — exactly a year after the French campaign really began, as Hitler and his generals prepared to invade Russia. Meanwhile, Italy, now an ally to Germany in their Axis alliance, was fighting Allied armies in Greece and North Africa, which made further demands on British military men and equipment.

RAF Fighter Command, still recovering from what was now being termed the day Battle of Britain, was still short of fighter pilots, and was now being asked to send pilots and aircraft to the battle zones in the Middle East, which also included the strategically placed island of Malta. And all the while, the Command was trying desperately to increase its overall number of operational squadrons.

In the spring of 1941, neither Britain nor the RAF had any way of knowing that the Battle of Britain Part II would not begin with the improved weather. That the RAF fighter pilots had staved off the air assaults of the previous summer, did not necessarily mean that the Germans would not try again in 1941. Perhaps some of the senior commanders suspected it through various intelligence sources, but to the men in the fighter squadrons, it could well turn out to be another summer of battles over southern England and beyond.

However, thoughts were beginning to turn to other ways of continuing to wage war on the Germans in early 1941, and many seemed keen to discuss ways of taking the war to the enemy. This is often stated in history books but again, hindsight needs to temper this view with reality.

Firstly, Fighter Command was and had been designed as a purely defensive arm. When Sir Hugh Dowding began to create Fighter Command in the late 1930s, with a future war seeming very possible, there were few who envisaged that France and the Low Countries, not to say Norway, would fall to the Germans. If war did come a second time, it would probably be very similar to World War One, being fought out on the Continent, with other fronts created in the Middle East, now that Italy was a foe rather than the ally she had been in WW1.

The only differing factor, apart from certain improvements in weaponry and armour, was that the aeroplane had improved greatly since 1918. There had been raids upon Britain during the 1914-18 war, by both airships such as the Zeppelins, and aircraft — Gotha twin-engined bombers. These had inflicted some hurt on both population and property, but now, 20 years on, the fear of heavy damage and large loss of life from fast modern bomb-carrying aircraft, was very real. The only glimmer of hope lay in the new monoplane fighters, the Hurricane and the Spitfire, whose performances far out-stripped the nice silver biplane fighters of the late 1920s-early 1930s. The other bit of luck was that German fighters would not have the range to escort their bombers over Britain, so the defending fighters should be able to ward off the raiders. That Bomber Command, who in the event of a war, might well be called upon to raid Germany, was convincing itself that its equally new bombers could fight their way through, seems now to be a laughable contradiction in air force thinking.

The 'fighter escort' theory, of course, changed quite dramatically with the fall of France, Belgium and Holland. Now a good part of southern England was in range of Germany's new and deadly fighter, the Messerschmitt 109, as well as the twin-engined Me110, although this aircraft had proved disappointing already over France.

Being, therefore, built and developed to defend, or if necessary, to support allied armies in a possible WW1 type battle-front, (eg, France) the Hurricanes and Spitfires were both short-range aeroplanes. Over either England or if operating in France, from French bases, they would be within radar and radio range of their parent units. If damaged in combat, the pilot stood a good chance of baling out over England, or, if operating over 'the lines' as in WW1, he may be lucky enough to glide back to his French base, or at least gain 'his' side of the lines before baling out.

Therefore, in the spring of 1941, with thoughts of 'taking the war to the enemy' being entertained, one needs to assess the practicalities of such a move.

First and foremost was the range. A Spitfire, in 1941 the RAF's premier front-line day fighter, operating from southern England would have only a limited combat radius once it had crossed the French coast. As the minutes ticked by, the pilot would not only be keeping an eye open for enemy aircraft, but would have the other eye firmly watching his fuel gauges. There were no 'friendly' landing places over there, and he had a very cold and uninviting English Channel to recross before gaining any home territory once more. The British fighter pilot would soon discover in full, just how much Luftwaffe fighter pilots had been up against with limited range when operating over England, and especially towards London. In the summer of 1941, the average time span of a sortie over France, from take-off to landing back, was around 1 hour, 45 minutes.

Flying over France also meant flying either out of range or certainly at extreme range, of British radar and radio. Both were improving all the time, but in early 1941, the greater the distance away from the radar stations along the south coast of England, so the Controller's ability to guide and warn accurately, diminished. Radio too might prove a problem at extreme range. The systems were simply not designed for these kind of operations.

Tactics too would have to be re-thought. Already the peace-time training in tactics had proved wholly inadequate in modern combat situations. It was a throw-back to the early defence thinking that enemy bombers only would be found, then the RAF fighter pilots could line up and attack without interference. Also, everyone had been flying around in vic formations of three aircraft. It looked very nice, and over a cloudy Britain, when squadron and flight commanders had to bring 12 aircraft up above cloud, little sections of three could each climb up and once in the open sunshine, hopefully still be together as a unit and quickly reform. It meant, however, that the two wingmen had to keep close station on the leader, and not so close attention on the hostile sky around them. So of 12 pairs of eyes in a squadron formation, only four were really scanning the sky, and at least a couple of them would also be watching the squadron commander's aircraft, in case he suddenly decided to change course, while naturally keeping radio silence. Radio in itself was new; the old biplanes didn't have it. Early in the war, some pilots thought it a bit cissy even to use the radio, just as some thought it cissy to use oxygen! But that didn't last long.

Becoming a little more offensive would be good for the forces' morale, good for the public morale as well. In addition, with the war in the Middle East starting to expand, keeping up some pressure over

France would help to force the Germans to keep men and equipment, especially fighter aircraft, in France, instead of sending them to support the Italians in the Mediterranean.

All this was in the minds of the HQ and Group Commanders, once it was suggested Fighter Command, as Air Chief Marshal Peter Portal, the Chief of the Air Staff phrased it, "started to lean towards France". It must also have been in the minds of the squadron pilots too. Without doubt they were keen to dish out some of what they had been taking, but many were professional airmen, like Paul and Micky Robinson. They knew not only their own but their equipment's limitations. There needed to be some serious discussions on the "how" and the "wherefores".

The aeroplane the Squadron was now flying was the Spitfire Mark IIa, which had started to replace the old Mark Is in February, although they still had some Mark Is on strength. In May, some of the new Mark Vb types would also begin to make an appearance.

The Mark IIa had an improved engine over the older Mark I, a 1,175 hp Merlin XII, an increase of 45 hp over the earlier model Merlin III. The Mark Vb would have the even better 1,470 hp Merlin 45. The 45 still had a single-stage supercharger but gave more power, running at a higher manifold pressure.

Armament for the IIa was still the basic eight Browning .303 calibre machine guns, four to each wing. Revolutionary in 1938 when the Spitfire first came into service it had proved its worth in the Battle of Britain, although German defensive armour had improved over the summer of 1940. Something better was needed now, something which gave a heavier punch — a 20 mm cannon. The Germans had cannon in their 109E fighter, developed by the Oerlikon company, as well as the 7.92 mm Rheinmetall machine-gun. The RAF had been experimenting with the Hispano 20 mm cannon since early 1940 but it was not until early 1941 that all the 'bugs' were ironed out. Until then the most serious problem had been jamming, but now the cannon was ready for full-scale action. RAF fighters used cannon from then on.

Each .303 machine-gun carried 350 rounds of ammunition, an improvement from 300 rpg in 1940, (total 2,800 for an eight-gun fighter, while total for a four-gun set-up was 1,400). With the arrival of the Mark Vb, its armament was four .303s and two 20 mm cannon. Each cannon carried just 60 rounds, each capable of tearing up an aeroplane or a ground target.

Each fighter pilot had just about 15 seconds of firing time before his guns were empty. With the average burst of, say two seconds, this gave the pilot seven or eight chances to hit his often fleeting target. Any bursts of longer duration soon emptied the guns.

In the Battle of Britain, the Spitfire usually had the edge on the 109, where the pilots were of roughly equal ability, especially at lower altitude. The advantage a 109 pilot did have over his RAF opposite number, was that with an engine with fuel injection, he could put his nose down and dive away, whereas a Hurricane or Spitfire pilot who tried to follow, had his engine cut out, when the centrifugal force drained the carburreter float chamber of petrol. The 109 also had a higher ceiling. But the Spitfire could climb faster, turn tighter, although the 109 had a better performance in a dive.

For the men of 609 Squadron, the summer of 1941 was about to begin. A whole new era of fighter operations was about to start, and Flight Lieutenant Paul Richey DFC was to be a part of it.

Being experienced professionals, Micky and Paul, along with Johnnie Curchin, soon had their heads together to see just how 609 were going to operate on the offensive. Paul had always looked at things in a very professional way, and Michael, although a trifle more flamboyant, was none the less sober enough to try and get things off to a good start.

Operating away from the comparative safety of the English coast was going to take some serious consideration. The Squadron had at least stopped flying in threes by this time. The 'finger four' which would be pioneered by the Tangmere Wing in the summer of 1941 had yet to be universally discovered and adopted, so in the spring, each squadron was experimenting with its own variations. As Roger Malengreau noted, Paul had already come up with his own tactical idea while a Controller, now he was able to put his ideas into practice. Paul told me about those ideas and how they were used:

> "When I eventually got back to air fighting in 1941, I found that although we had gone over to flying in pairs and fours, we were still flying a very rigid formation in 609. I had several discussions (rows) with Micky about this. We used to take off in three fours, climb up to the French coast, each section in line astern, four in front, four to the right and four to the left — but all flying in line astern.
>
> "Micky wanted these fours to stay very close to him and stay very close to each other. The result was, we were so busy with flying in this formation, that we couldn't see what was going on around us. This was fairly general throughout Fighter Command at this stage. In some ways we progressed from the absurd vics of three, but were still a little bogged down.

"Having already seen this in France I knew we must loosen up but we were a frightfully easy target, flying straight and level. Anyway, Micky went on leave for a fortnight and I managed to introduce my own theories. What we then did was that we had the leader's four in longish line astern at the bottom, gently weaving, then above him we had the second four, snaking from side to side across him. Above that was the third four, also snaking, in order to keep the two fours below always in sight. So as the bottom four weaved to the right for instance, the second four would turn left and then right so they could look down on the leading four, while the top four would be doing the same in sequence. So the whole Squadron would snake along very fluidly. Flying in this fashion we were never bounced over France in 1941.

"Later, Micky said to me, at the end of that shooting season, 'You were absolutely right, although I didn't say it at the time.' Even when he came back from that fortnight's leave he didn't say anything.

"But the 'Snake' as we called it, didn't catch on generally in 11 Group or the Command. The Tangmere Wing had quite a different thing; they had the 'finger four' formation under Douglas Bader and 'Cocky' Dundas, etc. We had, of course, learnt the pairs system from seeing what the Germans were doing. By 1940, they had pairs fighting down to a fine art. It took the RAF a bit longer."

John Bisdee also recalls 609's tactics in 1941:

"We soon invented a special flying style for Circus operations. We flew in three sections of four aircraft, led by the CO and the two flight commanders (or their deputies). On the way over to France, each section flew in a rough line abreast, stepped down from the leading fight. Once over enemy territory, each section went into line astern and weaved so that there were eyes looking everywhere. I don't believe we were ever 'bounced' while in this formation. It had a lot of advantages too:
a) each pilot was continually on the move and taking an active part;
b) the leaders felt safe enough to watch out for targets, particularly below. I can remember how we pounced several times on 109s below us, flying in line abreast, who did not see us until too late.
c) without loss of individual flying speed, we advanced over the countryside at the speed of the bombers, if we were escorting any.

"I don't know if any other squadrons used this manoeuvre, but

THE SNAKE

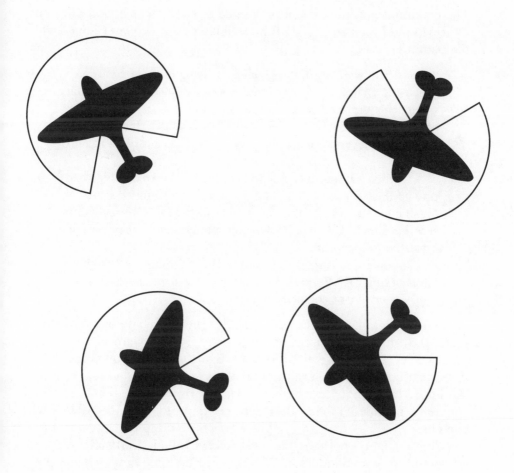

Each section of four formed a 'snake' — so that with three snakes one above the other, and the field of vision from each fighter, there wasn't much of the sky left uninspected.

I took it to Malta with 601 Squadron in 1942, but other squadron commanders asked me not to do it, as we scared them into thinking we were Messerschmitts.

"On Circus Operations, the various fighter Wings took it in turn to do the various escort and cover jobs. It may be that if a squadron only had Mark II Spitfires, instead of the newer Mark Vs, it would be given lower down roles."

The comment that the formation looked a bit Germanic, is confirmed by Raymond Lallemant, one of the Belgian pilots who later joined 609 that summer:

"It was Paul who began the practice of flying in three 'Snakes' to which the Biggin Hill pilots, and especially 609, attributed their success on the Spitfire V, an aircraft slower than those of the enemy. Each 'Snake' was deployed one above the other at intervals of several hundred feet and, whenever possible, against the sun.

"Each section was then able to keep a good lookout behind and protect their leader. In this way the whole sky could be searched for enemy aircraft, so that we never once were subjected to a surprise attack, EA invariably being spotted before they were in a position to open fire.

"The only disadvantage of these tactics was that, at this time, pilots of other RAF squadrons, seeing us fly in an unusual formation, assumed us to be hostile!"

As Fighter Command found out quickly, the Luftwaffe didn't always react to an offensive operation, especially if there were no bombers present. As the RAF realised in 1940, fighters on their own posed no threat, and defending aircraft only risked casualties for no real return. Therefore, whenever possible, a small formation of bombers was generally included in the 1941 Ops as bait, to lure the 109s into combat.

Adolf Galland, perhaps the best known of all Luftwaffe fighter pilots and air commanders in WW2, confirmed my views when I put questions to him about 1941 air operations over France. In 1941 he commanded JG26 on the Channel coast:

"In April 1941, Hermann Goring delivered a big presentation to the Air Force Commanders, in which he announced the re-opening of a second big Air Offensive against England in the spring. This meeting was held in Paris and when he had finished he talked privately to my friend Werner Molders, who commanded

JG51, and myself, asking about our opinion and remarks. We were not enthusiastic at all since our conditions were far worse than in 1940, at the opening of the Battle of Britain. Now we were fighting in North Africa and the Balkans.

"Goring then disclosed to Molders and myself that his announcement of a second part of the Battle of Britain was made by him with the purpose of camouflaging the forthcoming invasion of Russia. I well remember the terrible shock which hit me, because this would be the opening of a major second front. Goring was super-optimistic. He told us that Molders, with his Gruppen, would fight in the beginning of the Eastern campaign for about six weeks, while I, with JG26, should 'do the rest'.

"In the event, JG51 (Molders) did finally fight in the East and JG26 in the West, for the rest of the war."

I asked General Galland what his pilots thought about the RAF bringing the war to them, rather than them having to cross and recross the Channel, believing they would have welcomed this turn of events. I also wanted to know if Luftwaffe pilots were always able to choose to either engage the RAF incursions, or not, especially if bombers were not present. He confirmed:

"The average Luftwaffe fighter pilot did react positively to the chance to engage the RAF over France and could choose to do so or not but only until the beginning of the invasion of Russia. It soon became obvious to us that the RAF was being forced to help relieve, with offensive operations, the pressure on Russia. As a consequence, we fighter pilots were ordered to engage every RAF incursion of German-occupied territory.

"This was ordered then even against purely RAF fighter formations. When Blenheims and later Bostons started their operations with fighter escort, it was demanded of our fighter pilots to an even higher degree. It became mandatory to attack and to try and prevent attacks on German targets during daytime.

"The losses of JG2 and JG26 in these air defence operations in 1941 was very high, much higher than in the East. Fighting in the West was more difficult than in the East. This was partly compensated by a much higher value of personal air victories for awards."
[See also Adolf Glunz's comments in Appendix F. Ed]

Thus the scene was set for the Fighter Pilot's summer.

CHAPTER IX

TAKING THE OFFENSIVE

THE scene had begun to be set at the end of 1940. With something akin to schoolboyish enthusiasm it was suggested fighter pilots fly over to the French coast, and if they saw anything that looked German, shoot it up, then zip back to England fast. With the well known flair of RAF fighter boys, this seemed extremely daring and 'press-on', and over those early days a number of these sorties by the odd pair of Hurricanes or Spitfires, took place.

At first they were called Mosquito operations, someone's humour, no doubt, knowing that while they could not harm the might of the Wehrmacht very much, these 'mosquito bites' could be very irritating! Later the name was changed to Rhubarb sorties. Any number of such sorties were flown over the next couple of years, usually in poor weather, so that the pilots could use cloud cover for surprise as well as defence if they ran into enemy aircraft. Usually flown in twos, sometimes fours, anything was likely to be attacked. Trains, road transport, gun emplacements, troops marching along a road, or parading in some square. Occasionally an airfield might be risked, sometimes ships off the French coast, or barges on a river or canal. Some were more dangerous than others, but flying fast and low, even a lucky shot fired by a soldier's rifle could prove fatal. If lucky the pilot might manage to belly-in. If unlucky he would dive straight in!

The pilots occasionally got involved in these types of operations, but during the month Paul arrived, there was little action save for some patrols and another escort to a calibration Blenheim to Dunkirk. The month of May was to see a change in the Squadron's recent fortunes.

Once it had been decided to begin an offensive stance, provided the Luftwaffe didn't check-mate it all with further large-scale raids upon Britain, HQ Fighter Command's planning staff put together ways by which the day fighters could take on the enemy.

The first idea was to mount fighter sweeps by several squadrons of Hurricanes and Spitfires, which would sweep round areas of northern France, engage Me109s which rose to oppose them and shoot them down. There had been no pre-war training in operating in any larger formation than squadron strength — 12 aircraft, flying in their four vics (sections) of three or occasionally displayed in six aircraft (two sections) in echelon, although this seemed mainly for the benefit of camera men taking pictures of the aircraft in flight. The echelon was, however, a tactic, whereby two sections would peel off to make an attack, or as a formation in preparation for joining a landing circuit. Now the proposal was for anything from two to four squadrons to be formed into a 'Wing' and to operate in Wing strength.

This had to be practised, for it was not easy to arrange possibly three squadrons, totalling 36 aircraft, into some sort of manageable formation. It had been tried at the time of Dunkirk, when for the first time fighters had to operate away from UK air-space, off and over the French coast. The reason that made this necessary was the discovery that the British fighters were nearly always outnumbered when operating in just 12-man units, by anything up to 40-50 Me109s, who were escorting their bombers into the battle area. To counter this, 11 Group of Fighter Command, commanded by Air Vice-Marshal Keith Park, ordered groups of two or three squadrons to operate at the same time over the evacuation. Each squadron took it in turns to lead the Wing, the thought being that this would usually be a squadron leader, or certainly a senior flight commander, but things were never that straightforward. Battle casualties sometimes made it necessary for the squadron, and therefore, the Wing, to be led by perhaps a flying officer, merely because it was a particular squadron's turn to lead! So one had the ludicrous situation of, say, a flying officer leading 36 fighters, while two perfectly good squadron leaders trailed along with their own units.

Once, however, the Wing arrived off Dunkirk, they never operated as a whole, nobody had been trained or even thought about how that could be done, so generally the individual squadrons went their own way, which then defeated the object of massing more fighters to counter the larger groups of 109s.

The first real attempt by Fighter Command to mass fighters into a Wing and to train them to operate as such, was the famed Big Wing, organised by Air Vice-Marshal Trafford Leigh-Mallory's 12 Group, during the Battle of Britain. Keith Park's 11 Group took the brunt of the Luftwaffe's assaults, although he could call for support from both 12 and 13 Groups as necessary. When 12 Group were called upon, they generally found the enemy were already turning for home, or well on their way, and an additional squadron or two didn't make a great deal of difference.

Having more time to think about tactics, 12 Group felt that if they could get three Squadrons airborne, and fly over 11 Group's area in time, this mass of fighters should be able to inflict heavy casualties on a force of raiders. The squadrons chosen for this experiment operated from RAF Duxford, and were led overall by the dynamic air fighter, Douglas Bader, CO of 242 Squadron, who had lost both legs in an air crash in 1931. There has been much controversy on how the '12 Group Wing' was used, or might have been used, (or even, should it have been used) which we will not go into here. It is true to say that the concept was right, but circumstances were against it. Nevertheless, the concept was now to be tried in different circumstances, so that by early 1941, there were at least a few air commanders who had gained some experience of operating and leading multiple squadrons.

The fact that Leigh-Mallory was given command of 11 Group, at the end of 1940, and it would be his Group which would mount the main summer offensive over Northern France, helped, for his enthusiasm for Wing formations was now to bear fruit.

The main requirement now was for men to lead the new Wings. Douglas Bader was an obvious first choice, and he was given command of the Tangmere Wing in March 1941. The choice of wing leaders needed to be very selective. It had already been found that command by seniority in wartime was not necessarily the best policy. War flying — successful war flying — needed men who could command both in the air and on the ground, lead with an ability to assimilate the overall view of the operation, and be both aggressive but responsible — knowing when to retreat as well as attack.

Among the first wing leaders were men of proven ability as air fighters and air leaders. It was soon evident that one did not always lead to another. There were superb air fighters, men who could shoot well and fly well, and who built up a good score of victories, but who could not lead others in the air. Likewise there were those who could lead and command well, but just didn't seem to be able to shoot down many hostile aircraft. If they could do both then all well and good.

Two other early wing leaders were Sailor Malan, and John Peel. Malan had been leading 74 Squadron since the time of Dunkirk, and as already mentioned, he had scored around 20 victories. Being based at Biggin Hill, he got the Biggin Wing to lead. John Peel DFC, like Malan, was a bit older than most, 29. He had joined the RAF in 1930 and during the Battle of Britain had led 145 Squadron, scoring half a dozen assorted victories. He was given command of the Kenley Wing.

Hornchurch had a slightly different set-up. The Station Commander was Harry Broadhurst DFC AFC. He was even older — 35! He had transferred to the RAF from the army way back in 1926 but by early 1939 was commanding the famous 111 Squadron, having won an Air Force Cross in 1937, soon adding one of the early WW2 DFCs to this, for engaging an enemy aircraft in extremely hazardous weather. Taking command of Hornchurch at the end of 1940, he was not obliged to fly on operations, but he did. He often led his squadrons in 1941, effectively leading the Hornchurch Wing, although in June 1941 officially the Wing Leader was 25-year-old Wing Commander J R Kayll DSO DFC, who had commanded 615 Squadron in France and during the Battle of Britain. Joe Kayll had a dozen air combat victories.

North Weald Wing went to Wing Commander R G Kellett DSO DFC. Joining the RAuxAF in 1934 Ronald Kellett had commanded the Polish-manned 303 Squadron in 1940, receiving the Polish Virtuti Militari 5th Class in December. He had gained half a dozen victories, coming to North Weald from command of 96 night-fighter Squadron. One would have thought Kellet would have been the obvious choice to lead the Northolt Wing, where the Polish fighter squadrons were based. However, the 'Polish' Wing was led by Witold Urbanowicz, then aged 33. His first victory in the air had been gained in peacetime (in 1936), a Russian aircraft shot down over Eastern Poland. Making his way to England after the fall of Poland, he had flown with 145 Squadron in the Battle of Britain, then 303 Squadron. In all he scored 17 kills in 1940, being awarded four Polish decorations and the British DFC. (He would gain three more kills flying with the Americans in the Far East.)

These then would be the fighter Wings which would lead the way during the summer of 1941, in taking the new air war to the enemy. They would also be supported by similar Wings created in 12 Group, operating from Duxford or perhaps Coltishall, but who would fly down into 11 Group's territory to refuel.

The first operation actually took place as early as 10th January 1941, although a haze prevented it starting until just before noon. Three squadrons from North Weald — not yet officially a Wing — were led by the Station Commander, the legendary Victor Beamish DSO DFC

AFC, who was 38 years old, but an aggressive fighter from County Cork, who had entered Cranwell as a cadet in 1921. Although he had no need to fly operationally, that didn't stop him. When his boys were in the air, so too was he. He had a number of kills to his name and an even longer list of probables and damaged. Three squadrons from Hornchurch would also take part as well as three more from Biggin Hill, the latter providing a force in support of the others' withdrawal. Six twin-engined Blenheims were the raiding force, set to bomb dumps in the Foret de Guines.

These operations were given the name of 'Circus', which was generally a small force of light bombers from 2 Group, escorted by Hurricanes and Spitfires. The target was unimportant, but the RAF themselves had learnt during the latter stages of the Battle of Britain, that there was no sense in RAF fighters taking the air against German fighters, which on their own posed no threat to Britain. Due, of course, to the shortage of pilots and aircraft in 1940, Keith Park had soon ordered that enemy fighter sweeps should not be engaged, and only raiding forces which had bombers amongst them need be attacked.

The Germans had countered this in late 1940 by sending over fighters carrying bombs, sometimes escorted by other fighters. Once the fighter-bombers had dropped their small bombs, they then became the deadly Me109 fighter once more. The RAF didn't adopt these latter tactics, relying solely on a small bomber force to be the bait. And bait was needed if the Luftwaffe fighters were to be lured into the air and destroyed by escorting RAF fighters. That was the theory, anyway!

During the spring, following the first few Circus operations, some of which produced reactions from the 109 pilots, sometimes not, the overall plan of campaign gradually developed. Circus operations as such — each numbered consecutively — continued, but became a little more sophisticated. From experience, it was found that in addition to bombers and escorting fighters, the escorts needed to have very specific tasks if the bombers were to survive being the bait, and the maximum of hostile fighters were to be shot down.

From March onwards when the Wings really began to operate as Wings, each would take it in turn to be the Close Escort, Escort Cover, Cover Support, Extra High Cover, Target Support, Rear Support, and so on. This did to some extent depend on the equipment a Wing used. In early operations some of the squadrons still flew Hurricanes, and so they would generally be assigned as Close Escort. Later, when Spitfire Vs began to replace Spitfire IIs, the Vs usually got the higher escort work, while Hurricanes were taken from these operations and given other work. One useful task Hurricanes performed for a while was to patrol over the Channel or the Goodwins, to help with the withdrawal back to England, for on occasion 109 pilots might pursue RAF aircraft way out over the sea.

To explain the various Circus tasks is fairly easy. The Close Escort Wing would usually be two, sometimes three squadrons. Their job was to stay in close escort contact with the bombers and not drift away for anything. They were the final line of defence and responsible for the bombers' safety.

Escort Cover Wing, two or three squadrons, would, as the name suggests, give cover and protection to the Close Escort boys, while Extra High Cover — perhaps just one or the third Wing squadron, would keep watch from high up to help protect the whole lot from a high 'bounce'. If they couldn't or didn't engage, they should certainly be in a position to warn the lower squadrons of an impending attack.

Target Support Wing or Wings, would fly directly or indirectly to the proposed target area. They would not be part of the bomber/fighter formations, as their job was to be more free-ranging in and around the target area, hopefully reaching the target just ahead of the bombers in case the enemy Controller had guessed at the target and already sent some fighters to it, and they might also stay until the bombers had departed, fuel willing, hoping then to take on any straggling 109 pilots who had arrived at the 'party' area too late.

Rear Support Wing would give cover to the returning formation, by either staying just off the French coast — but out of AA range — or by sweeping just inland to engage any 109s which had headed for the coast with a view to attacking the returning Circus aircraft. There might also be a Diversion Wing, two or three squadrons sweeping inland near to the operation, hoping their presence would divert 109s away from the main 'Show'. Being totally free of the Circus, this Wing could engage 109s without being in any way tied to the Circus — a free hand — while at the same time, by splitting the enemy fighter force, the main Circus fighters would be able to deal more easily with the reduced numbers of 109s homed in on the bombers.

These then were the main tactics used by Fighter Command in the summer of 1941, although slight variations were adopted in the light of further experience. Sometimes for instance, it was deemed necessary for the target being attacked to be a little more important, where its destruction might be desired. When, therefore, there was a real need for the target to be bombed, and the operation was not mounted merely to lure 109s into combat, the operation became known as a

'Ramrod', rather than Circus. If the operation was against shipping in the Channel, off the French coast or even in a French port, the operation was called a 'Roadstead'.

There might still be a pure fighter sweep, without bombers, mounted in order to confuse enemy radar into thinking bombers might be present because they usually were. These sweeps, as well as the diversionary sweeps, would later be termed 'Rodeo' — a sweep over enemy territory without bombers. One last coded operation was the 'Jim Crow'. This was basically a fighter reconnaissance sortie flown over the Channel, or near the enemy coast, looking for enemy shipping, etc. Often this type of operation was assigned to a specific squadron, 91 Squadron at Hawkinge being the most famous. But any squadron might be asked to fly a Jim Crow mission, which might cover any form of reconnaissance gathering Op. The RAF used Jim Crow sorties towards the end of the Battle of Britain, its two pilots checking over an incoming raid, to ensure it was pure fighter, (ie, no bombers present) so that it could be ignored. The Germans appeared to use this tactic too during 1941, a pair of 109s often being seen high up, making no moves to engage anyone, and obviously reporting back to their ground controller that there were or were not, bombers present, or to confirm the direction and strength of the incursion.

For their part, the German fighter pilots were not fools. They might have realised that they had lost the advantage in the Battle of Britain, or perhaps more accurately, they had not lost, merely had not won! But they were still part of a victorious team which had defeated and conquered most of Europe and were winning in Greece, North Africa, pounding Malta, sinking shipping in the Atlantic, and so on. There was as yet no sign of them losing the war, far from it.

So why should they give the RAF the satisfaction of constantly engaging their puny forces of half a dozen Blenheims, closely protected by several dozen fighters, when there was no real reason to do so? What if some French factory or power station might be damaged or even destroyed, or a fuel dump or lorry park be bombed? Bombs were not falling on German towns or civilians in these small daylight pin-pricks, so if they did react, they only engaged if they saw they had an advantage. If the escorting Spitfires seemed a little out of their normal positions, then a quick pass at the bombers might produce a kill. If not, then, forget it. Only later that summer (as Galland has already mentioned), were the German fighter pilots ordered to engage at all times.

In 1941, the RAF pilots often reported the Luftwaffe pilots being non aggressive on some days, more aggressive on others. This all depended on how the German pilots saw the raid. There was no point in diving in with all guns blazing, shooting down one Blenheim and perhaps a Spitfire, if they might lose several Messerschmitts. The whole object was to inflict some hurt on the RAF group, with nil losses. That's how you win.

And if they wanted to be aggressive, then they could be and were. After all, they were now fighting over their own (if occupied) territory, so if they were shot down or damaged, they could bale out or crash land, without being captured as they had been when operating over England the previous summer. The positions were now totally reversed from that conflict, where the RAF fighter pilot if he baled out was usually back with his squadron within a few hours. Now if he was hit, he had to consider (if allowed the choice) either baling out and going 'into the bag' for the duration, or if he thought he might make it back before his engine stopped or fuel drained from a damaged fuel tank, could he get over that Channel? This stretch of sea was as forbidding to him as it had been to his German counterpart a few months earlier.

So there was a good deal to consider, not only from a commander's point of view but also from squadron level. The new wing leaders too had a tremendous responsibility suddenly thrust upon them, something which was totally new, and for which there had been little or no thought or training before the early part of 1941. Elevated from squadron to wing commander, he had now anything up to 35 lives as his direct responsibility (he being the 36th pilot).

He had not only to position his squadrons, flights and sections, but had to ensure each were in the best position for either defence or attack, help keep a watch on the hostile sky, and if battle was joined, try for as long as possible to keep some measure of control on his pilots, not just let them dive away after speeding 109s, which might expose and endanger the bombers. After this, if at all possible, he had to try to reform as much of his force as he could, either to continue with the operation, or to make a reasonable withdrawal without losing any stragglers to 109 pilots who were more than adept at picking off the slow, the inexperienced or the unwary.

As Paul Richey began to contemplate his return to operational flying, to see if he could once more face the enemy, following his near fatal experiences over France the previous May, all of the above was slowly about to unfold before him. At that moment, April 1941, he was with a quite successful front-line squadron, flying the most advanced British fighter aeroplane of the day, and soon to fly an even better one. He was a professional, among professionals and experienced amateurs. He knew he was part of a team fighting a deadly enemy, who themselves had a superb front-line fighter in the Me109E, as well as the even better Me109F which were beginning to appear, in a war which wasn't going to go away for a very long time.

The 109F looked very different from the 109E. It had rounded rather than square wing-tips, and the engine cowling was more stream-lined. Gone were the two tailplane struts which made the E-model so identifiable. Armament was changed in the first F-models. To make the whole craft lighter, all wing guns were removed. The F-1 carried two 7.92 mm MG17 machine guns in the upper cowling and one Oerlikon MG FF/M 20 mm cannon mounted between the engine cylinder blocks, firing through the propeller boss. In the F-2 model this latter gun was replaced by a Mauser 15 mm machine cannon which was electrically operated. The 109F began to re-equip fighter units in the spring, the first units to get them being the Stab (Staff) Staffel and the First Gruppe of Galland's JG26, in March.

Paul had survived France — just. Would he survive 1941? Would he survive the next few weeks? Would he survive his first combat since being shot down? He was now a Flight Commander, with men under his command, who would be looking to him for leadership, guidance, courage and inspiration.

There were other responsibilities too, other things on his mind. On 15th April Paul became a father, and Micky an Uncle. Teresa had given birth to Ann, in Stroud, during a blitz on nearby Bristol. As 609 Squadron's diary announced: "Birth of a daughter today to Flight Lieutenant Richey, who is the only member of the Squadron to have reproduced himself." Would he be around to see her grow? Have the chance to help shape her future? Only the immediate future and that first all important combat would tell. He had only to touch his neck, and see that still terrible scar in the mirror to know how lucky he had been last time.

CHAPTER X

IN ACTION OVER FRANCE

THE day Paul became a father, the Prime Minister, Winston Churchill visited Biggin Hill, not that Paul was at Biggin on this day. Benghazi, a port on the Libyan coast had just fallen, so the Prime Minister had more than enough on his mind. A couple of days later, Paul's brother flight commander, Johnnie Curchin, despite his rank and position, was ordered by the Station Commander, Group Captain Dickie Barwell DFC to attend a funeral. The unfortunate deceased, a pilot in another squadron, had been killed while slow-rolling at low level. Curchin had then been caught doing the very same manoeuvre — hence the punishment!

Syd Hill was proving to be quite a boistrous member of the Squadron, evidenced on several occasions, not least during one April evening's foray into London by Micky and his pilots. They had gathered at one of their favourite watering-holes, Prunier's, where Micky and Keith Ogilvie competed to see which of them could remain inverted the longest. One assumes there was some point of honour here! The boys then adjourned to The Suivi nightclub, but there were few who could remember what had happened here. Later, Hill, minus his jacket, wearing a canary coloured sweater, his hair dishevelled, was spotted entering Lyons Corner House, shouting impossible demands in a loud murky voice, then being eased gently to a seat by two loyal taxi drivers.

A few days later, 27th April, was Syd's birthday, which proved a good excuse for a party. A game of snooker degenerated into a game of hockey, using the balls and cues, followed by a duel between Hill and the Squadron Intelligence Officer, Frank Ziegler, using soda syphons; an event which quickly cleared the bar. The party then

adjourned to the pilots' off-camp living accommodation at Southwood, where later, Syd Hill was found lying flat on the floor of his
bedroom. Gently lifted onto his bed, his sole recollection was the sight
of the Station 'Spy', Flight Lieutenant de la Torre, with cap reversed,
shouting that he was the fire brigade, and that all fires and bombs had
been satisfactorily dealt with! Syd hopefully enjoyed his birthday; it
was to be his last.

Things became suddenly serious and very active on 29th April. In
three separate operations, the Squadron became engaged with
Me109s. In the morning they escorted Blenheims across the Channel
at zero feet, to attack four ships sailing between Dunkirk and Gravelines. During the attack six Me109s dived out of cloud. In the skirmish
which followed, several 109s were shot at and Sergeant G C Bennett
disappeared. Bennett had been one of the first NCO pilots to join the
Squadron and had been shot down and wounded off Dunkirk during
the evacuation. He had only just returned to the fold, now he was
missing — again off Dunkirk. This time there was no happy-ending.
Bennett had been killed.

Shortly after 2 pm the Squadron flew a patrol to Dungeness at
26,000 ft and had another skirmish with four 109s. Hill got a couple
of them on his tail, Keith Ogilvie firing not only at them but at Hill
too — which amused them both — later!

An hour afterwards the other Flight had a similar fight although
positive results were again impossible to assess. 'Duke' Du Monceau
had his first shot at a 109, but didn't see any hits.

May began. On the 4th, Paul saw his first enemy aircraft from the
cockpit of an aeroplane for a year. He led off his A Flight to patrol
above Mayfield and Dungeness. Over the latter, at 26,000 ft, they saw
two Me109s which attempted to lure the Spitfire pilots over the French
coast. Not to be drawn into any trap, Paul began to circle mid-
Channel, and soon the two 109s returned, bringing two pals with them!
You don't catch a veteran that easily. The four Spitfires and four 109s
circled each other at a distance, neither seeing the chance of any
advantage and soon the 109s headed back into France. The only firing
came from a flak-ship, then some AA guns at Dover, both of which
practised on the Spitfires.

Micky hit a 109 on the 7th but could only claim a 'damaged'. Micky
led A Flight in an escort to a two-seat Defiant, which was going to
spot the fall of shells from heavy guns at Dover, which would fire into
Calais. There was no radio link with the Defiant so Micky detailed
Roger Malengreau to broadcast any visual signs from the Defiant
crew. Later the Defiant broke off and went home, replaced by a

Blenheim which did not wait for the escorting Spitfires to take station. Malengreau however, kept with it at sea level where they were attacked by Me109s which scored hits on the Blenheim.

Meanwhile, four more 109s came headlong at the covering Spitfires which had now reached the location above the other two aircraft. Seeing the danger Micky pulled up his nose and fired at the leading 109 following it round until he was inverted. Seeing the other 109s begin to dive away, he throttled back and fired at them as they over-shot him. One appeared to be hit, going down at a steep angle with black and white smoke coming from it and shedding small pieces of metal. As he turned and looked down again, he saw a splash, thinking it was his 109, but in fact it was the poor Blenheim. The next day was Micky's 25th birthday — and what a day it proved to be.

Late in the day of the 8th, the usual 'stooge' patrol was flown, take off coming at ten minutes to five in the afternoon. These stooge patrols had to be mounted as 109s were using the south-east corner of England as their playground in the spring of 1941. They would nip across the Channel at either nought feet and try to shoot up something on the ground — quite often using RAF Manston as a prime target, or hang around at great height, hoping to bounce any RAF aircraft which might be struggling up to see what was happening.

Flying at 15,000 feet over Maidstone, Control spotted some activity on the radar, out over the Channel. The Germans appeared to have a pilot of theirs sitting in a dinghy, some 109s keeping him in sight and giving cover in case some British rescue effort came along. Indeed, an RAF launch had been sent out to investigate, but this was set upon by the 109s and by the time 609 Squadron had been vectored out over the sea, the boat was on fire with two Me109s circling around it.

Micky Robinson ordered Blue Section to remain as top cover, then led the others down but the 109s saw them and scooted off towards France. However, up above, Blue Section were attacked by more 109s, Blue 3, Sergeant Mercer, being hit. Undismayed, Mercer went after two 109s which dived by him, hit one with a burst of fire, seeing it dive vertically, trailing smoke. Down below, Red and Yellow Sections had reformed, only to spot a second rescue boat and more 109s. Leaving Yellow Section as cover, Robinson took Red Section, plus Blue 1 and for some reason, Yellow 4, down on the Messerschmitts.

Robinson immediately shot one into the sea, while Johnnie Curchin, Red 2, fired at two others, one of which also went into the water, while the second was hit and shot down by Sergeant Hughes-Rees (Yellow 4). Curchin's Spitfire was then hit by a cannon shell in the wing, but he got the machine home despite it being covered in German oil plus a jammed aileron. Blue 1, Tommy Rigler, shot down another while his No. 2, Goldy Palmer, chased two towards Calais, but then he heard a call over the R/T — "Beauty Leader being fired on!" Robinson had chased another 109 also to the French coast, shot it down into the surf, when he was attacked by nine more very angry 109s. Now out of ammunition, Robinson turned for home, Palmer coming to his rescue. Palmer saw a 109 lining up on his CO's tail. Firing twice, he saw hits on the 109, seeing the German's propeller appear to slow down but he was then attacked himself. He last saw the 109 gliding down, apparently out of control.

Meantime, Paul, heading Yellow Section, was dutifully keeping top cover as the scrap went on beneath them, and even though they themselves were attacked, several 109s veered away when they saw the covering Spits. Paul and his two companions even saw Rigler despatch his second 109, which went down in flames. As Rigler followed through some cloud he saw the wreckage burning on the water. Paul also confirmed seeing Rigler's first 109 go down, Rigler himself seeing a large patch on the sea which he believed was where his first victim had gone in.

As the Spitfires drifted back to base, news of the action had already reached Base HQ via the Duty Controller in the 'Hole' (Operations Room). The arrival of Micky over base confirmed it too, for he carried out two victory rolls, much to everyone's delight, although these should not have been the actions of a squadron commander. But then, this was Micky Robinson.

As the pilots landed, taxiing in to dispersal, the Station Commander and Wing Commander Flying, Barwell and Malan, drove up to welcome them back. When the scores were totted up, the following credits were given:

S/Ldr M L Robinson	Red 1	2 Me109s destroyed
F/Lt J Curchin	Red 2	1½ Me109s destroyed
Sgt T Rigler	Blue 1	2 Me109s destroyed
Sgt J Hughes-Rees	Yellow 4	½ Me109 destroyed
Sgt A G Palmer	Blue 2	1 Me109 probably destroyed
Sgt R T D Mercer	Blue 3	1 Me109 probably destroyed

Those involved in this famous fight were:

Red Section: Robinson (P7881), Curchin (P8264), Van Lierde (P7305), Seghers (P8270);

Blue Section: Rigler (P8422), Palmer (P7625), Mercer (P7734), Boyd (P8098);

Yellow Section: Richey (P8266), Malengreau (P8241), Du Monceau (P7834), Hughes-Rees (P8271).

What the 609 Squadron pilots couldn't know, but we now know, is that their opponents on this day had been Jagdesgeschwader No.3 (JG3). According to Luftwaffe loss records, they only lost three fighters on this day with another damaged. Damaged, that is, seriously enough not to be repaired at staffel (squadron) level. All had been the new 109F models, the three pilots who were shot down being Leutnant Gunther Poopel of the 1st Staffel JG3 (1/JG3), Leutnant Julius Heger of 4/JG3 and Feldwebel Gerhardt Grundmann of 3/JG3. The damaged 109 had landed at Etaples, being a machine of 6/JG3. JG3 also claimed one Spitfire shot down.

The German pilot in the dinghy had been Leutnant Karl Pones of JG3, shot down earlier by a 302 Squadron pilot. He had baled out but when finally picked up he was dead.

That 609 appears to have overclaimed during this fight was a fact of life. It is always difficult in the heat of battle to be certain of anything. At the speeds the fighter aircraft travelled, it was often impossible to retain any comprehensive idea of what had been happening. If one glanced away to ensure one wasn't about to be attacked, when looking again at the main action, all sorts of things might have occured. The more people involved, then the more conflicting were the reports. If one pilot shot at a 109 and later saw a 109 go into the sea, he might genuinely think it is his victim, when in reality it was someone elses; and a third or fourth pilot could very easily confirm seeing so-and-so shoot down a 109 which went into the sea. Thus with one 109 actually crashing, we might have two claims and two independent pilots confirming them. All the pilots could do was to report in good faith and hope the Squadron Intelligence Officer could sort it all out.

Two Spitfires had been damaged, Curchin's and Mercer's, the latter having been hit by a cannon shell which had exploded in the fuselage, splintering the perspex, one hole from which was found to be just an inch above Mercer's head.

Next day a telegram arrived from Leigh-Mallory — "Congratulations on a good day's work. Well done." Happy though the pilots may have been with the success of this air battle, all knew they had been in a fight. Most emerged a little more sober, realising too that the 109 pilots were no push-over, and the season had hardly begun. As if to emphasise the point, the very next day they lost Bob Mercer. Curchin led off his Flight on a Scramble, 109s again being in the air off the south coast. They spotted two Me109s, Curchin detaching Green Section to head them off. One began to circle west again, Syd Hill seeing his chance to attack. He fired off all his ammo in two long bursts which caused the 109 to dive vertically, leaving smoke, but could only be claimed as a damaged. Mercer, who had been so lucky the day before, just disappeared (P7305). They heard him over the R/T saying he was trying to put down somewhere, and in fact was attempting a forced landing on the beach at St Margaret's Bay. It seems he hit a rock, the Spitfire exploded and burst into flames — perhaps he even touched off a land mine. Was it yet another trap? Were other 109s waiting for some unsuspecting RAF pilot to chase after those two decoy 109s? Someone had picked off Mercer as he weaved below Hill. They must watch out for these situations.

May was hotting up. The next day, the anniversary of the start of the German *Blitzkrieg* in France, Paul led A Flight on yet another patrol just inland from the south coast. They were at 28,000 feet when they spotted four 109s with rounded wing-tips (109Fs) three thousand feet above them. The 109 pilots were at it again.

They turned and headed for France, keeping their height. Paul kept a watchful eye on them and the sky, and sure enough, one pair turned back, while the other two lurked in the background. The two formations circled each other some distance apart, but one eye was kept firmly on the two 109s further away. As the Spitfires and the two nearest 109s closed in, Bisdee edged near enough to make a sudden attack on one 109, but whether he hit it he could not judge for certain. There followed a brief exchange of fire with both 109s, then they were off.

Paul, ever watchful, and determined to learn from what he saw, reported that in his view, flying above 25,000 feet, the Spitfire was definitely outpaced and outclimbed by the 109F. But he had kept his head and had not been drawn into a tail-chase with the Messerschmitts, thereby leading his men into a possible trap.

Later that afternoon, Paul led another patrol to the Dungeness area, spotted four Me109s flying in pairs inland near Maidstone, but then lost sight of them. Keeping a careful watch, he picked out six more aircraft in the distance but couldn't quite make out what they were. The Controller said they were "friendly" but Paul had his doubts as their antics appeared odd. Later, Paul was so convinced they had been hostile, the Squadron Intelligence Officer asked Group if any British aircraft did act in the way Paul had described. Group signalled back — "Unusual antics observed probably friendly, probably Polish!"

One of the Belgian pilots, Francois de Spirlet, so nearly became the victim of another German trap on 15th May. An evening patrol by four aircraft of B Flight, somehow got mixed in with a bunch of Hurricanes, then de Spirlet saw the Hurricanes dive away and suddenly he found himself alone. Next he sighted a lone Me109 just flying along, a perfect target, thought the Belgian. Curving down behind the German he opened fire, seeing masses of tracer ahead of him. Sudden realisation that this couldn't all be coming from his guns, was accentuated when he noted that his starboard guns were not firing, due to an explosion in the wing. Then being conscious of his fighter taking other hits, he quickly rolled over, catching sight of four more 109s behind.

No doubt one of these gentlemen went home to claim a victory over a lone, stupid Spitfire pilot, who took the bait of a lone 109, but de Spirlet had been extremely lucky that the German's fire had not hit anything too vital. His engine sounded a bit rough but he managed to make an emergency landing at Eastchurch, despite the additional problem of a punctured starboard tyre. As the Squadron diarist recorded: "Tres dangereux Monsieur de Spirlet!"

The new Wing Leader, Sailor Malan, took the Wing out on a practise on 16th May, leading all three Squadrons along the Channel, 92 and 609 from Biggin, 74 from its satellite base at Gravesend. The temptation to show this strength to the Germans proved too great, Malan edging the 36 Spitfires towards the French coast, where isolated pairs of 109s were quick to disappear. That afternoon, Micky led his 609 on a patrol near Dover, circling round at 22,000 feet. Some enterprising 109s made a quick pass at the Spitfires, Bob Wilmet taking successful evasive action.

Micky left Paul and his Yellow Section as top cover, taking Red and Blue down after the 109s. Keith Ogilvie attacked one, causing it to trail smoke, half roll and dive at a steep angle, with the Canadian right behind, with Van Lierde his No.2 covering him. Ogilvie registered 450 mph in the dive, in which he used all his ammunition. Meantime, Van Lierde fired at a second diving 109 while Syd Hill, Red 4, attacked a third.

Ogilvie's 109 was reported crashed by the Dover balloon barrage, while Hill's was seen burning on the water, although Hill himself, having dived from 20,000 to 1,000 feet, narrowly missed hitting several barrage balloon cables as he pulled out and up.

Pilot Officer Joe Atkinson chased two more 109s, which then had the impudence to make a pass at Paul and his Section, who had kept station high over Dover. Richey and his wingman, Vicki Ortmans, broke in opposite directions, Ortmans getting in a quick burst at one 109 as it flashed by. Taking off after it, Ortmans' fire produced some black and white smoke but he could only claim a damaged as he broke off the chase near the French coast.

It will be noted that Micky usually gave Paul and his Yellow Section the top cover spot. Why? Quite obviously Micky had absolute trust in Paul's ability to watch and to protect the rest of the Squadron as they made the main attack. It says a lot for Paul; and Micky must surely have wanted only the best — and who better to look after you than your brother-in-law!? It did mean that Paul and his Section usually didn't get the chance to make a bounce and score in the initial clash, generally the best time to pick off a 109, but protection and safety were paramount.

Atkinson was in the action again the next day, during an A Flight patrol over Tenterden. They were then vectored towards Manston where some 109s were reported. Two or three Messerschmitts were indeed found and a skirmish developed. Atkinson was hit in the starboard wing by a cannon shell, heading down with the intention of landing at Rochester. However, as he made his approach, dropping flaps, only the port one came down which then stuck. Almost losing control of his Spitfire (P8241), Joe managed a forced landing in a ploughed field, which whipped off his undercarriage, and caused him to bump his head, but he was safe.

Circus 10 was mounted on 21st May; 17 Blenheims escorted by massed 11 Group fighters would attack an oil refinery at Bethune. Biggin Hill Wing's part in the plan of things was to provide Withdrawal Cover for the operation, Malan leading 609 along a patrol line between Gravelines and North Foreland at about 12,000 feet.

As the bombers and their closer escort winged their way back across the French coast, while 609 were flying in three extended sections in line astern, several Me109s flying in pairs and fours were encountered. In the ensuing fight, Malan damaged one 109, but could not engage it further as he suddenly found himself alone! Pilot Officer Mackenzie, covering the Wing Leader, blacked out and spun down, the other members of the section following him. Malan was then ingloriously chased by several 109s but escaped them.

Hughes-Rees damaged another 109, while Ortmans chased one down which was then engaged by four other Spitfires, one of which, flown by John Bisdee, fired a burst into it from vertically above. Almost at once he saw pieces of aircraft in the air and a parachute just behind him, thinking himself to have been hit. He broke off and made a rapid landing at West Malling, but he had not been hit. Later, as the fight was pieced together, he came to the conclusion that the bits of aircraft were of his No.2, Pilot Officer de Grunne, who failed to return.

If it was indeed de Grunne in the parachute, he was not rescued. Spitfires did follow it down until the pilot went into the sea, but although the position was radioed to Control, they had to leave the spot when fuel ran low. Rescue boats and Air Sea Rescue aircraft searched in vain. Matters were not helped by the fact that the Kenley Wing had three of their men in the water at this time, so there was a lot of sea to cover, but then again, de Grunne may have already been dead. John Bisdee recalls that day vividly:

> "I saw some Me109s way below us and ordered an attack; as there were no enemy aircraft above us the section headed down. As we began to close the gap I looked in my rear view mirror, and with some surprise, saw a mass of rubbish, which turned out to be de Grunne's Spitfire disintegrating. We lost interest in the 109s below, starting to circle round a bit to see if de Grunne had got out but we could see no sign of him. Later some Spitfires flew out to search the area further but nothing was ever found.
>
> "I believe he was the victim of wing failure. It was found with the fabric-covered ailerons of the early Spitfires, that in certain attitudes, the fabric tended to indent, causing the leading edge of the ailerons to rise slightly. But it was enough to catch the slip-stream which then flicked up the ailerons suddenly, acting just like an air-brake. Thus the wings began to be pulled back; the trailing edges of the wing-roots were crushed inwards, trapping the pilot's feet and ankles. So as the Spitfire disintegrated the pilot had no way of escaping."

The loss of de Grunne was a sad blow to both 609 and the Belgian contingent. He hadn't yet been able to get back into his stride since his return to operations. One of his last actions at Biggin before take off had been to rush back to the IO to retrieve his miniature lucky horse-shoe from his wallet. But today his luck had run out.

John Bisdee's recollections of the Spitfire problem is interesting, for Paul once told me:

> "By the end of 1941 quite a number of Spitfires had had their wings fall off. The Spitfire, in a dive, used to try to twist to the right and the faster you went, the more bank you had to put on to counteract it.
>
> "I was doing this one day over the Channel, with some bank on, when suddenly the aircraft banked left instead of keeping straight.

"So I took the bank off and looked out at my ailerons, seeing they were both 'up'. So something like this was happening, which helped pull either the aileron(s) off or the wings off. Anyway, I reported it but at about the same time a Spitfire test pilot had a similar experience and his aircraft broke up but fortunately he was flung out and he came to, dangling in his parachute. From that we then knew what was happening so I assume they managed to cure it."

Apart from these moments of drama, danger and excitement, there were, as ever, moments of light relief. Being so near the 'flesh pots' of London, it was tempting for the squadron pilots to get into town on many evenings. The Squadron at this time boasted two cars, a Humber Barouche and a Ford. Unhappily the Humber was written-off on 24th May when it was left smashed against a London lamp-post during a Squadron night-out, so to get the pilots all back in time for dawn Readiness, the Ford had to make two trips. So on this morning, Readiness consisted of the assigned pilots falling limply onto the bunks and camp beds housed at dispersal, sleeping it off until 9 am.

The day after this night-out, de Spirlet and Seghers became separated on a patrol so headed home. Long after they had landed and sitting comfortably in the sun outside the dispersal hut, it was discovered that two Spitfires of 91 Squadron at Hawkinge, and an Air Sea Rescue Lysander, had been sent out to search for them! Even more amusing to the two Belgians, was the later information that they had blithely watched the whole of 92 Squadron take off from Biggin, to help in the search, not knowing they were the cause of the flap.

Good news came with the arrival towards the end of May, of the first Spitfire Vb, complete with two 20 mm cannon. Micky took one of them up for a flight, returning to say he found it a delight. Another event which occured at this time was the arrival of Captain Cuthbert Orde, the portrait artist. He had been commissioned in 1940 to make charcoal sketches of the more famous of Fighter Command's pilots. On the 29th May he began his portrait of Paul, whom everyone was now calling 'Apollo' due to his classical good looks.

There is no doubt that Paul's fine physique and handsome features made it easy for the ladies to 'swoon' over him. Probably more often than it was good for him. Being a successful fighter pilot with the DFC added to the overall picture, for these were very much the heroes of the day, feted as Pop Stars are today. Most pilots, for their part, knew only too well, as did most other fighting men in war, that any day might be their last. This was even more true of Britain's operational

RAF men, who were daily torn betwixt the comparative safety and good comforts between operations, and the deadly combat in the sky which could happen at any time, whether over England, the Channel or Northern France. Unlike a soldier in a front line trench, where death and danger were constant, and could in some way be accepted, it was a different kind of strain to be one minute sleeping in a warm, cosy bed in a Mess, or having a beer in the local, the next being chased by a Me109, 20,000 feet up in the air.

Paul rather liked being admired by the opposite sex. True he was married, and a father, but he was still a man, if a young one. Everyone knew that Paul didn't put the ladies off, and it must have been awkward on occasions, with Micky being his brother-in-law, and close at hand. Quite a few of the pilots had met Paul's wife, not only through Paul but through Micky too. Some felt embarrassed by it all, feeling strongly that he was being unfair, to say the least. It was a problem for Teresa too:

> "I suppose I should never have married him if it hadn't been for the war. He wasn't marrying material but in the war people did a lot of strange things. I had no illusions as to what he was like, but later there were the children to consider. Paul certainly couldn't be trusted as far as women were concerned...
>
> "Whenever we went to dine in town, or anywhere else for that matter, we rarely, if ever, paid for a meal if we went into some expensive restaurant — there was never any bill for a fighter pilot, which again wasn't good for their discipline. And that went for Micky as well. But that was the way it was in those days."

The month of May ended with a party held at Orde's house at Edenbridge although the pilots of both 92 and 609, having been released due to poor weather, had raced to the Berkeley Club in London. It was only then that Micky and Paul remembered about the party invitation, which had started an hour earlier. Everyone hastily scrambled down to Edenbridge where they remained for most of the night.

With June came summer and long periods of good flying weather. 609 and the Biggin Hill Wing were soon to be in the thick of the action.

CHAPTER XI

THE SHOOTING SEASON BEGINS

JUNE began, however, with pea-soup fogs, thick haze and generally poor flying conditions. Fighter Command were now keen to begin their new offensive, perhaps thinking that if the Luftwaffe were about to return to a daylight campaign once more against Britain, offence would be the best form of defence. They would soon get the weather required, for in fact, the second half of June saw the start of a six week heatwave.

The month also began with the pilots starting to try their hands with the new Spitfire Vbs. There was also a new Station Commander, Group Captain P R 'Dickie' Barwell DFC, who at the age of 34 was not about to give up any chance to fly on operations despite his age and high position. Like Harry Broadhurst, Barwell had been among the first RAF fighter pilots to win the DFC, back in October 1939. He had led his squadron out over the North Sea to intercept German bombers attacking a convoy. In the scrap which followed, he shot down one and shared a second. In the Battle of Britain he had flown a few sorties while commanding RAF Coltishall.

The month of June was to prove successful for 609 and the Biggin Hill Wing but they didn't get off to a very good start. On the 4th, having already flown a late afternoon escort to a Roadstead operation, at just on 7.30 pm, the squadron took off to escort an Air Sea Rescue search aeroplane, looking for a downed pilot from 54 Squadron. On the way out another Lysander was reported heading out, so Paul and his section were detached to escort it, but they failed to make rendezvous.

Micky led the other aircraft in sections at 2,000 feet, but then spotted three Me109s above. He commenced a steep climbing circle towards them, while calling Paul to gain height and surprise the Germans from up-sun, but before this could be done, the 109s attacked. One Messerschmitt went after one Spitfire whose pilot was lagging behind and below the others. This was Vicky Ortmans who was having trouble with oil pressure and engine temperature. He took rapid evasive action, which caused the 109, as it tried to follow him, to break up.

Robinson meantime, began a dog-fight with a second 109, but the German was as good as Micky and neither could gain advantage over the other. Finally Micky decided to fly straight and level, enticing the German to come at him, whereupon Micky turned sharply, throttled back, then opened fire as the 109 overshot. The 109 began to trail smoke, turned onto its side and headed for the sea. He later saw a splash but deduced that this had to have been a Spitfire, not his 109.

Tommy Rigler, meanwhile, went after the third 109, shooting it down with a full deflection shot from below, then another 109 came at him, which was probably the 109 damaged by Micky, into which Rigler put another burst, knocking pieces off its wing.

Back at base, it was reported that 609 had been in a fight, and then the Spitfires began to drift back in ones and twos, a sign which confirmed they had been in action. When all had landed, there was a shock realisation that five were missing, but calls soon came in that four aircraft had landed at Hawkinge and West Malling, then another was down at Manston. That made 11 accounted for — one missing. A quick totting up of the heads revealed that Johnnie Curchin was not back.

It seemed impossible. Checking and re-checking later, taking into account times and observations by the Dover guns and balloon boys, it had seemed that the first aircraft to go into the sea had been a 109. The splash seen by Micky Robinson had been a Spitfire, as Mackenzie had seen a 109 dart between Curchin and his own Spit, before he spun trying to turn after it. So one of the 109s, presumably the 109 already hit and damaged by Micky, then Rigler, had managed a burst at Curchin's machine (P8204) and been on target. It was another blow to 609. Curchin had been well liked as well as being B Flight Commander. His great pal Syd Hill was very cut up about his loss. Joe Atkinson relates:

"Curchin and Sydney Hill were very very close friends and when Johnnie was killed, Sydney never really got over it. They were both very good scratch golfers too. Johnnie drank a lot. Sydney drank too but not as much as Johnnie. Probably the strain, but

however much Johnnie drank, he'd wake up in the morning, his
eyes would clear and he'd fly and was alright. Curchin once put a
bullet hole through one of the paintings at Southwood and it was
discovered that this had been the only valuable picture left in the
house."

B Flight was taken over by John Bisdee, and by the 9th, Paul's A
Flight had become operational with Spitfire Vb fighters. Then on the
11th another pilot was lost.

Sailor Malan led the Wing on a Roadstead sortie, 609 acting as top
cover to five Blenheims, but they saw no sign of the ship being
attacked as they ran into a couple of 109s, which bounced the second
pair of Blue Section — Ogilvie and Sergeant Guy Chestnut, a
Canadian. Chestnut's machine was damaged and he turned for home.
Meanwhile, Robinson and Bisdee tried to counter-attack the 109s,
Bisdee opening fire at one of them which obligingly flew right in front
of his Spitfire. Ogilvie also got a quick shot at one of them, but in the
scrap, the 109s made a pass at Robinson's Spit. Finding only one of
his cannon's working, Robinson broke off rapidly and joined up with
the rest of his men, as the 109s disappeared towards France.

Regaining the formation, Micky then saw glycol streaming from
Chestnut's damaged fighter, as the Canadian began gliding towards
the sea a mile from Ramsgate's cliffs. Micky urgently tried to signal
to Chestnut not to do so, but the NCO continued his attempt to get
over the clifftops, failing to make it. The Spitfire struck the cliff-face
just a few feet from the top. In fact one wing, which was ripped off,
landed on top of the cliff while the rest of the aircraft slithered down
the side, smoking.

Coastguards later reported seeing a parachute, and hopes were
raised that Chestnut might have baled out, but his body was found in
the wreckage. Whether the parachute was a mistake, or perhaps even
the pilot of the damaged 109, is not known. Guy Chestnut was buried
in Margate Cemetery.

What Fighter Command pilots in 11 Group began to term "the shooting season", began in earnest on 17th June. It was the start of a long
series of Circus Operations which were to continue almost without
respite for the rest of the summer. Circus 17 consisted of Blenheims
raiding Bethune and 609 shot down three Me109s for no loss, on the
way home. John Bisdee sent one down in flames, Ogilvie caused
another to blow up in the air, while de Spirlet caught one head-on,

which headed down, Micky Robinson then seeing a patch of foaming water where the 109 would have gone in.

This same June day saw the arrival of Jean Offenberg and Baudouin de Hemptinne, both posted in from 145 Squadron. De Hemptinne had one victory in his log-book, a Heinkel 115 floatplane he'd shot down in October 1940.

De Hemptinne was in action the very next day, flying as wingman to Sydney Hill. The Squadron were acting as rear support, along with 92 Squadron, to a returning Circus. From the start of their patrol along the line Gravelines to North Foreland, they saw 109s above them. Then Hill and de Hemptinne became separated, Hill going after a pair of 109s he had spotted off Gris Nez. Hill fired at one which appeared to start down and some pilots thought they saw something go into the sea. (Perhaps this had been a 109 from I/JG26 whose pilot had to make a forced landing at Sangatte, on the French coast, just along from Calais.) Hill and his Belgian wingman headed back to Dover then turned for Gris Nez once more, where they ran into several more 109s, but after some moments of inconclusive engagement, the two Spitfire boys headed north once more. It appears, however, that Hill's machine had been hit and as Hill began to glide towards Dover, de Hemptinne lost sight of him. What followed was almost a repeat of Sergeant Chestnut's loss. John Bisdee remembers:

> "Syd tried to get back despite being advised to bale out. He thought he could make it and very nearly did. He just failed to get over the coastal cliffs, the Spitfire falling in flames onto the beach below. The pilot was incinerated. His family asked to have his ring but it had melted in the heat.
>
> "At his funeral, as the party was moving to the cemetery, it had been arranged for two Spitfires to fly over low, in salute. Two aircraft duly arrived but they turned out to be two Me109s. Everyone scattered, leaving the coffin in the middle of the road!"

June 21st, 1941, saw Fighter Command's most successful day since the end of the Battle of Britain. Two Circus Operations were launched and 609 and the Biggin Hill Wing were in amongst the 109s. Keith Ogilvie shot down one over Le Touquet airfield, in full view of the German occupants, the enemy pilot taking to his parachute. Sergeant Bob Boyd sent another crashing into a field from 3,000 feet, and Vicki Ortmans attacked another which was making life difficult for a Spitfire pilot, but could only claim a damaged. Still, two destroyed and a damaged for no loss was satisfactory. In all that day, around 30 enemy aircraft were claimed shot down, one being the Kommodore of JG26,

Adolf Galland. He claimed two Spitfires and a Blenheim on the 21st, to bring his score to 70, but he was firstly forced down with a shot-up aircraft, and in the afternoon, had to bale out of another, hit by a sergeant pilot from 145 Squadron. On the afternoon sortie he had taken off alone — something which was not allowed, but he was the Kommodore! — and had made the mistake of following his 70th victory down to see where it crashed and paid the price. His 109 was shot-up, and he was wounded in the head and right arm. His fighter on fire, Galland headed down, unable to jettison the cockpit hood, but then, by sheer brute force, smashed it open and baled out. His 109 crashed at Billebrune.

Luftwaffe losses only indicate eight 109s lost with another two seriously damaged, during the day. The RAF claimed 30 or more. Most were from JG26, four being reported as lost over the Channel, one near Etaples, another over Samer. Two of those pilots in the Channel were picked up by British rescue craft and taken into captivity. One of the others shot down, but safe, was Galland's wing-man on the first sortie, Oberfeldwebel Hegenauer, which was why Galland had flown solo. JG2 lost one, shot down by a Spitfire near Etaples, with another 109 damaged. Galland's was the 8th loss. However, his reward was the news that he was the first recipient of the Swords to his Knight's Cross with Oak Leaves.

The very next day — 22nd June — came the news that Germany had invaded Russia. This was to make Fighter Command's summer offensive even more essential from Britain's war leaders' point of view. Very obviously the Germans had taken troops and aircraft from their occupied territories in France, Belgium and Holland in order to support their invasion in the east. It wasn't long before Joseph Stalin, the Russian leader, was asking Britain to help with supplies as well as opening a second front in France. However, it was clearly impossible even to consider an attempt at putting an invasion force from Britain onto the coast of France at this stage of the war. All that could be done was to continue with as many offensive gestures as possible, in the hope that it would tie down German forces in the west.

As we now know, the Luftwaffe retained just two major fighter units in the west, Jagdesgeschwader No.2 and Jagdesgeschwader No.26. JG2 took the western side of France, down to Cherbourg and Brest, JG26 the eastern end, covering Boulogne and the Pas de Calais, to the Dutch border. There was also one Gruppe of JG52 in Holland, where it operated until the autumn of 1941, and later one Gruppe of JG53 in the autumn. This gave the Luftwaffe fighter arm opposing the RAF, a paper figure of around 275 Me109s — if every one was serviceable.

In order to disguise the move to the eastern front, the Germans had kept up their daylight Me109 intrusions over southern and south-east England, as well as their night bomber offensive, at least until early May. Hitler had also had additional calls on his aircraft strength for the Greek campaign which his Italian ally couldn't fight without German help, and although Greece had now fallen, as had Crete, the Yugoslav partisans were creating additional problems, which needed men and aircraft to deal with them. Malta was still besieged and any successful campaign in North Africa would need air forces to fly against that island, to protect the lines of communication and supply across the Mediterranean.

Circus 18 was organised for the 22nd, 609 and the Wing acting as forward and withdrawal wing. 609 in fact flew in three independent sections at between 20-25,000 ft inland from Dunkirk. Blue 1, John Bisdee, spotted nine 109s flying down the coast from the Dunkirk area. Attacking, he set one Messerschmitt on fire, Sergeant Rigler a second with two others damaged, although he was himself shot-up and was lucky to make it back to Manston.

Paul's Yellow Section was engaged on crossing the French coast, and de Spirlet, Yellow 3, was shot down, Vicki Ortmans also being hit. De Spirlet glided out to sea for a while but then it was time to abandon his machine. He baled out with some difficulty, inflated his Mae West on the way down, then hit the sea. Twice he fell out of his dinghy — once while he stood up to wave — and was later picked up by a rescue launch, after an argument between the launch and a Naval gun-boat as to who should rescue him. With a 109 also damaged by Offenberg, this made it two destroyed and three damaged for one Spitfire lost.

Three 109s were lost this day. I/JG26 lost a 109E near Cassel, while III/JG2 lost a 109F near Calais, Leutnant Martin Adolf being killed. III/JG2 lost Uffz Wilhelm Scharf and his 109F between Arobouts and Capelle. The Stab unit of JG2 had another 109F badly damaged.

Next day, the 23rd, came Circus Nos 19 and 20, 609 being involved with both. The first was against Bethune, Biggin Hill providing all three of its squadrons as one of the Target Support Wings but 609 saw little sign of the enemy. Circus 20 was organised around six Blenheims from 107 Squadron, against Mardyck airfield.

There was haze up to 4,000 feet, but otherwise the weather was mainly clear, with good visibility above this height. This was one operation where the Me109 pilots reacted well, and managed to get through the fighter screen to shoot down two of the Blenheims. The Biggin Hill pilots crossed the French coast as a Wing near Hardelot flying between 25-27,000 ft. They encountered a formation of 15 to 20 Me109s which were attacking the Polish 303 Squadron, which was part of the Escort Wing. Jamie Rankin led his 92 Squadron down and they shot down three 109s, including one by Rankin, with one more probable and one damaged.

No.609 Squadron, however, were having radio problems, failing to receive Malan's order to assist 92, continuing their course towards St Omer, then completing the sweep back to Mardyck. Only then did Paul see two Me109s near Hardelot, coming down behind them. He yelled a warning, but Bob Wilmet's Spitfire caught a burst and he dived away, landing safely at Hawkinge. Then two more aircraft came in as they crossed out by Le Touquet, but Paul, seeing they had white spinners (RAF fighters generally had white/duck egg blue spinners), did not identify them as hostile until they began to fire. As he yanked the stick over, a bullet went into his header tank, covering his canopy with oil.

Throttling back, he kept a keen eye on his instruments but managed to coax his Spitfire (W3240) back across the Channel, landing back at base without trouble.

On the 24th, the day was mainly spent entertaining four Press photographers while the pilots waited for a call for action. For most of the day, the pilots were photographed, staging bogus cricket matches and hay-making parties, events in which 609 boys would never dream of becoming involved, but so long as the Press liked it....

Late in the day came a call to participate in Circus 21, so the pressmen's wait was rewarded by seeing and photographing some of the Wing pilots taking off. Within the hour they were skirmishing with Me109s over the French coast, 609 scoring three probables and one damaged for no losses. Circuses 22, 23 and 24 followed during 25/26th June, but they saw little of the enemy. On the latter date, Malan ordered 609 to remain over Gravelines at 27,000 feet and although they edged down a little way, they were still way above some fighting that was going on below, so came home empty handed. The next day, however, Paul got some hits on an enemy aircraft for the first time in over a year. It would be a great feeling.

June 27th; Circus 25, against the Fives-Lille Steel and Engineering Works. Lille was quite a distance for Spitfire pilots flying with just 80 gallons of fuel! Some of the pilots thought so too and they were right. It was nearly twice as far inland as St Omer, Desvres, Cassel or some of the other targets they had been to. Even Bethune was pushing it. This was long before the advent of the long-range external fuel tanks which could be jettisoned if a combat situation arose. However, ...

Six Blenheims each from 18, 21, 139 and 226 Squadrons in 2 Group were to provide the punch — 24 in all. Fighter Command's 11 Group would provide the escort as usual, with a little help from 12 and 13 Groups:

Escort Wing — 71, 306, 303, 308 Squadrons, from Northolt and North Weald;
Cover Wing — 74 and 609 Squadrons, Biggin Hill;
Extra High Cover — 92 Squadron, Biggin Hill;
Target Support — 603, 54 and 611 Squadrons, Hornchurch;
— 145, 610 and 616 Squadrons, Tangmere;
Diversion and Support — 19, 65 and 286 Squadrons, 12 Group Wing;
Rear Support — 41 (13 Gp), 258 and 1 Squadrons, Kenley.

Weather was reported as thick haze up to 9,000 feet, with clear skies above, and the bombers made rendezvous with their escort squadrons over Martlesham, at 7,000 feet, just on 2100 hours. The Biggin Hill Wing left North Foreland at 2125, approaching Dunkirk at 18,000 feet, crossing over the enemy coast, learning that the bombers had been three minutes early so were some way ahead. Malan headed inland and made contact with the bombers and close escort over the target. By this time 74 Squadron were at 20,000 feet, and were dived on by several 109s. The Squadron turned to engage and although they claimed one probable, they lost three pilots.

The 609 pilots, with just nine men, led by Paul, with Malan making up the 10th (ie: five sections of two) were again experiencing radio problems as they tried to contact 74 Squadron and were hindered too by thick haze. Malan headed back with his 609 boys to the coast on the southern flank of the withdrawal, trying to bring several 109s to combat but only a few brief skirmishes resulted, in which one Messerschmitt was damaged. Paul saw two Me109Fs coming in from behind. Paul turned to meet them but they quickly began to dive when they saw the Spitfires, then three more 109s came at them. Turning sharp left to get behind them, Paul followed one down as it spiralled towards the coast. Staying with it, he watched as the 109 pilot began to straighten out his dive, then Paul jabbed the gun button firing two short deflection bursts from 300 yards. A hit! Glycol coolant started to stream from the 109 but as it was now heading down extremely fast, Paul decided not to waste his precious height. Breaking off and upwards, his last sight of the 109 was as it continued down in a near vertical dive. Offenberg confirmed seeing the glycol trail from the fighter.

Offenberg and Ortmans both had undetermined scraps with 109s, but at least 609 suffered no losses. Due to their combats, Paul and Vicki Ortmans both had to land at Manston while Du Monceau and de Hemptinne put down at Hawkinge. Malan and the rest landed at Biggin.

Piecing together the fight in which 74 Squadron had been badly hit, it seemed that they had crossed the French coast at 20,000 feet north of Dunkirk and were almost immediately attacked from above by a bunch of 109s. Flight Lieutenant C H Saunders engaged some of these and damaged one, being later credited with a probable. When the Squadron straggled back, the three missing men were known to be the CO, Mungo-Park, Pilot Officer W J Sandman and Sergeant C G Hilkin. Sandman, who had often flown as wingman to Malan, and Clive Hilken were both taken prisoner, but John Mungo-Park was killed. 74 Squadron was then taken over by Squadron Leader S T Meares, who had been a flight commander with 611 Squadron over at Westhampnett. Biggin was almost a home posting, for Stan Meares had been born just up the road, in Sidcup, Kent.

Malan led nine of 609 again the following day (28th), the Squadron only being able to achieve nine serviceable aircraft. This time it was a Circus to the Commines Power Station, the Wing acting as Target Support. Several Me109s were encountered on the way back, Malan shooting down one — his 30th victory — while the only 609 pilot engaged was Paul. A 109 came down on his tail and it took some extremely tight turning to reverse the situation. Paul hammered off some cannon shells at it from 250 yards, forcing the 109 to dive away inland, weaving like mad. Again fuel shortage made it necessary for Paul to lob down at Manston.

That night, the squadron diarist recorded, the pilots departed for a place called The Nuthouse, in London's Regent Street (an appropriate name some might say), where "the appalling atmosphere of this so drugged the pilots that they did not get back until 05.00 hours."

Good news came on the 29th, however, in the shape of awards of the DFC for John Bisdee and Keith Ogilvie. Their citations appear in the Appendices. On the last day of the month, Paul was back in action once more and shot down a 109.

CHAPTER XII

CIRCUSES AND SWEEPS

IN conjunction with Bomber Command's No.2 Group, Fighter Command HQ prepared details for Circus 27 to be organised for Monday June 30th. The target was to be the power station at Pont-a-Vendin, three miles to the north-east of Lens. 2 Group would supply 18 Bristol Blenheims; ten from 18 Squadron based at Oulton, near the Norfolk coast and eight from 139, which was based at Horsham St Faith, just to the north of Norwich (today's Norwich Airport).

Once again 11 Group of Fighter Command would mount the escort, with support from 12 Group:

Escort Wings — 303, 306, 308 and 242 Squadrons, Northolt and North
                Weald;
Target Support — 54, 603 and 611 Squadrons, Hornchurch;
                74, 92 and 609 Squadrons, Biggin Hill;
Diversion — 1, 258 and 312 Squadrons, Kenley;
Rear Support — 145, 610 and 616 Squadrons;
                65, 266 and 485 Squadrons, 12 Group Wing.

Nineteen fighter squadrons, comprising approximately 230 fighter aircraft, of which 120 would be in direct contact with the bombers, while the others created diversion and helped support the raid's withdrawal back over the French coast and the Channel.

The weather was fair, with some slight haze but cloud above 20,000 feet. That high cloud would give the escorting fighter pilots some problems, especially the top cover boys. At Biggin Hill, Sailor Malan called his three squadrons into the briefing room in the early afternoon, as the Circus was to be flown that evening.The way the Wing organised and balanced things, 609 would be taking on the top cover job, with 74 and 92 below. The Biggin Hill pilots took off at 5.30 pm, 609 putting twelve aircraft up, the pilots being:

SL M L Robinson	W3228
FL P H M Richey	W3240
FO K Ogilvie	W3115
PO V Ortmans	W3241
PO I Du Monceau	W3254
Sgt J H-Rees	W3239
Sgt K W Bramble	W8640
PO R Malengreau	X4666
PO P MacKenzie	W3368
Sgt R Boyd	W3187
Sgt A G Palmer	W3373
PO J Offenberg	W3173

The eighteen Blenheims flew down from Norfolk and made rendez-vous with their close-escort fighters over Clacton on the Essex coast, at 7,000 feet, just on 6 o'clock, then headed out over the Channel, crossing the French coast at Gravelines, two thousand feet higher. They met heavy flak fire from the town. One bomber of 139 Squadron, with a mechanical defect, aborted and flew home.

The formation droned on, some of the fighter pilots noticing that the airfields at Bethune and Lille appeared empty of aircraft. Were all the 109s waiting for them somewhere?

Meantime, the Hornchurch Wing had formed up over North Fore-land, then headed for Gravelines, slightly ahead of the bombers. Just a few miles inland, 603 Squadron, flying at 18,000 feet were attacked from above and behind by three pairs of Me109s, which came at them in line astern. The leader of 603 had no alternative but to break into them but in doing so his squadron became detached from the others as they then dived to evade. However, one section of the Squadron engaged four 109s, with a fifth flying behind, and shot down one of them, but in the melee, one Spitfire disappeared. To the target and back, 603 saw any number of 109s, mostly in small formations — all with height advantage — but they seemed singularly disinclined to come down and fight. Perhaps the 109 pilots could see they were not in direct support of any bombers, so were leaving well alone.

The Blenheims reached the target at 6.34 pm, to be met by more heavy flak. They released their bombs, five crews seeing hits on the ground west of the power station, while six other bombers dropped bombs on a large factory at Hisnes, a few miles north-west of the primary target, scoring two hits. Then they were turning for home. More 109s edged in and there were a few skirmishes between the target and the coast. The Poles of 303 Squadron saw a bunch of 109s weaving just above but owing to their slow escort speed were unable to pull up to attack. One pilot did try a burst but he saw no results of his fire. Near the coast four 109s tried to make an effort to engage the bombers and 306 headed them off, one Pole damaging one of the Messerschmitts, his fire hitting the cockpit area.

As they had neared the target, the Hornchurch Wing pilots saw six 109s diving across in front of them from west to east, travelling very fast, in an obvious attempt at splitting up the Wing still further, but the Wing Leader kept his pilots in check and the ploy failed. As they then headed back to the coast, four more 109s made a stab at 54 Squadron although the manoeuvre seemed more designed to induce the Spitfire pilots to turn back into France and follow, but this too was ignored. Reaching Gravelines once more, 54 then spotted two 109s cruising along the coast at 2,000 feet. 54 were anxious to engage, but the bait seemed too tempting. Further checks on the sky picked out nine or ten more 109s above and to the left, so it was a trap. One of the German pilots slanted down at the Spitfires but the RAF pilots were ready, one firing into the 109 which turned away rapidly, slightly damaged.

All this time, the Biggin Hill Wing, having made rendezvous with the bombers and escort wings ten miles to the east of North Foreland, had flown high above them to Gravelines, crossing into France at between 23-28,000 feet. They too saw the many small formations of 109s, most of the way from St Omer to Lens, and many more on the way back again. 74 and 92 found none near enough to have a go at, but being up high, 609 were attacked at extreme range by "nibbling" attacks. Quite obviously the 109 pilots had no intention of mixing it, but hoped that they could disrupt the Spitfire sections sufficiently for them to cut out a straggler or two. This was confirmed by later reports of seeing ten 109s up-sun, but which, in the end, made no attacks at all.

Afterwards, the 609 pilots estimated seeing in the region of 40 Me109s at various times, and at such heights as to be obvious that they had been scrambled well in time for them to climb above the Circus aircraft. Then two 109s made a lunge at 74 Squadron, Micky Robinson chasing them away, before getting behind five 109s he saw stalking Blue Section. The 109s scattered but not before Robinson had damaged one. Meantime, Blue 4, Sergeant Hughes-Rees, turned on one of the attackers, fired and saw it go down leaving a trail of black smoke, and crash.

Over the Foret de Nieppe, the Squadron followed Malan down to investigate aircraft seen below, Paul, leading Yellow Section, seeing four Me109s to his left trying to work themselves in behind the Spitfires. Pulling up, Paul and his No.2 — Vicki Ortmans — turned back and each selected a 109. Ortmans knocked some pieces off of his target, while Paul got behind the other. Firing a number of bursts, the 109 pilot made violent left and right hand turns, then flames started to come port side of the engine. The 109 flattened out, slowed down then went into a spiral, spewing oil. As Paul pulled out, Roger Malengreau, Yellow 3, followed the 109 down for about nine thousand feet, firing at it as it tried to flatten out again. The 109 finally dived again, well over the vertical, then the Belgian lost sight of it as his engine began to fail through fuel starvation in the carburettor.

Linking up with other Spitfires, Paul saw six 109s diving in formation from above and behind. After a bit of a dog-fight, Paul found himself alone, diving for a patch of cloud at 800 feet near the Foret de Clairmarais. Getting down to almost ground level, he then saw two 109Es diving onto his tail while a third — the leader — came in and opened fire from his starboard quarter. Paul pulled his Spitfire up into a violent climbing turn, a side-loop bringing him onto the tail of the latter 109, into which he pumped two long bursts of cannon and machine-gun fire, which caused the German pilot to half-roll and dive vertically at full speed. Paul watched it go, believing it impossible for the pilot to pull out at such a height and at such a speed. Meantime, the other two 109s came at him but he succeeded in evading them, then headed home at tree-top height.

Paul, being Paul, took the time to search the French countryside, so when he made his report, he was able to tell Frank Ziegler, the Intelligence Officer, that he saw "...no cars on the road, no barges on the canals; no cows or sheep in the fields, only horses — and several horse carts." He also noted that there was a large cargo ship off Fort St Phillippe (Gravelines), and an RAF rescue launch with two or three figures in Mae Wests, 10 miles from Ramsgate!

Malan engaged 8 to 10 Me109s and claimed one destroyed, last seen going down completely enveloped in black smoke from the engine which was on fire. Flight Lieutenant B E de la Torre, the Senior Intelligence Officer at Biggin, later assessed the results of the show as being four Me109s destroyed, one by Paul, one probable, shared by Paul and Roger Malengreau, and one damaged. Paul had expended

116 cannon shells (leaving just four in each gun) and 760 rounds of .303 ammunition.

Fighter Command claimed a total of six 109s destroyed on this operation, with two more probables and three damaged, for the loss of one pilot. It had certainly seemed as if the German fighter pilots were studiously avoiding any major engagement with the Spitfires, although they did seem anxious to try and draw off small numbers of RAF fighters by providing tempting decoys. They maintained height advantage as 609 themselves had witnessed, hoping for the chance of a hit-and-run attack to pick off stragglers. The Spitfire boys would need to watch themselves.

The Squadron's successes for the month of June were noted as being 14 destroyed, five probably destroyed and seven damaged, for the loss of Johnnie Curchin DFC, Sydney Hill and Sergeant Guy Chestnut.

The numbers-game, of course, was all-important for it was Fighter Command's 'raison d'etre'. Yet the Command were losing overall. Although the pilots were claiming a goodly number of Messerschmitts shot down over France, in truth, the number actually being destroyed were far less than claimed. Over the period, for instance, 14 June to 4 July 1941, JG2 had lost 15 aircraft, JG26, 33, total 48, with another 33 damaged. Fighter Command for the same period had lost 80 aircraft and 62 pilots, although it had claimed 214 German aircraft destroyed, 84 probably destroyed and 95 damaged.

These inflated figures — they were known to be inflated by the air commanders, because Ultra intercepts constantly monitored German requests for replacement aircraft each day, so knew the approximate losses — were allowed to stand for purposes of morale. Just as they had been allowed to stand during the Battle of Britain. Fighter Command's AOC, Sholto-Douglas, knew only too well that if his pilots were scoring so well, they would be knocking out the Luftwaffe fighter force every month! But the offensive against the Luftwaffe was costing the Germans dearly in pilots — 32 killed and five wounded in this period — but at a terribly high cost in RAF lives, of two to one.

The pace did not let up. In fact from the 1st to the 12th July, not a single day passed which did not see 609 heading across the Channel and into France, at least once, sometimes on as many as three occasions. The weather became extremely warm in early July, but when it abated from the middle of the month, only then did some respite from operations commence.

The month began quietly enough with an event-less sweep over the French coast on the morning of the 1st. Circus 29 the next morning went to bomb the power station at Lille, Biggin's squadrons acting as Escort Cover to 12 Blenheims. Again the 109s stayed away, just the odd few being seen on an airfield — not in the air. In the afternoon three Blenheims were escorted to bomb shipping off Le Touquet, but the only hostile element was some gunfire from the coast.

On the 2nd of July, 609's first French pilot arrived, Sous-Lieutenant Maurice Choron, who, as already described earlier, turned out to be an old friend of Micky's. Choron had been a flying instructor on his native Corsica, and Micky had met him there during one of his pre-war trips to the Mediterranean. It was the start of an association for the two former acquaintances which would last until 10th April 1942. Raymond Lallemant also joined 609 at this time, another of those gallant band of Belgian pilots so closely linked with the Squadron. In fact, 'Cheval' Lallemant would one day command 609. He was later to record:

"July 1941 brought us a new pilot to the Squadron, the first French pilot, or rather, the first Corsican. Maurice Choron was another crystalisation of the marvellous past of Michael Robinson, our CO. In fact it was during the last years of peace, in 1937, that Michael, who was already a pilot in the RAF, and who owned a Puss Moth — a tiny touring plane built by De Havilland, crossed Europe and landed at Bastia, Corsica, where he met Choron the instructor at the aeronautical club of that island. Those two totally different men shared their passion for flying in a reciprocal friend-ship which was going to seal their destiny for ever. As Frank Ziegler was to write in his history of the squadron: 'Choron was certainly the happiest pilot I knew and with his repertoire of French songs and a guitar, he was able to maintain a festive atmosphere from dawn onwards.' He was soon designated No.2 to Robinson and was to remain so, literally so, until his death, for in a final fight with the enemy together, they faced their 'last enemy'.

"When the war began, Choron was a reserve Sergeant Pilot, and mobilised to serve as an instructor. Choron was furious not to be in a fighting unit while his old friend was serving in 87 Squadron. But after the Dunkirk period, Choron arrived in England, responding to the call of General de Gaulle. As soon as he had arrived in London, Maurice looked for his friend, who, as the CO of 609 Squadron, asked Air Ministry to let the Frenchman join him.

"From that day he was Michael's No.2. Michael would no longer be seen without him — a formidable pair. Furthermore, in order to carry out with brilliance, his difficult role, he followed him in all circumstances like a shadow, thus ensuring the cohesion of the group and its readiness for combat. It is also true that a leader such as Michael could benefit from a wingman of the class of Choron, so even in his later position as Wing Leader, when Michael would lead a flight of another squadron, he continued to have Choron as his No.2."

Cheval Lallemant had been under training in the Belgian Air Force when the shooting war began on 10th May 1940. When the Germans bombed his airfield at Wevelghem, the place was devastated, their aircraft destroyed where they stood. After the collapse he and others made their way to Morocco, and in July sailed from Casablanca for Gibraltar, then to England in a British freighter. On the way he had met up with Pyker Offenberg, Boudouin de Hemptinne, Ivan Du Monceau and Vicki Ortmans' brother, Christian.

Once in England, Cheval completed his flying training, then posted to 609 Squadron along with several of his former friends he had met on the journey to England and war. He would win the DFC and bar, Belgian and French Croix de Guerre, and command 609 in August 1944.

Micky Robinson drew first blood for his Squadron in July, on the 3rd — in fact he scored twice in two different shows. Target for Circus 30 was Hazebrouck's Marshalling Yards, Biggin being the Support Wing. Weaving in fours at 22,000 feet, nearing the target, a single Me109F was seen 5,000 feet below. Taking his section down, Robinson opened fire from astern of the Messerschmitt, who seemed to be taken completely by surprise. Hit, it broke up and was then seen burning on the ground.

That afternoon 609 provided escort to Circus 31 to the same target. This time, rather than a lone 109, Robinson spotted 9 or 10 109s when over St Omer, 3,000 feet higher, about a mile ahead. At the same moment he saw two 109s below. There was enough space for it not to be a trap, so Micky led his Red Section down for the second time that day. The 109 wingman saw the danger and rapidly dived away, Micky closing in on the leader. The German pilot had started a turn, but Micky had no difficulty in turning inside the turn, fired but missed. A puff of smoke from the 109's engine showed that the German pilot had opened up his engine to full boost — what the RAF termed as "using one's Ha-Ha gas!" The 109 climbed rapidly, Micky firing at great range. Suddenly the 109 seemed to stop in mid-air, allowing Micky to fire the rest of his ammunition into the 109 from dead astern, having to break away quickly to avoid collision. The 109 went down half inverted, pouring out black smoke and in a left hand spiral. He then lost sight of it but Red 4, Hughes-Rees, watched it further and saw its wings come off and crash.

Luftwaffe returns show two losses on this date. One was Hauptmann Rudolf Bieber of I/JG26, flying a 109F-4 and shot down near St Omer. Was this the lone 109 — a captain having a look round on his own? In his log book, Micky later noted the 109 to have been a "stooge!". The second loss was none other than the Geschwader Kommodore of II/JG2, the German 'ace' Hauptmann Wilhelm Balthasar, who had seen action in Spain, gaining seven victories, and had added a further 23 during the French campaign. Micky had noted in his log that this 109 pilot was "not such a stooge!" Was this Balthasar, holder of the Knight's Cross of the Iron Cross, with Oak Leaves?

The Germans confirm his loss near St Omer, another saying he crashed at Aire, which is between St Omer and Hazebrouck, and that his 109 had lost a wing. John Hughes-Rees had reported seeing the 109's wings pull off. Victor in 47 combats (40 in WW2), Balthasar, who was 27 years old, had received the Oak Leaves just the day previously, only the 17th German to be so honoured. In fact he was only the second fighter pilot to receive the coveted Knight's Cross.

While Robinson had been shooting down this Me109, his No.2, Du Monceau, fired at another 109 seeing smoke come from it, while Paul, once more leading Yellow Section, spotted a vic of 109s 1,000 feet below. As he was about to attack, his No.2 thwarted the surprise, by going after another 109 and taking Yellow 3 with him. Paul had to go to the rescue when Yellow 3 was in turn attacked by a 109 with its side painted red from nose to rear of the cockpit.

Circus 32 was flown on the 4th, 12 Blenheims against the Khulman chemical works and power station at Chocques, three miles west of Bethune. The escort comprised:

Close Escort: — 71 and 242 Squadrons, North Weald Wing;
Escort Cover: — 74, 92 and 609 Squadrons, Biggin Hill Wing;
Target Support: — 54, 603 and 611 Squadrons, Hornchurch Wing;
                          145, 610 and 616 Squadrons, Tangmere Wing;
Rear Support: — 56, 65 and 601 Squadrons, 12 Group Wing.

Weather was reported as clear over the Channel and coast, but 9/10ths cloud could be expected over the target area, Bethune being some way into France.

Bombers and their escort met-up over Southend at 2.30 pm, and headed for France, crossing the hostile coast at Gravelines. During the run across France some 109s tried to get at the bombers but they reached Bethune unmolested. Cloud covered the target so bombs went down instead on the railway junction at Aire, although results could not be observed due to the cloud. On the way back, one Blenheim was hit by flak and had to ditch in the sea off Gravelines.

During the way to the target, the Biggin Hill squadrons, led by Sailor Malan, and with Group Captain Dickie Barwell as his No.2, crossed the coast at 2.49, with 92 to the left, 74 to the right and 609 above. 109s soon appeared and began to congregate at the rear of the RAF formation. Their attacks began as the target came up, diving under the Spitfire to stab at the bombers from the rear. The Wing was able to thwart most of the attacks but after the turn from the target things got a bit hectic and the Wing got caught up with some of the Close Escort aircraft.

Malan and Sergeant Adolf Pietrasiak DFM, a Polish member of 92 Squadron, shared a 109E destroyed, then Malan blew apart another 109, and damaged yet another. Barwell also claimed a probable and a damaged, while Micky Robinson claimed another also damaged.

Paul, Yellow One, saw the bombers turning for home as he saw too several Me109Fs manoeuvring behind and above. One came down at him but it broke away to the right when Paul turned into it. He followed, firing two short bursts of cannon and machine gun fire, which produced glycol, but not wanting to be enticed away from the bombers, broke off pursuit and headed back. He then saw two 109Fs diving very fast on his left, going for a section of 74 Squadron. Paul called a warning, and as the other Spitfires broke, one Messerschmitt tugged after the leading one as both went into a very steep left hand turn, climb and dive.

Paul curved in after the 109's wingman, giving him three short bursts, following the 109 as the pilot put it into a left-hand climbing turn, then banked beyond the vertical. It began to leave a trail of brown smoke and Paul observed smoke still pouring from it when it was last seen. Almost at that moment, Paul saw a large streak of glycol in the sky ahead of him, then saw an open parachute with a figure in black overalls at the end of it, and then he saw a Spitfire heading down just off Gravelines, followed by a patch of foam in the sea.

Back at base, the score appeared to be six 109s destroyed, four probables and 10 damaged for the whole show. One of the Luftwaffe losses was Leutnant Hans Gerlach of II/JG2, killed in his 109F-2 near Bethune. Two Spitfire pilots were missing, one from 74 Squadron — and one from 609 — Keith Ogilvie.

Ogilvie had been leading a Section and had seen the 109s attacking the bombers so had turned after them when he was hit. His port aileron floated away, a huge rent appeared in his wing, and he was pushed forward onto the gunsight and instrument panel. With blood all over the place, his engine stopped, it was time to get out. Wounded in the arm, he came round in a field and was taken prisoner, eventually ending up in Stalag Luft III. Later, he was among the party of RAF officers who got away in the Great Escape, in fact he was one of the last out before the tunnel was discovered. Two days later he was recaptured and was among the fortunate ones not to be shot as 50 of the others were.

One irony was that Ogilvie was due for some well earned leave in a few days time. He had flown on every operation since June, a record shared by Malan and Vicki Ortmans — all three having also been in action during the hectic summer of 1940. Ogilvie now had an extensive leave, as a guest of the Germans. Not that the boys at Biggin knew if he was alive or dead, not until, that is, Lord Haw Haw himself broadcast the fact six weeks later. Obviously the Germans regarded him as quite a catch.

CHAPTER XIII

WAR IN THE SUN

JULY was to see Paul in the thick of the summer fighting and on the receiving end of mixed fortunes. Even though he had flown on six Sweeps during the first four days of the month, he was again out on the 5th during Circus 33 to Lille. Biggin's Wing flew Target Support, and although routine and uneventful, the Spitfire pilots had a change of bomber to escort. Rather than the usual twin-engined Blenheims, they had three large four-engined Short Stirlings, each having the bomb capacity of around six Blenheims. Fighter Command was trying to make the enemy react to their incursions, just as Galland had noted, now that the war in Russia was going badly for Britain's newest ally.

The only problem 609's pilots had this day was fuel shortage. With the bombers being able to stay airborne longer than Blenheims, so the escort had had to stay up longer. This sort of problem would have to be tackled if escorting Stirlings was to continue. It gave 609's Adjutant and Intelligence Officer some anxious moments back at Biggin as the sky continued to be silent after the usual 1½ hours, at which time fighters were usually landing back. After two hours the silent sky seemed ominous of disaster, and those on the ground began to wonder if everyone had been shot down. Only then did word come that the Squadron were queueing up to land at Manston or Detling, with petrol warning lights glowing. Paul landed at Manston after 1 hour 45 minutes, flying back to Biggin after refuelling.

Two operations were flown on the 6th; a Roadstead in the morning, a Circus in the afternoon. Paul was on both. On the Roadstead, 609 and 74 escorted three Blenheims to attack shipping reported steaming north-east from Gravelines, but no ships were found. Circus 35 was once more directed against Lille, and once more it was Stirlings — this time six of the huge bombers.

About twenty pairs of Me109s were seen on the way to the target, and their pilots attempted the usual trick of trying to decoy the Spitfires away from the bombers. 609 had several brief skirmishes with the 109s without result, especially on the way out and between St Omer and Gravelines, Roger Malengreau and Pyker Offenberg were bringing up the rear. Malengreau had slipped behind a little — 500 yards or so — which was an invitation for a 109 pilot to have a go. Offenberg saw a 109 slip down behind his Belgian comrade and a snap burst caused glycol to stream from the damaged Spitfire — then the engine stopped.

The 109 curved away as Offenberg called a "M'aidez" (Mayday), and the rest of 609 closed up to protect their stricken pilot. Malengreau coaxed his Spitfire out over the Channel and somehow managed to glide all the way back, re-crossing the English coast at 2,000 feet, then crash landed down wind, ending up in a hayfield. As the Spitfires circled, Malengreau stepped out and waved that he was alright. As he said later, the worst part of it was all the oil and glycol sloshing about in the cockpit.More recently, Roger Malengreau remembers:

> "On July 6th I had a narrow escape when a Me109 blew my engine to pieces near Dunkirk (Gravelines). The fire went out and my engine as well. Michael Robinson recalled the whole squadron to protect my attempted return and flew next to me while I was gliding and made signs — my R/T had gone too — to give me an idea of the speed to keep. I just managed to make the cliffs and crash landed near Dover. Michael nearly had to do the same thing as having flown all that way with flaps down, he ran out of petrol, luckily within sight of Hawkinge.

Once again Paul landed away from Biggin, putting down at Hawkinge too, after 1 hour 40, his fuel almost gone. He took his responsibilities seriously and along with the others, had stayed with Malengreau for as long as possible. As Paul finally landed back at Biggin, he was seen immediately to climb from his Spitfire and fetch his bathing costume from his office, and depart for the swimming pool. The next day he so very nearly had an enforced swim.

Circus 37 on the 7th July was an attack on the Potez repair works near Albert, by four Stirlings with Biggin's squadrons flying Escort Cover at 13,000 feet. For 609 at briefing, there was some apprehension, for Albert was a hell of a way; almost to Amiens and certainly the furthest south they had flown. To compound this, the bombers turned up six minutes late, forcing the Spitfires to circle and wait, thereby wasting precious fuel.

However, the raid seemed to take the enemy by surprise for nothing blocked their path prior to the target, and 109s that were seen did not show up until the journey back. Nearing the French coast, Offenberg saw a ship convoy with a couple of escorting Messerschmitts, low down. Whether these were in fact more decoys is not certain, but as they sheered off, more 109s came down on Offenberg's section just off Le Touquet. Sergeant Evans was attacked by two 109s; the first one zoomed past and down, but the second one hit the Spitfire with a burst of cannon, setting the Spit's engine on fire. Meantime, Offenberg went after the first 109, following it down in a steep dive until he had to pull up to avoid the water. The 109 pilot appeared to misjudge his dive, for as the Belgian pilot looked down, he saw a large splash right among the ships.

Sergeant Evans, however, was trying to extricate himself from his burning fighter, and did so at 10,000 feet. As he floated down under his parachute, his dinghy pack became detached and blew away, so he finally splashed down in just his Mae West, only two miles from the convoy, although they made no attempt to pick him up. Evans became disorientated and began to swim manfully towards the coast which he took to be England rather than France. The Air Sea Rescue boys were alerted and later a Lysander and some Spitfires found him and dropped a dinghy. He had just about settled into this when a rescue launch arrived from Dover and picked him up. He had splinters in his leg and hand but otherwise was OK. 74 Squadron had also lost a pilot who was also picked up by ASR. Moose Evans, a burly Canadian, would soon return, later be commissioned and become one of 609's long serving characters.

Paul landed back at base and as he taxied in knew he was almost out of petrol after 1 hour 55 minutes flying time. It had been a long show. Considerable damage was reported to the target, which was located in totally new territory for all of 609 with the exception of Maurice Choron, who confirmed that before the war he had flown over 150 hours from the nearby French airfield.

The second Circus of the day — No.38 — took place that afternoon and was in more familiar surroundings; the Kuhlmann Works at Bethune. Paul had to fly another Spitfire after his morning's effort, so took W3313, taking off at 1425 pm. Several 109s were seen but none made any effort to interfere with the raid, but on the way back Paul was again in trouble. He suddenly found he was running out of petrol and by mid-Channel his engine began to stutter and cut-out — then it stopped. He headed down towards Hawkinge but in the final approach had to make a rapid forced landing when a number of Hurricanes appeared and landed ahead of him.

Back at Biggin, the Wing was visited by Winston Churchill and the AOC of Fighter Command, Air Marshal Sir Sholto Douglas. Paul meantime had flown back to base in another Spitfire, then took his old W3240 up for an hour's aerobatics, but the next day, he and his favourite Spitfire would be back in trouble again.

July 8th saw an early start. The previous evening the Wing had been warned of a dawn show, and Circus 39 was up and running by 0536 am. Three Stirlings were going to bomb Lens, with the Wing acting as Escort Cover.

Once over France, a lone Me109 flew along level with 609 for a short distance, then broke away as it fired off two Verey flares. Whether the signal had any significance can only be guessed at, for no follow up attack by other 109s developed. As the target was reached, the bombers and fighters came under heavy flak fire, and one of 609's fighters was rocked by a near miss. One of the Stirlings was hit and went down, being seen to crash into a factory building, but then three 109Fs dived through the formation. Over Lens, as Paul turned to engage, there was an ominous sound from his engine. It sounded serious.

Some scraps developed with the 109s, John Bisdee firing at one while escorting one of the other Stirlings. The 109 suddenly flashed right in front of the B Flight commander, but John did not see if he hit it or not. Micky Robinson blasted another, which shed some pieces and trailed smoke, the same 109 which had just attacked Sergeant Hughes-Rees.

John Hughes-Rees had just been attacking another 109 which he saw flick onto its back, go down and disintegrate before it hit the ground. He was then hit by heavy fire from another 109 from behind and his oil pressure disappeared to zero. He turned sharply, looked up and saw the 109 begin to circle over him, the pilot obviously looking to see if he had a kill. Hughes-Rees lifted the nose of his fighter and hosed off a long burst, which brought a bright flash on the 109's starboard wing, putting the enemy fighter into a spin. He then headed his Spitfire for the coast but as he reached the sea his engine seized when at 9,000 feet, so it was again a case of gliding home. He didn't make it, and finally had to plop his Spitfire onto the water without flaps as his hydraulics were also out. As the fighter began to sink, he was out on the wing, but his dinghy burst. However, he was lucky to have got the fighter down without serious injury to himself — better pilots than him had not been so fortunate in ditching a Spitfire. He was picked up by a boat a couple of hours later, but by then he was unconscious so knew nothing about it.

All this time Paul had had his own problems, once his engine began to play up. He quickly dropped below the bombers, turning to head for the coast. His section followed, realising his problem and knowing they would have to protect him from enemy fighters if spotted. Nursing his rough engine and losing oil he reached the French coast, crossed the Channel and thankfully put down at RAF Hawkinge. An inspection revealed a broken piston ring and just half a gallon of oil left, but he'd made it.

Flying back from Hawkinge after minor repairs, Paul was flying W3241 that afternoon on Circus 40, which fortunately for everyone, proved nothing more than a 'stooge' mopping up job with nothing to mop up.

The next day he was in W3241 again while his W3240 was repaired. Circus 41 asked for three Stirlings to raid Mazingarbe, near Bethune, the Wing acting as extra high cover.They reached the target three minutes ahead of the bombers. As they had crossed the coast by Ambleteuse three red flak bursts heralded their arrival which was obviously a signal as various patrols of Me109s quickly appeared. However, none made any attempt at attacking, and the Spitfires were certainly not going to be drawn away from the bombers.

Over the target, 92 Squadron did go for one group of 109s but 609, flying behind them at 30,000 feet, stayed in position, making it virtually impossible for 109s to get at the Stirlings. On the way back, however, a brief fight developed. John Bisdee and his Blue Section spotted a couple of Me109s which appeared to be patrolling over two small boats off Le Touquet, 2,000 feet below them. Covered by the others, Bisdee and Offenberg dived. The 109 pilots saw them and started to turn but the one Bisdee latched onto evidently lost his bearings by some thick haze which blotted out the horizon. In any event, Bisdee had no problem holding him and after a few short bursts, the 109 began to trail thick smoke, falling upside down into Le Touquet Plage where it crashed.

There were changes at Biggin in July. 74 Squadron was rested and sent to Acklington, 72 Squadron moving down from Acklington to take their place. 72 was commanded by Squadron Leader D B F Sheen DFC. Desmond Sheen was an Australian, and had fought in the Battle of Britain. Indeed, except for a brief period he had been with 72

Squadron since June 1937, rising from junior officer to squadron commander.

Micky had been acting Wing Leader for some time now and had led the Wing on occasion. Sailor Malan was getting tired so Micky began to lead on Malan's days off. He led on 10th July.

This date saw Circus 42, with another three Stirlings, this time going to the Kuhlmann chemical works and power works at Chocques, near Bethune. Close Escort was provided by North Weald and Northolt Wings, while Biggin Hill took the High Cover slot. Target Support was the job of Hornchurch and Tangmere, Rear Support, Kenley and the third Northolt squadron. 10/10ths cloud was expected over the Channel up to 1,000 feet, haze up to 12,000.

The Biggin Hill squadrons' job was to sweep the French coast between Hardelot and Le Touquet, then fly with the bombers half way to the target before breaking away towards Gravelines and Calais. This would be 72 Squadron's first show with the Wing but they didn't get off to a good start; in fact the Wing didn't get off to a good start either.

The 609 pilots and aircraft were:

SL M L Robinson	W3238
FL P H M Richey	W3240
FL J D Bisdee	W3371
PO M Choron	W3117
PO R Malengreau	X4666
Sgt R Boyd	W3187
PO W Sanders	W3315
PO I Du Monceau	W3254
PO P Mackenzie	W3372
PO E Seghers	W3173
Sgt K Bramble	W3307
Sgt A Palmer	W3373

Take off came at 1115, and rendezvous with the Stirlings from 7 Squadron, Bomber Command, was made over Rye at mid-day but before that happened, Jamie Rankin's radio packed up and he landed at Hawkinge to have it seen to. Due to a misunderstanding, two sections followed him down. Later, some 109s were understood to be over the Channel and the three of 92's pilots who had also landed were Scrambled but only one saw anything and he was promptly shot down and baled out. Luckily he was picked up by a drifter in the Thames Estuary.

Meanwhile, 72 Squadron became disorientated in haze and lost contact with the rest of the Wing, so proceeded to Hardelot on their own, at 28,000 feet and crossed into France. Between Fruges and St Omer they were attacked by two formations of Me109s and two pilots were picked off. Heading back to the coast, another pilot began to straggle and before he could catch up, he too was picked off by a pair of 109s. The others got back, landing at Coltishall, Norfolk!

While all this was going on, 609 and what remained of 92 had crossed out over Rye and as they went over the French coast, could see numbers of 109s all over the place. Way below they could also observe the bombers and their escorts, seeing too, one Stirling (N6017) hit by flak from Boulogne. It was not a pleasant sight watching the huge bomber turn over onto its back and plunge into the sea, even though three or four of the crew managed to bale out first.

Up above, 609 found 15-20 Me109Fs and both formations began to circle each other, but the Spitfires showed superior manoeuvrability and succeeded in getting behind the 109s. It seemed so easy that Micky Robinson concluded they were inexperienced and certainly showed little inclination to fight. Some of the 109s began to dive away inland while others pulled up into the sun. Micky went after one, missed with a deflection shot, but began to chase it down as it dived. He was about 1,000 yards behind, firing from this range until black smoke began to appear. They were now some 30 miles inland from Le Touquet and Robinson noted his indicated airspeed as being 450 mph. Suddenly the 109 increased its angle of dive and both wings ripped off. Victory number 12 for Micky.

Paul and his Yellow Section went after three 109s, one breaking off immediately, but the other two were pursued as they went down in shallow dives. Paul fired three bursts at one of them which began to leave smoke which he took to be boost. The 109 began to turn, Paul firing again, but then he saw aircraft overhead and broke off. In the event, the aircraft proved to be Spitfires. However, two other 609 pilots watched the 109, reporting its propellor almost stopped and stating that they thought the smoke was glycol, so Paul was given a "damaged".

As they reformed, Paul's Section saw three more 109s 3,000 feet above and behind, whose pilots began to show considerable signs of tactical experience. First one would dive and when it climbed again, all three would come down below and behind the section, trying to climb up beneath their tails, but Paul thwarted their efforts each time by turning back into them. This happened several times, but Paul, Malengreau, Du Monceau and Bramble kept up their defensive manoeuvres until the 109s gave up and left them. Paul was once more short of fuel after this action, and had to refuel at Detling after 1 hour 45 minutes flight time.

Paul made special mention of the German pilot's tactics at the end of his combat report, which began:

"I was Yellow One of 609 Squadron, Sweeping St Omer area and Gravelines for withdrawal of our bombers from a target at Chocques. Shortly after crossing French coast at Boulogne, sighted 109s ahead; three Me109Fs passed over formation on the left, going in the opposite direction at same height. Yellow Section turned left as EA did like-wise and circled to get on their tails. After about one circle, No.3 EA broke out of turn to the right. S/Ldr Robinson and remaining two EA flew straight, in very fast but shallow dive. I fired three bursts at left hand aircraft at long range and saw him emit slight black smoke which I took to be boost. I later fired again as EA climbed to right, then broke away into the sun on sighting many aircraft above. (Later identified as Spitfires.) Yellow Three and Red Three both reported seeing EA I fired at with propellor almost stopped."

Special Report on subsequent engagement, submitted as example of enemy tactics:

"Three Me109s sighted behind Yellow Section at 3,000 ft above. I led Section in a steep left hand climbing turn as No.1 EA (enemy aircraft) started to dive towards our tails. Other two EA started to dive but pulled up again as No.1 went below us and then regained his height in a steep climbing turn to the left. EA were now right above us and 2,000 ft higher. They circled as they continued to turn and then all dived very fast below and behind us in an endeavour to come up underneath our tails. This manoeuvre was foiled by turning and EA regained height. Manoeuvre repeated unsuccessfully twice more but on the third time, EA continued down very fast to the ground and could not be overtaken."

In all the Operation netted 11 109s destroyed, three probables and four damaged; at least that is what was claimed. However, several Spitfires and pilots were lost. Apart from those of 92 and 72 already mentioned, the Hornchurch Wing lost four although they claimed five 109s, while Tangmere lost three for two destroyed, two probables and a damaged. The Stirling had been lost because instead of hitting the French coast at a point five miles south of Hardelot, they went in just south of Boulogne, getting caught out by the flak from that well defended town. Despite the losses, the operation was deemed successful! With casualties about even, the war of attrition was not being won, and it appears that the Luftwaffe only lost three 109s on this date with four or five others damaged.

One of the lost aircraft was a 109F-2, flown by the Kommandeur of I/JG26, Hauptmann Rolf Pingel, an 'ace' with 26 victories including four achieved in the Spanish Civil War. He was foolhardy enough to chase the two remaining Stirlings back across the Channel only to be hit by return fire and his 109 so damaged that he had to force land in a field near Dover[1]. Apart from becoming a prisoner, Pingel had presented the RAF with its first virtually undamaged example of the new F model 109. This was later test flown by the RAF and in fact, Micky and Dickie Barwell, Biggin's station commander, visited Farnborough a couple of weeks later to look over the 109 themselves.

Paul got his old W3240 back for Circus 44 on the 11th. This was a Diversionary Operation by three fighter Wings prior to Circus 45 taking place, planned for implementation 45 minutes later and designed to catch the 109s back on the ground refuelling after taking off for the first show. The three Wings were, Biggin Hill (72, 92 and 609), Kenley (485 and 602), and 12 Group Wing (65, 266 and 452). The only bait for the Germans was a lone Blenheim of 60 Group acting as decoy.

The day started, however, with a visit to Biggin, by Mr P Frazer, the New Zealand Prime Minister, who had a bevy of military officers, pressmen and photographers in tow. Finally a briefing was held, with 609 little knowing that they were about to have their most successful day since 8th May. The pilots and aircraft were:

SL M L Robinson	W3238
FL P H M Richey	W3240
FL J D Bisdee	P8699
GC P R Barwell	
Sgt R Boyd	W3241
PO W Sanders	W3315
PO E Seghers	W3173
PO I Du Monceau	W3245
PO P Mackenzie	W3372
PO M Choron	W3117
PO R Malengreau	X4666
Sgt K Bramble	W3307

[1] Shot down by Stirling W7433 (PO C J Rolfe.

The Blenheim operated independently from Biggin Hill, gaining
height to 9,000 feet on a course to Manston via Eastchurch. It left the
Manston area at 1435 to fly back to base. Meantime the three Wings
made rendezvous over Manston at 1435, the Biggin squadrons having
taken off at 1350. However, the Biggin squadrons were diverted by
9/10ths cloud and found themselves over Essex, so turned over the
Thames Estuary, then proceeded across the Channel, going over the
hostile coast seven miles east of Dunkirk at 1450.

On commencing their Sweep, inland, there were obviously many
109s about, many black specks being seen way off to the south, trying
to get up-sun off Gravelines. They were manoeuvring to put themselves into a good position when the Spitfires had to fly home. So the
Wing Leader — Micky — decided to head straight for Gravelines and
as they approached, three formations of ten 109s suddenly appeared.
609 had turned with the Wing at Cassel, whilst flying at 27,000 feet,
and also spotted these 30-40 109s climbing up through cumulus cloud,
no doubt responding to the Blenheim's ethereal vibrations.

Micky turned his fighters to fly parallel to the coast, still 15 miles
inland, gradually converging with the 109s who appeared not to have
spotted the higher Spitfires. The 109s were in three groups in line
astern and the first was allowed to fly by unmolested, then Micky
ordered Paul's Yellow Section of 609 down onto the second bunch
while he winged over with his Red Section to go for the third lot.

Paul made the bounce, and in doing so achieved some fine team-
work, using the R/T to give orders and warnings with such good effect
that the Section stuck together during three consecutive engagements.
Paul lined up one Messerschmitt and used up all his cannon ammunition at close range, which went down pouring out black smoke after
making an initial attempt at climbing. He then pulled round onto a
second 109, only to find it being pursued already by Blue Section.
Breaking off they used the speed of their dive to climb up towards
four more 109s. Leaving the nearest pair to Du Monceau and Malengreau, Paul attacked and damaged both the other 109s with frontal
and rear quarter attacks. His No.2, Sergeant Boyd, destroyed one and
damaged another Messerschmitt, shattering the canopy and probably
killing the pilot of the one he destroyed. Du Monceau probably
destroyed another which he saw turn onto its back and fall sideways
out of control. Sergeant Bramble, Yellow 4, damaged yet another.

Red Section also got in a good surprise attack, Micky Robinson
shooting down one fighter from dead astern, seeing the pilot bale out.
He then followed another down in a steep dive from 27,000 down to
10,000 feet, firing his machine guns all the way. Just as he was

despairing of running out of ammunition, his No.2, Dickie Barwell, who had stuck with him in the dive, opened up with cannon and machine guns, setting the 109 ablaze, its pilot also appearing to bale out. In the same dive, Barwell, without losing Micky, had also damaged a 109 on the way down. Red 3, Seghers, attacked a 109 going after a Spitfire and it too rolled onto its back and poured black smoke, then was surprised to see a parachute open. This made it four destroyed, two probable and five damaged for no loss, although Luftwaffe losses do not confirm such a high loss rate.

As the pilots landed back at base, it coincided with a visit to Biggin of Lord Trenchard, the Father of the RAF, a man, some noted, with as many rings on his sleeve as rows of medals on his chest. 609 were of course, cock-a-hoop after their air battle, and Trenchard was pleased to chat to most of the pilots and certainly shake hands with them all. In the midst of this, Sergeant Moose Evans who had been wounded a few days earlier, arrived in a Magister, and was also introduced despite his crutches.

It was back to France on the 12th for Circus 47, which was scheduled as a repeat of the previous day. A special Blenheim was again put up, by 75 Wing, but this time there was little reaction from the Luftwaffe — perhaps they twigged what was going on. Just two Me109s came close enough to be engaged and Micky Robinson performed his hat-trick in three sorties by knocking one down.

Rendezvous had supposed to have been made at Southend with the Kenley and Northolt Wings, Biggin being high cover, but the RV did not happen so Micky led the three Squadrons across into France at 27,000 feet over Gravelines, where they broke into fours, stepped up. After about 20 minutes, 92 Squadron dived onto some supposed 109s which turned out to be Spitfires, while Micky latched onto two 109s seen diving after them. He fired a long burst at the second 109 at long range, as the leader sheered off, leaving his No.2 to dive in an even steeper dive. Knowing his engine would cut if he followed by steepening his own dive, he rolled over onto his back and hammered into the 109 while inverted, thus keeping his carburetter from draining of petrol. (The 109s had fuel injection, but the RAF fighters had not got that yet.) Closing quickly he fired again from 50 yards dead astern despite his windscreen starting to frost over, and saw pieces blast away. Then the 109's hood came away followed by the pilot. He was so close that he ducked involuntarily at the sight of the opening para-chute, then the canopy banged into his tail fin, but luckily did no damage.

The day ended with a visit from two Belgian pilots who just a few days before had escaped from occupied Belgium in a Stampe SV4 two-seat biplane, very much like a Tiger Moth aeroplane. The Stampe had not been flown nor had the engine been turned for over a year, but a group of men worked on it, got it airworthy, bought petrol on the black market from a German soldier and headed out from Brussels to freedom.

The two were former Belgian Air Force pilots, Mike Donnet and Leon Divoy. They landed on the Thorpe mud flats in Essex, although they had a bit of a time trying to convince the local police who they were and where they had come from. Both men later flew with the RAF, Mike Donnet winning the DFC and commanding 64 and then 350 Squadrons. He later became Lieutenant General Baron Donnet CVO DFC CdeG. He knew Jean Offenberg, the latter inviting him and his companion to visit the Belgian contingent in 609, at Biggin. They told their amazing story to a captivated audience and were pleased to find so many former friends operating with RAF Fighter Command.

The recent hot July weather faded at this time, and several rain storms brought the heat-wave to an end and restricted operations. Paul also went on leave and such was the problem that two of the three squadrons began to be released for the day. On the 13th it was thought to be a good day to celebrate the recent achievement of the Biggin Hill Sector scoring the 750th victory of the war. Luckily the sun decided to come out in the late afternoon, so the celebrations continued in more equable temperatures on the Mess terrace overlooking Biggin's famous valley.

The pilots of 609 were nothing if not keen on parties and outings, and being so close to London, and having two socialites like Michael and Paul, things were usually organised when the slightest chance arose. Roger Malengreau recalls:

"One afternoon the Squadron was released early with nothing foreseen for the following morning. As usual Michael suggested that we all go to London in his staff car, the Belgian barouche and another car, and as usual, to meet up for a night cap at 'The Suivi' between 11 am and midnight.

"On arrival at the night club, Michael found a message ordering the squadron back to Biggin Hill immediately as an operation was planned in the early morning. Unfortunately the three pilots who borrowed the cars had not come back. OK, said Michael, and ordered four taxis. When we arrived back at Biggin Hill the taxi drivers would not accept a penny for the fares.

"So later in July, a party was organised for our kind drivers, their wives and a few friends. It was a real good do and as a souvenir our guests presented us with an old fashioned taxi steering wheel which up to the late 1980s still decorated the Station Commander's office."

While away, Paul missed Circus 48 on the 14th, Micky bagging yet another 109F, which brought his personal total of claims to 15, but then more bad weather stopped ops once more, or cancelled them at the last minute. On the 18th 609 escorted three Blenheims on a Roadstead, meeting up with 222 Squadron's Spitfire on this cloudy day. 609 never saw a thing, although there was a ship and a couple of flak ships too. In the event all the Blenheims were shot down.

The good news of the day was that Micky Robinson was told he had been awarded the Distinguished Service Order, a very popular award which heralded a few drinks. He tried to celebrate the next day on Circus 51, but could only manage to damage a 109F, one of several that made determined efforts to get at the three Stirlings bombing Lille. Again came the sight of one of the huge four-engined bombers going down in flames, after being hit by flak from the coastal defences.

Paul had returned and was able to join the Wing on Circus 52 on the 20th, but it was a complete waste of time. No flak, no fighters and no target seen to bomb. It was estimated that some 10,000 gallons of petrol had been used for this show and as one pilot remarked, he couldn't get two gallons for his car! To add to this man's hurt, the Squadron were then Scrambled to 15,000 feet over Horsham, as 109s were reported hovering over Le Touquet, but nothing happened so another 500 gallons was sucked up by the Merlin engines for no return.

Circus 54 followed on the 21st, an early morning operation which began at 0745, but 609 were without the CO and most of the Belgian pilots who had gone off to London to be invested with the Belgian Croix de Guerre. Thus Paul led the Squadron, Biggin acting as escort cover wing with 609 on the top at 23,000 feet. Little was seen, although a few 109s did sniff around, but one pair got in close enough to pick off Sergeant Bramble who began to lag behind — fatal over France. Recently arrived Sergeant Van Shaick, who despite his Belgian sounding name was a true Brit, got into a scrap and damaged two 109s although his Spit was badly shot-up too. Two other 609 pilots escorted a Stirling home, limping along on three engines. Ken Bramble was later reported dead by the Germans, and buried in Merville Cemetery.

B Flight was released when everyone got back, only to find then that Circus 55 was called for the evening, 609 being then only able to supply six aircraft with pilots. The Station and Wing Leader brought this to eight, so it was this reduced number which helped escort three Stirlings to Mazingarbe, Biggin being one of the Target Support Wings. But the show was called off due to heavy cloud when half way to the target.

While all this activity had been going on, Micky with Offenberg, Vicki Ortmans, de Hemptinne, de Spirlet, Wilmet and Seghers, had been invested with the Croix de Guerre by the Belgian Minister of Defence in the Belgian National Government in London, M. Camille Gutt.

The next bit of real excitement came on Wednesday 23rd July, Circus 59 with six Blenheims to a target at the Foret de Eperlecques, just north-west of St Omer, and Circus 60 — again to Mazingarbe, with six Blenheims. The first show went off without much problem, Biggin providing Escort Cover but saw little or nothing. Only one of the Target Support Wings got into a fight with some 109s, claiming three but losing four pilots themselves.

The 36 Spitfires of the Wing led by Malan, with Group Captain Barwell too, took off for the second show of the day at 1940. They had orders to act as one of the two Target Support Wings, one squadron to fly in fours at 27,000 feet in the Bethune area, while the other two, also in fours, were to fly west of the target, up-sun, at 28-30,000.

Malan headed out, finding a shelf of cloud stretching down the Straits between 26 and 30,000 feet, so he tried to fly around it but he found it would take the Wing north of Dunkirk so he headed for Calais which they crossed at 28,000.Soon afterwards sixteeen Me109s were seen in the St Omer area, so Malan turned to engage but they rapidly dived away so he reformed. Several more formations were encountered and a general dog-fight began.

The target area was reached while this fighting continued, and over it six 109s dived down from 30,000 feet and 72 Squadron were forced to make a turn. It was then noticed that 609 had lost contact. Unknown to Malan, two of 609's pilots had been forced to abort due to faulty oxygen gear, Du Monceau had had undercarriage problems and when he'd sorted this out, had tagged onto another squadron. Finally, Dickie Barwell found his R/T had failed, so signalled he was returning. As so often happens, the rest of his section misunderstood his actions and followed him. This left Paul with just four other pilots to represent 609.

Paul himself was having trouble with his R/T, losing touch with both the leading squadron and the Wing Leader. Malan had called to 609 to engage some 109s but Paul was unable to hear properly and then lost sight of the other Spits in some haze. Having become separated, he orbitted south-east of the Foret de Nieppe while trying to spot where everyone had gone, but then five or six Me109s came screaming down at them from astern. Paul saw the danger and turned his men into them, his quick reactions foiling the attack, then they were climbing up into the sun. As they did so, two Me109s appeared and crossed their bows at close range, surprisingly turning away when engaged. After several bursts of fire from the quarter, with one Messerschmitt taking violent evasive action, Paul saw it begin to spew oil, while his No.2 saw bits coming off it, while Blue 2 saw the 109 suddenly flick and invert in a way no pilot could have manoeuvred while under any sort of control at such a speed. The 109 twisted down, a pilot in 72 Squadron seeing the pilot take to his parachute. Meanwhile, Sergeant Goldy Palmer, Red 2, knocked pieces of the other 109 and claimed it as damaged.

The main Wing formation made a fighting retreat to the coast, Malan damaging one 109, while Wing pilots claimed two 109s destroyed to add to Paul's. One 72 Squadron pilot failed to return. It had been quite a scrap but Paul had brought his small unit home without loss. He landed back at 2115, after a flight of 1 hour, 35 minutes in W3187.

German losses for the day amounted to three destroyed with two more crash landing after being damaged by fighters. Only two of the losses were E-models, whose pilots were Unteroffizier Alfred Barthel of II/JG26 and Gefreiter Ernst Kramer of III/JG26.

Next day he was back in W3240 for Circus 61, which was cancelled and then turned into a Roadstead, with torpedo-carrying Beauforts going for a large merchantship and five flak boats. While the Beauforts dropped their 'fish' the Spits strafed the flak ships, but all the torpedoes missed, so that was that. A couple of 109s joined in and Paul manoeuvred with one and some of the pilots saw a splash and thought he had hit the sea, but it was another 109. Only one 109 was attacked, by Brian Kingcome of 92 Squadron, and as all the British aircraft returned, Kingcome was credited with a 109 destroyed.

Paul missed Circus 61 when this was reactivated that afternoon, but Micky got into a scrap with some 109s and scored a probable and a damaged, while Tommy Rigler claimed a destroyed. The day also saw awards of the DFM to Palmer and Hughes-Rees.

There now came a move, from Biggin Hill to Gravesend, which was not welcomed by the Squadron, but had to be endured. The only redeeming feature was that the pilots would be living in Cobham Hall, a stately home of Tudor vintage belonging to the Earl of Darnley, who lived in one wing. There were plenty of 16th century beds and furniture to enjoy as well as floral lavatory basins, classic columns and Old Masters to view. Before that happened, however, Lord Robinson invited the Squadron down to tea so Micky led his flock down on a cross-country flight to Hullavington, the Squadron having been released because of 'non-op' weather.

They returned well watered, or perhaps well-tea'd, although judging from the amount of hilarity amongst the returning pilots, they seemed to have had something more in keeping with the continuing celebration of Micky's DSO.Roger Malengreau remembers this event:

> "One day in July, we were released for the afternoon and Michael suggested that we do a little cross country reconnaissance. The whole Squadron took off and landed at Hullavington. We were picked up by car and driven to his parent's home. We had a typical English tea and something a bit stronger just before leaving. We flew back in and out of clouds and with his bird's instinct, broke cloud just above Biggin Hill and made a low fly past in perfect formation over Sailor Malan's office. I don't know if Group approved but Michael could get away with almost anything."

No sooner was 609 at Gravesend, than Micky gave them the sad news that he was leaving the Squadron. Sailor Malan was finally being taken off Ops — with a victory score of 35 destroyed or shared destroyed — and Micky was taking his place as Wing Leader. While everyone was pleased about his new elevation, it would be hard to see him go, the only consolation being that he would still be leading them, even if in another guise.

The new CO was to be Squadron Leader George 'Sheep' Gilroy DFC, a flight commander from 603 Squadron at Hornchurch. As the news also came of the award of a bar to Paul's DFC, some wondered why he had not been given the Squadron, but the orders had been made, Gilroy arriving post-haste on the 29th. Gilroy, described as a slightly dour but kindly Scotsman, had flown in the Battle of Britain and had around 9 victories. He had shared in the destruction of the first enemy plane to land on British soil in WW2, a He111 forced down over the Firth of Forth back in October 1939.

Thus as August began, 609 started a new era, as did its former CO, now promoted to acting Wing Commander. For Paul too time was running out, his Fighter Pilot's summer coming to an end.

CHAPTER XIV

GOODBYE 609... GOODBYE MICKY...

JOHN BISDEE became tour expired at the end of July, his place as leader of B Flight taken by Jean Offenberg, the first Belgian fighter pilot to receive the British DFC. Micky Robinson also led his last Sweep with 609 — in the garden of Cobham Hall! It involved much hurdling of the ancestral yew hedges, while both Micky and Ziggy Ziegler lost their trousers, much to the surprise of Ziggy's wife who had been left neglected for two hours in his car.

As August began it was a difficult time for Paul. Several people thought he should have taken over from Michael, with whom he shared both his operational and social ideas. Both men had worked hard developing fighter tactics over the recent difficult months operating over France, and 609 would have welcomed him as leader; Paul thought he should have got the Squadron too, but it was not to be.

Michael tried to champion Paul's elevation too, and so did Frank Ziegler, 609's famous Intelligence Officer. Ziggy even took the bull by the horns and mentioned the fact to no lesser being than Air Vice-Marshal Sir Trafford Leigh-Mallory, the AOC, when the great man attended a party at Biggin on the occasion of Sailor's departure, but before Sheep Gilroy had been formally promoted to 609. All that Ziegler got for his pains was a sharp reprimand for daring to suggest to the AOC who he should appoint as his squadron commanders.

It was rare, although not unheard of, for flight commanders, however good, to take over a squadron especially in the early war years. The RAF still adhered to its pre-war thinking of promoting from outside the individual unit, although it had by this time ended its method of promoting by service rather than by experience. Whether

Paul would have been a good CO of 609 was not at issue. It was (a) a question of was it right, from Command's standpoint, and (b) if Paul really did need a rest, wasn't it better to give him a less taxing task pro-tem.

Paul was about to begin his fourth month of operational flying since returning to 11 Group, but Michael deserved a rest too. He'd been at it almost non-stop since the Battle of Britain, and now he was to lead a Wing of three squadrons. In the event, Michael was soon to be rested, his appointment being something of a stop-gap, and reward for his considerable prowess in the summer air fighting over France. Paul would soon be admitting he was tired.

Meantime, the war continued, with Gilroy in charge of 609. On operations now, however, 609 had first to fly up from Gravesend to Biggin for briefing and have their petrol tanks topped up, fly the Op and then fly back to their home station. Paul flew Circus Ops on 4th August, 5th August, 6th August and 7th August. In fact on the 7th he flew three.

The first of the 7th was a Lysander escort soon after first light, landing back at Manston. The Lizzie crew were searching for a dinghy in which it was hoped the crew of a bomber would be sitting. It was Paul who spotted the Verey Flare and smoke signals, then located the dinghy, seven miles north-east of Calais. As the aircraft circled, heavy flak fire came from the French coast as a rescue launch arrived to pick up the men, then Me109s were reported. They too arrived and there was a brief skirmish as the Spitfires headed for home, Maurice Choron hitting one which limped away smoking.

Op No.2 for the day was Circus 67, between 1040 and 1215, during which Rigler and Sergeant P Nash each claimed a damaged. Then at 1650 the Wing provided High Cover to Circus 62. Over France Micky probably destroyed a 109, but another almost got Paul. The target for six Blenheims was St Omer. If the RAF thought the Germans would react, they were right.

The problem was that the bombers couldn't find the target, but the Wing penetrated via Dunkirk, almost reaching St Omer before several gaggles of Me109s were found both above and below. Some engagements began but the Messerschmitts, generally, once in trouble, tended to pull away with superior speed.

Paul later admitted he was flying sloppily on this occasion and was lucky to survive the next half an hour. He was having some icing problems which may have distracted him a little, but he was suddenly pounced on by what he later described as "a gaily coloured 109" which put a burst into his engine, smashed his glycol tank, and he promptly lost all his coolant. He immediately went into spin, seeing nothing but smoke and glycol, and quickly thought it was time to step over the side, but then discovered he was unable to release the pin of his safety harness.

Recovering from the spin, he then had to evade another attack from a 109, then somehow nursed his Spitfire towards the French coast. His No.2 told him he was leaving a thin trail of smoke, as his engine began to overheat, then came the decision to try to make it back or to bale out now. He had more than 30 miles at best of open sea, and although the Air Sea Rescue people would be alerted, he could still have a major problem. He knew perfectly well that with his engine coolant gone, he would very soon be forced to shut down his engine, or risk a fire right in front of himself.

Paul, characteristically, decided to make a try for England. That he made it was due to 75% skill and 25% luck. Nevertheless, Paul, being Paul, decided to write a report on how he got back, in order that other pilots might read it and learn — and perhaps, decide to stay with their aircraft rather than bale out into captivity. His report was later reproduced in a 11 Group Fighter Command Tactics Memorandum. These informative documents were distributed by Victor Beamish DSO DFC AFC, who was Group Captain (Operations) at Group Headquarters:

11 Group Tactical Memorandum No.10.
Special Report by Flight Lieutenant Paul Richey DFC & bar, Circus 62 flying with 609 Squadron, attack received near St Omer. 15-20 Me109s at 25,000 feet.

(1) I was Yellow 1 of 609 Squadron taking part in Circus 62, 7 August 1941. Having failed to rendezvous with the main formation of the Biggin Hill Wing, proceeded to carry out a "SPHERE" entry at Dunkirk and flying over St. Omer with the intention of leaving France at Cap Gris Nez. 609 was top squadron, 92 middle and 72 bottom, and heights were originally from 25-28,000 feet.

(2) Over St. Omer many 109s were sighted far below against cloud and 72 led by Wing Commander Robinson, attacked. 92 lost height by diving and then circled for some time, followed by 609 Squadron. If I may suggest it, I think 92's tactics were mistaken, for both height and speed were lost and nothing gained. In addition the stepped-up formation of 92 and 609 were messed up and generally confused, while the Huns were able to gain height and time and get up-sun with a good view of what was going on.

(3) I was troubled with ice on my hood and windscreen. I was

also very bored and cold and was flying sloppily. While my attention was concentrated on a formation above me, I was shot-up in no uncertain manner by a gaily coloured Me109 diving from behind. My glycol tank was pierced and all my glycol lost. I throttled back and went into an involuntary spin. I could see nothing but smoke, glycol etc and could not recover from the spin which became very flat. I opened the hood to bale out but had great difficulty in removing my harness pin, I think because (a) I did not look at what I was doing, and (b) I was experiencing a lot of 'G'. When I got the pin out I was slowly deciding which side of the cockpit to get out. The smoke abated and I decided to stay in and try to recover, by winding the tail wheel fully forward and using considerable strength on the stick, I did so. (The tail was damaged.) I dived for cloud and the French coast, weaving, and was attacked by another 109 which I evaded by turning violently and entering cloud. My "Maiz-dez" was answered immediately over the sea on Button 'D' and was given a vector.

(4) I was unable to use the vector because of having to weave and control the aircraft. Half way across the Straits at 1,000 feet I tried my engine and was able to use it to the English coast by cutting down boost and revs to a minimum. I had great difficulty in doing up the straps again because of instability of the aircraft which necessitated strong forward pressure on the stick, but succeeded after five minutes. I was comforted by the sight of many rescue launches and buoys and by the Hurricane low cover off the Goodwins. On a fast belly landing at Manston with a still smoking aircraft I found the fire tender very prompt. I would like to stress the following points for the benefit of young pilots:

1. Slackness in the vicinity of the Huns is easy but usually fatal.

2. A Spitfire will last long enough without glycol and even practically without oil, if revs and boost are reduced to an absolute minimum.

3. The sea is much more hospitable than German occupied territory. It is well worth risking attempting reaching it. The chances of rescue are excellent.

4. Do not try a slow forced landing, with damaged control surfaces.

Paul got down at Manston at 1850, but W3240 was badly damaged. He had been flying it almost exclusively since it arrived on the Squadron from No.8 MU on 28 May. It was now taken off to be repaired at Hamble and was not fit for further service until October.

It eventually went to 121 Eagle Squadron at the beginning of November, being finally struck off the RAF's charge in January after being seriously damaged in a crash.

Many years later Paul was to describe the incident during a television interview:

> "I was shot-up badly from behind. I didn't know, but my radio wasn't working and at 26,000 ft, it happened to be very cold that day and I had ice on the outside of the hood. I saw something flashing up in the sun and was watching this, when suddenly there was a whole lot of popping and banging and sparks, and so on, and there was some chap about 30 yards behind me, pumping stuff into me.
>
> "I went into a very quick turn and went into an involuntary spin. All my glycol came out and I thought this was it, I've probably got to bale out. I tried to get out of the spin, couldn't, so opened the hood and undid the straps, when I suddenly remembered I had a date for dinner at the Ritz that evening, so I'd better have one more shot.
>
> "So I had another go and got the Spitfire out of the spin. But then I had the difficulty that the aeroplane was practically uncontrollable and the first thing I did was to look behind, to find the German still there firing at me. So I managed to lurch into a cloud, flying very crazily, because the Spitfire wanted to loop all the time and so I recrossed the Channel in a series of swoops. I was losing height all the time, with the engine getting hotter and hotter, and eventually I had to decide, when I was down to 1,000 feet, do I bale out now and be safe, hoping I'd be picked out of the Channel, or do I try and get over the cliffs.
>
> "I thought, to Hell with it, I'll try to get over the cliffs, which I did, and parked down, as it happened, at RAF Manston. My wheels wouldn't come down and the aeroplane caught fire on the ground, and I jumped out in a hurry when it crunched to a halt. The fire engine arrived and a man pointed a foam nozzle at the fire, but nothing came out. Then I saw him look into it, whereupon it began to work, drenching the poor chap, which gave me a little light relief."

Paul's time with 609 was now drawing to a close. He was to fly just two more operations with the Wing, on 12 August, in Spitfire W3238. Circus 69 and Circus 70 were scheduled for the morning, the first to St Omer aerodrome, the other to the power station at Gosnay, laid on for a diversion for a 2 Group operation. These two shows were different in that they each had six Hampden bombers from 5 Group rather than Blenheims or Stirlings. Biggin Hill provided its three squadrons to act as Escort Cover Wing, but it was a pretty feeble affair, with just one Me109 damaged, at the cost of three Spitfires lost, two by the Tangmere Wing, one by the Kenley Wing — both of which were flying Target Support. Paul was in the air from 1110 to 1245. A few 109s were seen and Paul was attacked twice, first by a trio of very bright, new-looking Me109Fs and later by a lone 109 but no shots were exchanged. His last show, Circus 72, was a sweep and escort to Blenheims of 226 Squadron to Le Trait that same evening, 1715 to 1800 hours, which in the event was a bit of a flop and an anti-climax. Again a few 109s were seen but 609 didn't get near enough to engage. Only de Spirlet had some excitement, being fired on by flak from Calais as he came upon two 109s below some cloud, so quickly went back up into the cloud. Micky Robinson landed at Gravesend after this operation to have a drink with his old Squadron. A feature of Micky's sorties now, is that he had appointed Maurice Choron as his permanent No.2, no matter with which Wing squadron Micky flew, which made the intelligence reports somewhat confusing.

The Squadron MO, Flying Officer Lawrence, now recommended that Paul be rested. Since joining the Squadron in April he had flown on some 53 fighter Sweeps and Circus operations, as well as a number of other sorties. This sort of flying takes its toll, for not only did it mean an average of 1 hour 45 minutes in the air, generally with some sort of action over France, but it entailed two crossings of the English Channel, the one coming back usually with one eye on the fuel gauge. As a flight commander, he also needed to be alert, not just for himself, but for the men who he was leading and who relied on him for their safety. It is a measure of the man that while flying at the head of A Flight or on occasion the Squadron, he had never lost a pilot.

He now took the promised command of Sailor Malan's old 74 Squadron, which was still on rest up at Acklington. Not that the announcement was either welcome or totally diplomatic. A party and dance had been arranged at Biggin on the 17th August, on the occasion of Malan officially handing over to Micky, the job of Wing Commander Flying. The party was a good one and the AOC also came, who suddenly announced that Paul was posted to command 74, which was not greeted with any great joy by either Paul or 609.

As Paul described it:

"We were nearing the end of the 1941 'Season' of Sweeps and so on, and Leigh-Mallory came to a do at Biggin Hill, when Micky

Robinson had just been promoted to Wing Leader. Micky had wanted me to take over 609 but Victor Beamish, who was Group Captain Ops at 11 Group HQ at the time, came over to me and said L-M wants to talk to you. L-M said, 'We're going to give you a Squadron, Paul. We were going to give you the American Eagle Squadron [No.71 Eagle Squadron, RAF manned by American volunteers] but I think you need a rest and so I want you to go and pull 74 Squadron together before they fall apart. Immediately you tell me their ready, let me know and we'll get you back into 11 Group straight away.' So some days later, off I went to Acklington."

Before Paul left Biggin there was a bit of a party laid on by the Belgian Headquarters at Eaton Square, in London.The venue was to be the Pinafore Room at the Savoy Hotel, which as it turned out, was quite a sumptuous affair, with ample wine and liquor laid on. Getting everyone back to Biggin was a bit of a headache, Frank Ziegler taking Peter Mackenzie, Duke Du Monceau, Paul and wife Teresa, in his car. The three pilots immediately crashed out in the back, which was a bit of a nuisance for Frank, as only Paul knew the way back by road. Lost in the environs of Blackheath, in south-east London, Frank tried to get Paul to help with directions, but all Paul achieved was to get out of the car, 'liberate' the globe end of a crossing beacon he found lying in the gutter, climb back in and with the orange ball on his lap, go back to sleep.

More was to follow. Two policemen stopped Ziggy's car and their torches picked out the slumbering men — with the beacon globe — and were so amazed they could hardly give direction themselves. Arriving at the Dicken's Pickwick Leather Bottle Hotel in Cobham village, where Paul and Teresa had booked for the night, they were unable to gain entry at so late — or early? — an hour, so Ziggy and Mackenzie smuggled the couple into Ziggy's double-bedded room in the Cobham Hall Mess. Later they had to smuggle them out again, but not before an amazed batman was called to serve breakfast to a married couple in the Intelligence Officer's bed!

Paul said his farewells to everyone before he finally left for the north. 609 had been and would continue to be a wonderful band of pilots and ground staff. Micky, of course, said his farewell to his brother-in-law, whom he had always tried to get near him. Now they were departing and separating for good. They would never fly together again.

Paul's brother flight commander, John Bisdee, had already left at the end of July, and would see action on the island of Malta in the spring of 1942. He received the DFC just as he left. Of the others, there were mixed fortunes. John Hughes-Rees would be commissioned but would die in a crash at Fayid in April 1943 as a Flying Officer. Bob Boyd was also commissioned and was killed in action flying with 41 Squadron in September 1943, also as a Flying Officer. Goldy Palmer didn't survive 1941, being lost while still with 609, in October. On the same day as he went into the Channel, Vicki Ortmans was also shot down and taken prisoner. Vicki's brother Christian had also arrived on 609, just about the time Paul left. He and Paul would know each other better, later, Christian's destiny being entwined with that of Paul.

Of the other Belgians, Eugene Seghers rose to become a flight lieutenant, and win the DFC, only to die with 91 Squadron in July 1944 while attacking a V1 flying bomb. Baudouin de Hemptinne was killed over France with 122 Squadron in May 1942, while Jean Offenberg would be killed in a collision in January 1942 when on a training flight with 609. Francois de Spirlet was killed in a take-off accident with 609 in June 1942. 'Duke' Du Monceau would survive the war with the DFC and several Belgian decorations, and the highest score of any of the Belgian fighter pilots. He became a Colonel in his native airforce after the war.

Paul duly arrived at RAF Acklington to take over 74 Squadron on 23rd August, with the rank of acting Squadron Leader. The incumbent CO, Squadron Leader S T Meares DFC left to command No.71 (Eagle) Squadron — the unit Paul was so nearly sent to command. Stan Meares would be killed in November in a collision with one of his American pilots. Paul's two flight commanders were Flight Lieutenant Scott and C H Saunders. Paul could count himself lucky to have been given command of the 'Tigers' at this stage of his career, when most other tour-expired pilots might have expected a period as an instructor, or even worse, the job of "flying a desk". However, it was something of a rest as 74 were out of the front line and indeed, went further from it at the beginning of October when it moved to Llanbedr, on the west coast of Wales. Paul was also notified about this time that he had been awarded the Belgian Croix de Guerre, for his work with the Belgians in 609 over the summer. It was a singular honour and one he was proud of. However, things were about to change for Squadron Leader Paul Richey.

When recuperating from his injuries received in France, Paul had written up his experiences with 1 Squadron from the beginning of the

From top right clockwise:

1 Sergeant A G 'Goldie' Palmer DFM, killed in action 21 October 1941.

2 Sergeant R T D Mercer, killed in action 9 May 1941.

3 PO Count R G C De Hemricourt de Grunne, killed in action 21 May 1941.

4 PO Jimmy Baraldi, affectionately known as 'Jimmy the Wop'.

5 Sergeant Hughes-Rees DFM, killed in a flying accident in 1943.

6 Sergeant RJ Boyd, killed in action with 41 Sqdn, 6 September 1943.

Top: Visit by Winston Churchill to Biggin Hill, 7 July 1941. Seen here with Air Marshal Sholto Douglas, C-in-C Fighter Command. Note petrol bowser refuelling PR-M, for 609 had only just returned from Bethune (Circus 38). In 1942, Paul would be working for Sholto at Fighter Command HQ.

Bottom left: Another 'top brass' visit, this time ACM Hugh 'Boom' Trenchard, on 11 July. With him is Group Captain P R 'Dickie' Barwell, Biggin's 'operational' Station Commander, and Micky in shirt-sleeves. This time 609 had just landed from successful Circus 44, Barwell and Micky having bagged 109s.

Bottom right: SL Jamie Rankin DFC, CO of 92 Squadron which shared Biggin Hill in 1941 and was part of the wing.

Top left: Paul in 1941, with something to smile about - he was on ops!

Top right: In contrast, Micky looking sombre. Back from a gruelling sortie over Northern France.

Bottom left: The ever-smiling Vicki Ortmans …

Bottom right: … and his brother Christian, who would travel to India with Paul.

Top: Maurice Choron (left), Micky's loyal wingman, with Raymond Lallemant.

Middle: Wing Leaders RAF Biggin Hill, Sailor Malan and his successor, Micky Robinson. Mess party, August 1941.

Bottom: Fighter Command's adversary: the Me109F.

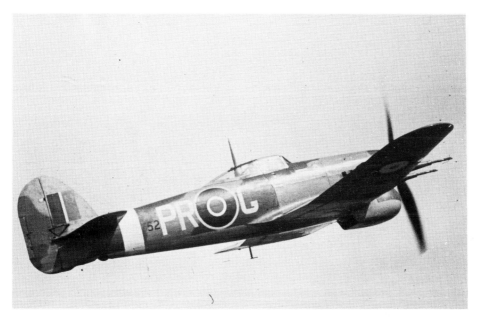

Top: Paul flying his Typhoon PR-G (R7752), as CO of 609 Squadron, 1942.

Bottom left: Francois de Spirlet, killed in a tragic accident.

Bottom right: Flight Lieutenant Joe Atkinson DFC, Paul's senior flight commander on 609 Squadron in 1942. Note black and white stripes under the wings to help identify the Typhoons from FW190s to coastal AA gunners.

Top: Paul with his men, 609 Squadron, 1942. (At top l to r); FO R J H Roelandt, FO P Raw DFC, FL J C Wells DFC, FO R Lallemant DFC, FS S H Spallin & Sgt A R N Davis. (Standing): FO Doc MacKechnie (MO), FO J G Astbury AFM, FO T A Yates (EO), FO E H Tidswell (adj), FL Joe Atkinson DFC, Paul, FL Jean de Selys DFC, FO R H Payne, FO J Solak, FL Frank Zeigler (IO). In front PO Mony van Lierde DFC, FO J G F Renier.

Middle: The FW190 which landed by accident at Pembrey, 23 June 1942, photographed by Paul the next day.

Bottom: The luckless Oberleutnant Arnim Faber, of III/JG2, who presented the RAF with a perfect example of the FW190. Paul spoke to him at Pembrey, the German taking a keen interest in Paul's Typhoon.

Top: Paul when OC 165 Wing, with the Supreme Commander SEAC, Lord Louis Mountbatten, Comilla, Eastern Bengal 1943.

Middle: Paul introducing the American Major General George E Stratemeyer, OC Eastern Air Command, USAAF, to his Wing squadron commanders at Imphal in 1944, (l to r): Stratemeyer, Paul Richey, SL C P N Newman (34 Sqdn), SL G J C Hogan DFC (5 Sqdn), SL G May DFC (42 Sqdn), SL H G F Larsen (28 Sqdn) and SL D Winton DFC, 155 Sqdn.

Bottom: Max Aitken DSO DFC, using Paul's back in order to sign autographs during the ceremony of the unveiling of a railway engine of the Battle of Britain Class, named '601 Squadron', September 1948.

Top: Paul seated in the cockpit of his Vampire F.3 at North Weald, during his period of command, 1950-52. Note squadron leader's pennant marking by cockpit. (Probably VT800.)

Middle left: A smiling Squadron Leader Paul Richey DFC, while with 601 Squadron, 1950.

Middle right: Although both had fought very different wars, Paul is seen hear talking to Group Captain Whitney Straight CBE MC DFC, at a post-war function. One thing they did have in common, they had both flown with 601 Squadron.

Bottom: Diana and Paul, in the South of France, 1964.

war until he was wounded. It formed the basis of a book, in which B
T Batsford Ltd, of North Audley Street, London, W1, took an interest
and agreed to publish. Paul was pleased, as most would-be authors
are, to have someone agree that they can write, but the problem was
the authorship. As an operational pilot, Paul did not feel inclined to
have his name emblazoned on the book cover, modesty notwith-
standing. There would be enough friends who'd pull his leg unmerci-
fully, when they did find out, without having his name publicized
openly. It was also the trend in those early war years for authors of
war books who were still in the 'front line', to have their books
published anonymously for one of several reasons, so Paul agreed with
Batsford, that the book would have no author name at all. It was
merely published, in September 1941, as Fighter Pilot: A Personal
Record of the Battle of France.

At Fighter Command Headquarters one morning, the C-in-C, Air
Marshal Sir William Sholto Douglas KCB DSO MC, strode into his
office with a copy of Paul's book under his arm. As he said his good-
mornings, he threw the book down on the desk and said he wanted
to know who had written it.

The P-Staff Officer apparently telephoned Batsford, demanding in
the name of Sholto Douglas, to know the author of the new book, and
Batsford had little choice, or desire, not to disclose who it was. So
"name, rank and number" was duly given to Sholto Douglas. Paul
told me:

> "While commanding 74 Squadron at Llanbedr, we had the new
> airfield all to ourselves, which was very nice, for there was no
> station commander or much admin staff about as yet, so we could
> generally please ourselves.
>
> "We were heavily into our training programme, and I had
> kicked out a few people who were proving useless, and then we
> were sent a signal that Sholto Douglas was going to visit the
> Station, which was rather a curious place to come to — for him.
> He duly landed and I had all the boys paraded in a Nissen hut, but
> almost from the minute he arrived he showered me with questions
> for about an hour, and even if I wasn't sure of the answer, I gave
> him one.
>
> "Then he went off and the next day came my posting to Fighter
> Command Headquarters. I quickly rushed off in a Spitfire to RAF
> Valley, which was our Sector HQ, and saw Group Captain John
> 'Doggie' Oliver DSO DFC, and told him I didn't want to go, being
> far too interested in my Squadron, but there was nothing he said

he could do about it. He thought, in fact, I was very tired. He knew, of course, that I had only recently baled out of a Spitfire near the airfield, but that had nothing to do with tiredness.

"Well, I asked Oliver if I could go in and talk to the AOC, which I then did. The AOC said he was pleased to know that I didn't want to leave him and his Group — which wasn't exactly what was in my mind — but he advised me not to fight it. So off I went to Fighter Command.

"I heard later that what had happened was that Sholto had gone into his morning conference with a copy of my book under his arm, and threw it on the table, saying to his P-Staff chap, Geoffrey Ellis, that he was to find out who had written it and wanting everyone in the HQ to read it. When they discovered who had written it, and told Sholto, he said, 'I want that man in my Headquarters.' So that was why I was unable to wriggle free."

But what about this 'recent bale out'? On the afternoon of 10th October, Paul was flying a Spitfire IIA — P8184 ZD-J (only front-line units had Spit Vs), back from RAF Valley. He told me:

"I was preparing to land when I found that I'd got one wheel stuck up and the other stuck down. I tried to get both wheels up again but found the lever had jammed. I thought that landing on the airfield, which had runways built on sand, would prove dangerous, believing that immediately the wheel-less wing lost speed and touched the ground, I'd be pulled off into the sand and probably turn over, and there might be a fire.

"So I thought — it's only £5,000 — so did three practise runs over the airfield heading out to sea, and everything seemed all right, so finally I baled out at a certain point, letting the Spitfire head out to sea so it would not land on anyone. As I came down I reckoned I'd drift in onto the airfield and was just about to do it but one of my pilots had taken off to assist me, and he came flashing by and I had to rapidly drop just short of the boundary, into a field."

His landing was a bad one. Seeing a stone wall surmounted with barbed wire below him, he tried to sideslip, landed on his left foot and jack-knifed his left knee with the full weight of his body on it, badly damaging the knee joint. As the Station hadn't yet got a Medical Officer, Paul did not have his injury attended to until early November when he saw his family doctor when posted to Fighter Command.

So posting orders were made, and Paul left 74 on the 7th November, 1941, his place taken by an old friend from 1 Squadron, Pete Matthews DFC.

I never asked Paul much about his time with Fighter Command HQ, perhaps there were many, as I thought, other interesting things to talk about, which, in retrospect, is a pity. No doubt he helped plan and disseminate, even try to dictate, some of the tactics fighter squadrons should adopt, based on his experiences while operating from Biggin Hill. What Sholto Douglas had liked in Paul's book was the obvious ability of this young man not only to be able to think and understand such things as tactics and air fighting, but also to write them down. Paul did write a number of reports which found their way to the squadrons, but whether they always or if ever, had his name on them is not certain. One of them was a paper he wrote on Fighter-Bombing of Shipping, which was issued by FCHQ and also promulgated overseas. Paul did admit to me that he didn't like the job much:

"After I'd been there about a month I went to Sholto and said I didn't like the work and may I go back to the Squadron? He said certainly not, I want you here for six months! However, each month for the next five months I would go back to him and ask to be allowed back to a squadron. Finally he said, 'Look, if you come to me again, Paul, and ask to go back to a squadron, I shall be extremely annoyed, but I promise you that the day your six months are up, and if you still want to go to a squadron, come to me and I'll let you go.' So, needless to say, on the very day my six months was up — I think it was on my birthday, 7th May — I went to him. He asked me what I wanted to do, and where I wanted to go.

"It just so happened that one of my recent jobs at Fighter Command HQ was to select the three squadrons which would be the first to equip with the new Hawker Typhoon fighter, and select their base airfield. I had finally chosen 56, 266 and my old 609, mostly on the basis of experience, standard of flying and availability. I also knew that Sheep Gilroy was due for a rest and about to be posted.

"So I said to Sholto that I'd like, if possible, to take over 609 Squadron, having heard that their CO was about to go on rest. Also, as 609 had just got Typhoons, I'd like to be with them. Sholto said OK, and I was sent as a Supernumerary to 56 Squadron, and then, when Gilroy got his posting, I was in the chair. So I came onto Typhoons, a decision I was to regret! It was an interesting aeroplane but I rather regretted not going back onto Spitfires."

When he made his decision, about the Typhoon and his posting, the new aeroplane had good potential as the RAF's 'new' fighter. Built primarily as a replacement for the Hurricane, it promised great things, but in the event it was too heavy for altitude air fighting. Although it was already proving a bit of a problem aeroplane, Paul undoubtedly thought it was just early teething troubles, but the desire to get back onto an operational unit, and having stage managed a return to 609 which he had helped to get Typhoons, had set the course he was to follow.

However, before all this happened, disaster had struck both the Robinson and Richey families. Micky was killed.

Micky had remained leader of the Biggin Hill Wing for just a few weeks, being rested at the beginning of September. During this period he brought his personal score of victories to 18, with four probables and eight damaged. Quite a record. Dickie Barwell gave him an 'Exceptional' assessment in his flying log book. From Biggin, Micky went to RAF Manston as Station Commander but then in early October he was given a post as Aide to the Inspector General of the RAF. He held this job until the beginning of 1942 when he was made leader of the Tangmere Wing, which, while something Micky might have been pleased about, put him back onto operations after less than four months of rest.

True he didn't fly very many Ops in those winter months, but he was on call and had a tough schedule of work, helping to train and plan for the spring with his three fighter squadrons, especially now that the Germans had their new Focke Wulf 190 fighter, which had started to make things difficult for the Spitfire Mark Vs as 1941 ended.

The Wing had hardly got into their stride when the fateful last sortie was flown — 10th April 1942. It was a High Cover Fighter Sweep, Micky leading 41, 129 and 340 (Free French) Squadrons. A Rodeo was being flown by 12 bomb-carrying Hurricanes against the harbour at Boulogne in the late afternoon, while Tangmere's fighters would be sweeping behind the town to engage any fighters that tried to engage.

Paul told me of the occasion the news arrived:

"I was flying Sholto about all over the place at this time, in a Vega Gull of all things. We had left Fighter Command on a four-day tour of the West Country. At one airfield we were at, I was sent for, being wanted on the telephone in the control tower. By the time I'd got there the call had been cut-off and I didn't think any more about it. However, when we got back to Hendon, having got into Sholto's Rolls-Royce to drive back to HQ, I remember saying to Sholto, how extraordinary it was that some chaps have the hell shot out of them time and again, come back and carry on, whereas another chap will never have a bullet in his aeroplane but suddenly will not come back — just disappear. Sholto agreed. I continued that Micky had never had a bullet in his aeroplane.

"When we got back to HQ at Bentley Priory, I found a note on my desk to say that Micky was missing. Sholto rang through to me immediately, for he had a note too. He told me to go off at once to Teresa."

Paul was stunned, and so was the C in C. Paul knew he should go home but there were more immediate things to do. For one thing he had to make sure everything was being organised in case Micky had come down in the sea. He made several calls to Tangmere and was told that the Air Sea Rescue boys were out searching and that rescue boats were standing by. It was now early evening, and news may come in at any moment, so he delayed his trip home until the next day. Unfortunately, by then, still nothing had been heard, so instead of bringing hope and good news to Teresa and to the Robinsons, he had no news at all.

Determined to find out all he could about Micky's last operation, Paul went down to Tangmere and interviewed everyone involved. He also found out that little Maurice Choron, Micky's faithful No.2, had also failed to return. Still no news came from the ASR squadrons, and although there was every chance he was in his dinghy somewhere in the Channel, it was beginning to look bad. How could this have happened to a man like Micky?

No. 41 Squadron was led by acting Wing Commander P H 'Dutch' Hugo DFC, who had only recently been promoted and was about to take up a Wing Leader post (in fact he then took over Micky's Wing), while 41's new CO designate, Squadron Leader J C Fee, flew in Hugo's section to get some experience. Squadron Leader R H Thomas led 129 Squadron, while Micky flew with 340 Squadron with its CO, Squadron Leader Philippe de Scitivaux, (Charles Jean Marie Philippe de Scitivaux de Greische, to give him his full name), who had previously been with 615 Squadron. It was 340's first ever operation.

Later, Paul was to write the following report on the events of this fateful day:

On the afternoon of Friday, April 10th, 1942, Wing Commander Robinson took off at the head of the Tangmere Wing with orders to carry out a sweep behind Boulogne. The Wing Commander was leading No.340 (Free French) Squadron on their first operation of this kind. The Squadron flew in three fours, the Wing Commander leading the first and lowest four, and Captain Duperier leading the second four, which was above and behind the first. The third four was above and behind the second. The remaining two squadrons of the Wing were stepped up above and behind No.340.

2. The French coast was crossed without incident, No.340 Squadron being at about 18,000 feet. Shortly afterwards one or two odd pairs of Me109s were seen below and travelling in the opposite direction (ie: west). The Wing turned north about twenty miles inside Hardelot (south of Boulogne).

3. They soon sighted (a) a large number of aircraft above them (identified by the Wing Commander as friendly), and (b) a pair of Me109s about 5,000 feet below on their left and going in the opposite direction (ie: south). (This was approximately between St.Omer and Boulogne, ie: 20 miles inland). The Wing Commander immediately half-rolled and dived after them, calling up and saying, "Come on, we are going down on these." He was followed by his No.2 (Lieutenant Choron) his No.3 (Squadron Leader de Scitivaux, CO of 340) and his No.4 (Lt de Labouchere). Captain Duperier had difficulty in following with his section because of the suddenness and violence of the Wing Commander's manoeuvre. The third four failed to follow for the same reason and lost contact. The two top Squadrons, who stayed up as top cover, also lost contact and did not engage.

4. In the dive, Captain Duperier sighted four FW190s diving behind him. He promptly pulled out of his dive to one side, followed by his three [men]. The FW190s continued their dive at great speed, and although Captain Duperier tried to catch them, he could not. By this time he had lost contact with the Wing Commander's four. He subsequently patrolled the area to the coast, turning inland again and eventually returning to England after a long combat over the sea in which his four were attacked seven times from above by four FW190s. He also saw and heard certain things as related below.

5. Lieutenant de Labouchere, the Wing Commander's No.4, who was the only one of this section to return, says that the section kept well together in spite of the violence of the Wing Commander's manoeuvre and followed him down close behind on to the two Me109s. Before the range had been closed, however, it was seen that there were four 109s flying in two pairs, and not a single pair as previously thought. The Wing Commander's four therefore split into two pairs, the Wing Commander and his No.2 (Lieu-

tenant Choron) attacking one pair and the Wing Commander's No.3 (Squadron Leader de Scitivaux) and No.4 (Lieutenant de Labouchere) attacking the other.

6. Lieutenant de Labouchere says that while firing at his 109 he lost sight of his leader (now Squadron Leader de Scitivaux). He thinks he shot his 109 down, but failed to find his leader or the Wing Commander and his No.2 again. He saw a number of dog-fights going on (this was probably the Polish Wing, which had engaged in this area about three minutes before the arrival of the Tangmere Wing). He saw a large number of aircraft in the distance which he thought were Spitfires but joined up with five nearer Spitfires in case they were not. He returned to England with these Spitfires.

7. Captain Duperier, Lieutenant de Labouchere, and several others of 340 Squadron, heard several transmissions while the above events were taking place. These started shortly after the Wing Commander's original attack and were as follows.

8. R.T Conversations. (a) Lieutenant Choron: "Michael, I've got him smoking!"

(b) Wing Cmdr Robinson: (calmly) "OK, Maurice, you're doing fine."

(c) Lieutenant Choron: "Michael, where are you? I have lost you."

(d) Wing Cmdr Robinson: "Re-form over Calais."

(e) Lieutenant Choron: Distress call and "I am going down," or something similar.

9. The Polish Wing meanwhile, had climbed to attack about 30 FW190s from below, shooting down 8 or more without loss to themselves. They report seeing a Spitfire going down in flames.

10. The remainder of the French Squadron report seeing a Spitfire spinning down out of control and another diving vertically with two FW190s on its tail. They also saw a dinghy in the sea off Le Touquet drifting in-shore. It was first seen 6 miles out and last 2 miles out.

Conclusions.

11. The following points should be noted:—

(a) Although the French Squadron was in the main inexperien-ced, the pilots who took part in the above events had had con-siderable experience of fighter sweeps during 1941.

(b) The Wing Commander's action in carrying out a sudden and violent manoeuvre for the sake of two Huns, and with a Squadron on its first operation, may be considered rash.

(c) Captain Duperier did very well to bring his section back intact.

(d) The R/T conversations indicate that Lieutenant Choron shot down his 109, lost the Wing Commander, and was later shot down himself. Also that the Wing Commander was in full control of the situation, though evidently alone, but probably made a mistake when he ordered a re-form over Calais, which was some 40-50 miles north of the position of the fight; he probably (though not certainly) meant Boulogne, which was nearby and well within sight.

(e) There is some likelihood that the aircraft seen above just before the Wing Commander dived, and identified by him as friendly, were hostile and that the 190s that attacked Captain Duperier's section in the dive were some of them. These Huns may have attacked and accounted for the Wing Commander, Lieutenant Choron and Squadron Leader de Scitivaux, all of whom were evidently alone by that time.

(f) The three Spitfires seen in difficulties (one in flames, one spinning, and one diving with two Huns on its tail), may only have been two seen by different observers at different stages (eg: the one seen in flames by the Poles may have been the one diving followed by two Huns seen by the French a few seconds earlier).

(g) The dinghy off Le Touquet was probably (although not by any means certainly) Lieutenant Choron's and the occupant, if any, is almost certainly a prisoner. (It was impossible for the British to pick it up, and a message was sent accordingly to the Germans.)

(h) There was a very strong westerly wind, which probably drifted the dinghy ashore. It would also blow a parachute well in-land from the French coast or over the French coast from mid-Channel unless a bale-out were made low down. Further, it would undoubtedly induce the Wing Commander to land in France if his engines were damaged.

(i) The Wing Commander had always said that he would head inland over France if there were any risk of not reaching England.

P H M Richey. S/Ldr
25 May 1942.

Even at this date, it was obvious that Paul and others were still hoping that Michael had indeed flown inland before either baling out or para-chuting down, and may yet be safe and with the French Resistance or at any rate, trying to evade capture. Only time would eventually show that nothing like this had happened and that Micky had gone into the Channel — hopefully with his Spitfire. Hopefully, because Maurice Choron, who had indeed ended up in his dinghy, was later reported dead, having died of exposure in the rubber craft which earlier had seemed to be his saviour.

Nearly 10 years later, Paul was to annotate this report, in biro, with the following:

> 1. S/Ldr de Scitivaux was later reported Prisoner of War. He was wounded and descended by parachute.
> 2. Lt de Labouchere is still Missing, presumed killed in action.[1]
> 3. Lt Choron's dead body was, shortly after the combat, reported by Radio Paris to have been recovered from the sea. He had died from exposure. There was no report from official German sources.
> 4. There has never been any news of W/Cdr Robinson.

Oddly enough, Paul was wrong in the make-up of Micky's Red Section on this day. The Squadron Operational Record Book shows the four sections were as follows:

Red Section	Yellow Section	Blue Section
WC M L Robinson	Cdt P de Scitivaux	Capt B Duperier
FO M Choron	S/Chef R Darbans	Sgt Debac
Lt R Mouchotte	Lt F de Labouchere	Lt J Schloesing
S/Chef Guignand	Lt A Gibert	Lt J Fournier

Therefore, Paul reporting that Micky, Choron, de Scitivaux and de Labouchere were in one section is incorrect. This is confirmed also by Bernard Duperier's book *La Veille Equipe*, wherein he records that Rene Mouchotte flew as Red 3 with Sergent Chef Guignand as Red 4. Mouchotte, leader of A Flight, would normally have flown as Yellow Leader (as Paul had done in 609) but as Micky was leading 340 and therefore Red Section, Philippe de Scitivaux had deposed Mouchotte, relegating him to Red 3. Duperier also confirms his section as himself, Debac, Schloesing and Fournier (the latter two incidently, would both command 340 in the future).

So, either the Squadron had got mixed up slightly in the air, or Micky had led down not a whole Section (Red) but just Red and

---

[1] This would indicate the fact that Paul knew that Francois de Labouchere DFC CdeG, was officially reported missing on 5 September 1942 during a fight with FW190s.

Yellow Sections ie: Micky and Choron, de Scitivaux and de Labouchere. A small point, but one made for the sake of accuracy.

Duperier's book also makes excellent reference to this operation, especially the last moments on the ground following the briefing. He noted:

> "Having given his orders Michael Robinson reminded us that the call-sign to use in all radio communications is 'Michael' and we all came out of his little office and got back into our cars. He took a book and calmly went to an armchair in the sun; despite myself I admire the amazing calm of this great man.
>
> "The last memory that I have, at the moment Philippe was driving off, was of this young man in his battle dress of fine grey-blue serge, a silk scarf round his neck, sitting in a linen armchair, on the green grass which surrounded him. His face had a total serenity and you couldn't read from the way he was that he was about to enter into a savage battle. But his silhouette disappeared from my eyes as the car jumped under the foot of de Scitivaux, towards dispersal."

Then a little later:

> "Suddenly the Wing Commander's plane let out a cloud of smoke which quickly vanished. One by one all the aircraft of 129 covered themselves briefly in smoke and dust raised by the wind of the propellors. Then 340 began to start up.
>
> "Already on the northern edge of the airfield, Michael's Spitfire, with the initials 'M-R'; to his right is a Spitfire of 340, that of Maurice Choron which is drawn up near the Wing Commander's. I see Robinson looking round, checking that all seems ready; his scarf floats in the slipstream. He raises his right arm to the sky and his gloved hand indicates the imminence of departure. De Scitivaux and I repeat the signal to our Sections and then Robinson's hand goes down. It is 5.10 pm, the Gruppe Isle de France sets off for the first time."

The Tangmere Wing had, on 12 April, made rendezvous with the Polish Northolt Wing at Beachy Head and together they had crossed the French coast at Le Touquet at 20,000 feet and almost immediately a dog-fight had started. Micky had ordered 129 Squadron to stay as top cover as the fighting began, and he led his section down. They were not engaged, and only 41 saw some brief fighting, claiming three probable FW190s, for the loss of one pilot and aircraft — Flight Lieutenant W Palmer, leading 41's Yellow Section.

Rene Mouchotte recorded in his diary (published in Britain under the title of *The Mouchotte Diaries* in 1956, and originally as *Les Carnets de Rene Mouchotte* in France):

"A total lack of opposition from the coastal batteries at once put me on my guard and immediately I heard a concert of shouts: 'Look out! A 109 behind you! Ten 109s in front. We're attacking.' Then the voice of Wing Commander Robinson, magnificently calm, speaking to us:

" 'Buck up, chaps, we're going to have some fun!' Then we went into hell, attacked from below, while four Focke Wulfs fell on us from behind, out of the sun. Our Squadron was the centre of the whirlwind.

"There were shouts on all sides. De Scitivaux dived suddenly, turning to port; followed by my Number Two, I kept close to him. Looking over my shoulder, I saw four 109s diving; we were in the best possible position to be shot down.

"Our speed was terrific. I used both hands to pull the stick back and to fly straight up to deal with them, which gave me the worst black-out I have ever had. I hoped to make the Huns turn tail or at least change their plan, thus allowing de Scitivaux to continue the attack on his Boche — which I hadn't spotted. As soon as I could see again, I was flying almost vertically and just had time to glimpse a 109's tracer coming from above. Our two planes had just missed each other, but his bullets and shells both missed their mark. I never saw de Scitivaux again.

"A score of Focke Wulfs passed very close, apparently without seeing us. They were painted dark green. ...I saw swastikas, then Spits, dived after one of them, it vanished, I pulled out.... Nothing!

"I was all alone with my inseparable Number Two. Still cries of, 'Look out to port! Attack to starboard!'

"Then the most pitiful thing of all, a very calm voice, 'Maurice here, I'm baling out, see you soon!' That was agonizing... The most terrifying air battle I had ever seen was over, after fifteen long, sweating minutes.... Robinson, de Scitivaux and Choron are missing, three of the best fighter pilots there are..."

It was the fighters of JG26 who engaged this operation and in total they claimed five Spitfires destroyed. The Geschwader had now fully re-equipped with Focke Wulf 190 A-1 and A-2 fighters, the last of the 109Fs going in early April. The pilots who claimed this day were:

Hauptmann Joachim Muncheberg, Kommandeur of II/JG26;
Oberleutnant Wilhelm Ferdinand Galland, of 5 Staffel;
Oberleutnant Kurt Ebersberger, Kapitan of the 4th Staffel;
Unteroffizier Adolf Glunz, of the 4th Staffel;
Unteroffizier Karl Willius, of the 2nd Staffel.

'Wutz' Galland was the brother of Adolf Galland. Each of these pilots were proven aces with JG26, with, respectively, 135, 55, 27, 71 and 50 victories by the war's end. Only Glunz, however, was to survive the conflict. All but Ebersberger would win the coveted Knight's Cross.

One of the later arrivals among the Belgian pilots in 609 was Raymond Lallemant, who arrived on the Squadron in July 1941. He recalls:

"I flew very little, unfortunately, with Michael Robinson but inherited the great respect and admiration my Belgian friends had for this famous CO and Wing Leader. I never understood why his tactics and strategy were not imposed on other squadrons due to the excellent results achieved and the relation between victories and losses. He had wonderful 'panache' as a brilliant fighter leader.

"In the air it was always 'Michael', although always 'Sir' on the ground despite the familiarity in flight or state of the sobriety of a party. Michael always took his pilots to London after a hard days action and was always proud to be with them. Very often, in order for everyone to forget the losses, he would say, 'Tonight, London is the form,' — giving them a rendezvous at the Ritz.

"The Squadron's call-sign was 'Beauty' and in the air, Michael would say over the radio when beginning an attack, 'Michael and his pretty boys going down!'

"He and Choron were an inseparable duo. These two were totally different men but shared spontaneously their passion for flying in a reciprocal friendship which in the end sealed their fate for ever.

"From the start he was Michael's No.2 and Michael would rarely be seen without Maurice — a formidable pair. In order to carry out with brilliance his different role, Maurice followed him in all circumstances like a shadow, thus ensuring the cohesion of the group and its readiness for combat. It is also true that a leader like Michael could benefit from a wingman of the class of Choron, so even in his position of Wing Leader, if Michael led the flight of another squadron Choron would still be his No.2.

"Maurice was of course full of friendship and gentleness, with a quickness of spirit and a sense of communication with determination and willingness to win. All this gave him a certain radiance and incontestible authority merited by his attitude as a war pilot."

Teresa was staying at Stanmore with her Mother when news of Micky's loss came. Sholto Douglas, Teresa recalls, also rang Lady Robinson. Teresa also remembers that: "Paul was more affected by Micky's death than anything she had ever seen. No doubt about it."

Donald Caldwell, who has made a detailed study of JG26 records:

"No 340 Squadron was attacked by Muncheberg's II/JG26. Wutz Galland was flying with Muncheberg's Stabsschwarm, and it is probable that either this pair or the 4th Staffel's Ebersberger/Glutz pair got Robinson and Choron, with the former pair somewhat more likely, but there is no proof either way.

"I think aircraft from both I and III/JG26 fought 313 Squadron, and claimed two Spitfires. Total Jagdwaffe losses were two II/JG26 pilots killed, probably by the Poles; no additional aircraft were damaged."

CHAPTER XV

GOODBYE FIGHTER COMMAND

PAUL officially took over command of his Squadron on 1st June 1942, at Duxford. The Duxford Station Commander was Group Captain John Grandy DSO, and the Wing Leader, Wing Commander Denys Gillam DSO DFC AFC. The other two Squadrons, were 56, which had been commanded by another old pal from 1 Squadron days, Prosser Hanks DFC, but now by Squadron Leader Hugh 'Cocky' Dundas DFC, and 266, commanded by the Rhodesian, Squadron Leader Charles Green DFC.

One of the prolonged 'teething' troubles of the Typhoon was that the tail tended to drop off at awkward moments — eg: in the air! Several pilots were killed in this way, and with no one surviving to give any clue as to why, all that could be done was to strengthen the tail assembly and hope. There were also problems with carbon monoxide coming into the cockpit which necessitated continual use of oxygen masks, and the Sabre engine had really been forced into service before passing all its trials.

Only when one pilot finally had a tail break off while he was taxying on the airfield, did the reason manifest itself. Paul told me:

> "Apparently it was the bushing, concerning the mass weight balance situated in the tail. The mass weight balance was on an arm with the bush at the pivot. The bushing was just rimmed out, it wasn't a properly fitted bush and when the thing got a bit of vibration on it, it would waggle about and the vibration increased — and became harmonic — and caused it to snap. When it broke, the elevators just went up and caused the tail to break off as they hit the slipstream, especially in a dive — and the Typhoon, if

nothing else, could certainly dive. The shock invariably knocked
out the pilot.

"The tail problem usually followed a half roll and a dive, then
pulling up. I think once you put the loading on the elevators, that
did it. In my view it was a disgrace to have put the Typhoon into
operations with these problems still unresolved."

Paul's initial task upon joining 609, along with Gillam and his brother
squadron commanders, was to try and get the Typhoon Wing
operational and overcome the various problems inherent with the new
aeroplane. As we now know, these were very largely overcome, but
the main cause for concern was that the Typhoon was never going to
be a competitor of the Spitfire as a day fighter. Despite its four 20 mm
cannons which could certainly knock down any German aircraft, it was
just too heavy an aircraft to duel high in the sky over France with
either Me109s or FW190s.

For a while it even looked as if the Typhoon might be relegated or
scrapped altogether, but what the Duxford Wing pilots did find, once
the aeroplane didn't either choke them or put them into the ground
minus the tailplane, was that while no good for high altitude combat,
it did have very good handling quality at low level.

Its emergence as a low level, ground-attack fighter and fighter-
bomber came at a time when just such an aeroplane was needed. Not
specifically as a fighter-bomber, that would come later, but as a low
level opponent for the Luftwaffe's latest tactic, that of flying hit-and-
run raids upon targets along the south coast of England.

Meanwhile, 609 under Paul tried to do their best with their new
aeroplane. Paul's A Flight commander, the job he had had the
previous year, was the long serving Joe Atkinson, who had risen from
junior bog-rat to flight lieutenant. Joe was amazing everyone by the
sheer length of service with 609. Somehow, officialdom had forgotten
him and having joined the Squadron in November 1940 was still going
strong — 20 months later. In fact nobody finally noticed until April
1943, by which time his 'tour' had lasted an incredible two and a half
years. Of his two COs, Joe remembers:

> "My view about Michael was that he was a first class squadron
> commander, mainly because he was a real professional and it
> was his job. Of course, he was a considerable socialite; this was,
> however, very much secondary for his flying mattered most to
> him.
>
> "I think I understood Michael; I don't think I understood Paul.
> They were both devout Catholics and this meant a lot to them.

I think Michael was, perhaps, more profound than Paul. Paul was also a professional. He thought about tactics for instance. I remember Hal Tidswell, our Adjutant, once commenting about the difference between Michael and Sheep Gilroy. Michael, he thought, was always anxious to know what his powers were in certain eventualities — what he should do if he lost contact with Group and so on. Whereas Gilroy just took what came along and dealt with it. I thought Michael was a very thoughtful person and very decent. He was first class and a much kinder heart than Paul. I think there was a streak of ruthlessness in Paul.

"I once stayed with Michael, when his Mother had a house near Hullavington. They seemed a very close family and of course, his younger sister married a chap who became Lord Hunt. I recall once, Michael asking me to fly down to Warmwell in the Squadron's two-seater to collect him after spending a weekend with Libby Hambro. He showed me where he'd been staying on a map; the house was called Milton Abbess. He said that on Monday, if I could fly down, locate the house, fly very low over it, he would then know I was there, then the family could drive him to Warmwell to meet me. It was an enormous great house, owned by the Hambro family (it later became a school). I remember Libby was a very attractive young lady. But then so were all Michael's lady friends. Paul had girlfriends too.

"Paul had a very good relationship with Michael. I remember Michael saying that he didn't think Paul had been sufficiently recognised for what he did in France. He admired Paul. He had been a fine athlete at school and I think Michael saw his good points and I'm certain there was never any bad blood between them.

"My impression, by 1942, when Paul returned as CO and I was his senior flight commander, was that Paul wasn't the dashing young man he had been. He was still responsible and it mattered to him that he was the CO, but he didn't intend to get himself killed.

"I think Paul realised after Michael's death, that he was very mortal. I am sure it affected him very much. If someone like Michael could be killed, then anyone could. We all knew that of course, but Michael's loss brought it home, especially to Paul.

"It was also a time when the Typhoon had a bad reputation — tails coming off and so on, and Paul was very conscious of this. He was a very rational sort of chap and I remember him saying once that if you got a puncture taking off, you ought to bale out.

The machine didn't matter but the pilot's life did. He made it clear
he would bale out."

I am certain Joe was right in that Paul had suddenly realised after
Michael's loss that it could happen to anyone. Paul himself had had a
couple of narrow escapes during the latter period of his time with 609
in 1941, as well as that bale-out with 74 Squadron, all of which must
have affected him. Not that he would have let it interfere with his
duty, he was far too professional for that, but there is little doubt that
he would be more careful from now on.

The Typhoon had still not been cleared for operations, which frustra-
ted everyone. Pent up emotions were let loose in mess parties and
other escapades, such as Paul's braces being suspended from the 20
foot high ceiling following a 'human fly' act by Flying Officer Jean
Creteur. Paul would also become aggressive late at night, leading
raiding parties on those who had decided to retire early.

The Station received a visit from the Duke of Kent on 9 June 1942,
and he met all the pilots. When he came to Paul's men, he, as CO,
introduced each man to the Duke who shook each hand warmly.
When it was the turn of Pilot Officer Giovanni Dieu, Paul mentioned
that the Belgian had been a test pilot in his country before the war.
"I was an instructor," corrected Dieu as he shook hands. Afterwards,
Paul took Dieu to one side and said, "Next time I say you were a test
pilot, Dieu, you *were* a test pilot!"

On the evening of the 18th, so the Squadron diary records, 609 did
much drinking in the Ladies Room of the Mess (the only lady on the
Station being the Station Commander's wife, Mrs Grandy), in honour
of a visit — due to being weather bound at Cambridge we are told —
of Wing Commander Jamie Rankin, Squadron Leader Brian Kingcome and other 72 Squadron 'types'. Major, the Marquis of Kildare
was carried to bed by Paul and Francois de Spirlet, and in going up
to bed himself, Paul preached a sermon to an imaginary congregation
from half way up the staircase. The night was then made hideous by
the braying of his clarinet.

There were other moments of mirth during June. Paul, still very
keen on swimming as he had been at Biggin, took the boys to a pool
at Royston on the 21st — a hot day — following much flying practise.
As the diarist recorded: "Pilot Officer Roelandt (Belg) became a bit
of a cynosure [attracted notice!] owing to a hole in the front of his
bathing costume."

And on the 22nd — "Battle School at Holkham for ground target shooting. CO appropriately gets top score. Other pilots succeed in knocking some tile off the roof of a house with spent cartridge cases [20 mm], one narrowly missing a man working in the garden."

Fighter Command were now really up against the Focke Wulf 190 fighter which had begun to appear over France in the autumn of 1941 and very soon had the edge over the Spitfire V. Pilots in 11 Group were taking even heavier losses when engaged with this new German fighter, and everyone was dying to get their hands on a captured one. There had even been a couple of schemes put forward to steal one, one such coming from Paul himself when he was still at Fighter Command. He told me of his plan, which he talked over with Sholto Douglas:

> "On one of our tours round, I said to Sholto that I had a plan to get our hands on a FW190. He asked what it was and I said my idea was to send up one of our captured Me109s, with some bullet holes knocked in it, make it look a bit battle weary, stick a German speaking RAF pilot in the cockpit wearing a captured German flying jacket — with an RAF uniform underneath in case he was caught — and send him out to land at a German airfield where 190s were based.
>
> "He'd taxi in to where the 190s were, let off a stream of German, say he was a Colonel so-and-so, and wanted a new aeroplane as there was a heavy raid coming this way. With any luck, an airman would deftly see him into a Focke Wulf, show him the nobs and taps, and he'd take off and head for home.
>
> "Sholto, rather to my surprise, didn't laugh. In fact he didn't even answer and seemed to be deep in thought. Finally I asked what he thought and he said he'd think about it. I even said I'd like to do it myself, but didn't think my German was good enough. It was some years later that I learnt that Jeffrey Quill and a commando pal of his, had also come up with a plan to steal a 190 but in the event everything was saved by a 190 landing at Pembrey."

This event took place on 23rd June. Spitfires had been in action with enemy fighters off Cherbourg and some 190s had followed the Spitfires back and a brief scrap had taken place south-east of Dartmouth. One lone 190 had then headed over Exeter, mistook the Bristol Channel for the English Channel and, short on fuel, landed at RAF Pembrey, near Swansea. Much to the pilot's chagrin, he found himself a prisoner, not back in France, having presented the

RAF with a perfectly good, totally undamaged FW190A-3 fighter.

The luckless pilot was Oberleutnant Arnim Faber, Adjutant of III Gruppe of JG2, and he landed at 8.35 that evening. No sooner had the news got about than Group Captain Grandy, Paul, and Philip Lucas, Hawker's test pilot who was at Duxford helping with the conversion of pilots onto the Typhoon, were heading down to Pembrey. Paul, still with his Fighter Command hat on, was dying to see it and borrowed Frank Ziegler's Leica camera to take some pictures.

Arriving at Pembrey the next day, Paul recounted:

> "When we flew down to Pembrey that day, the FW190 really opened our eyes. We met the pilot, and showed him our Typhoons, so we were all hoping he wouldn't escape and tell his chums what the Typhoon was like, but when we saw the 190, we all felt like hiding the Typhoons away somewhere!
>
> "We gave the Focke Wulf the once over; it was a beautifully designed thing and all the electrics I recall, had one enormous plug, instead of having to connect up all the bits of electricity that we had which seemed to take days to fix. The cockpit layout was superb and it had all the flying instruments on one panel and the engine instruments on another which was set below it, so it didn't stare at you in the face all the time, and the pilot didn't get confused over the dials. Therefore, the pilot had one bank for flying, the other just for checking.
>
> "Everything in the cockpit was faired so you didn't cut your hands on groping for levers as we did in our aircraft. All the switches and levers were logically arranged, as they are in the modern car, instead of seemingly random — where they can find room for them — as we did. I think it must have been the best fighter of the war.
>
> "I remember too, that Arnim Faber suggested to everyone that if he was given a small drop of petrol he would gladly take off and fly round the airfield and show us all what it was like. Good try."

Upon his return, Paul flew over to Fighter Command with a set of the photographs he had taken, who then demanded use of the negatives. In the next Intelligence Summary produced by Fighter Command, the full details of the 190 were made available.

There were still a number of Belgian pilots with 609 but one was lost in tragic circumstances, on 26th June. It was Francois de Spirlet, the commander of B Flight. The episode also gave an insight into Paul's complex character. Paul told me:

"We lost a flight commander on take-off — Francois de Spirlet. The chap formating on him was on his left, Cheval Lallemant. There was a tyre burst and the two aircraft collided. De Spirlet's tail was cut off and his aircraft went straight in and burst into flames, while Cheval, who was his best friend, they shared a room together, could only watch. The poor chap was in a state of shock when pulled from the wreckage of his own aeroplane. He was lucky to be alive himself. I was on a 48-hour leave in London, but I rushed back. Cheval was alone in his room and wouldn't see anyone and was apparently through with flying.

"I left him until the next morning but he still wouldn't come out so I went in to see him and said, come on Cheval, you've got to come and fly with me. I eventually persuaded him that he should and I made him take off in exactly in the same position he'd had with de Spirlet. I had my No.2, Christian Ortmans, on my right and the three of us took off. Of course, once in the air, Cheval stayed about 500 yards away for about a quarter of an hour. I kept calling him in closer, then closer still, until he eventually finished up in very close formation. We then did a very nice formation landing and he never looked back; in fact he got a DFC and bar by the end of the war and later commanded the Squadron.

"The Typhoon we found, did swing on take off. In fact I brought out a written order for the Squadron, on how this should be counter-acted. The way was not to bring up the tail too soon. Everyone was brought up to get the tail up as quickly as possible to accelerate fast, but the Typhoon swung before it got proper speed because of the torque. The thing to do was to take off with the stick more or less central, start the take off run with the stick not back but central so that the tail didn't come up straight away. Then, when you got enough speed on — enough speed to keep the thing straight — then let it come off the ground."

Naturally, Cheval Lallemant remembers this episode very well, and says of the incident:

"Since April we had been at Duxford where we were flying a great brute of 17 tons called the Hawker Typhoon. This was a completely new type of aircraft, both as to fuselage and engine, but was running into difficulty and causing us so much trouble that people spoke of scrapping this formidable 3,000 hp fighter. And not for the first time, as this Hawker prototype had previously flown as the Tornado, fitted with a Rolls-Royce Vulture engine, and had been withdrawn from production after a number of engine failures.

"I know something about this because in 1943 I was assigned to duties as an instructor during a rest period, but the C-in-C Fighter Command, having by some strange chance learned of this, found me a place as a test pilot at the Luton factory of Napiers and Son, Ltd, makers of the famous Sabre engine. It was there that I gained an insight into the reasons for the hold-ups in the development of this wonderful new conception, an engine without tappet-operated valves.

"The chief test pilot did little flying himself, and used flying techniques which were out of date. For example, on approaching to land, he throttled his engine right back which was entirely contrary to our own practice on operations involving large formations while engaged on offensive sweeps. On return to base, we had to observe a strict landing drill, requiring a powered approach, whereby aircraft were brought down on the runway in swift succession, so that very often the runway would be used by 12 Typhoons at a time. Under these procedures, any malfunctioning of the engine on the approach could result in a serious accident. And I must make clear that, at that stage, a flat-spot [ie: in engine performance meant that if the pilot pushed the throttle control forward 1, 2 or 3 millimetres, nothing happened and it was very often necessary to push the lever forward another 1 or 2 millimetres before the engine picked up.] in the throttle control was liable to alarm the pilot by interfering badly with proper use of the engine.

"So, despite all the Typhoon's advantages, such as being the first British fighter faster than the German fighters, there was talk in high places of putting our Squadron back onto Spitfires. Our CO, Paul Richey, a fighter pilot of great experience, had sized up accurately the qualities of our new aircraft and the use to which it could be put on operations. He made every effort to push things forward and to influence the climate of opinion about the proper operational role of this aircraft. It was, furthermore, thanks to Paul Richey that the Squadron was moved south in September 1942, to Biggin Hill first of all, so that we could try our luck against the equally well known Focke Wulf 190.

"That June morning when I was involved in a terrible accident, four Typhoons, led by Francois, were about to take off in tight formation with Christian on his right, myself on his left and Bob Wilmet on Christian's right. Half way down the runway, Francois' left tyre exploded and with slow inevitability his aircraft swung towards mine. There was a frightful crunching shock...

"That evening Paul came to see me and talked me into flying with him the next day. I got to the airfield where Paul took Christian and me for a training flight. Christian flew regularly as Paul's No.2. There was nothing special about the pre-flight briefing except that we were told to fly in close vic formation, one on each side of our leader. My only worry about this related to the flat-spot in the throttle control. We made a particularly good take off though the Typhoon was lumbering and clumsy on the ground. Paul led us to above 3,000 feet in a series of steep climbing turns and we proceeded to describe figures of eight, banking very steeply towards, and sometimes beyond the vertical so that we seemed to be flying upside down. I am not sure exactly what we were doing because I had complete faith in my leader and did not take my eyes off him long enough to gauge what evolutions we were performing. Indeed, it was only when we looped the loop that I realised what the leader intended.

"He made us execute several loops in succession, while changing formation. Paul was a first-class leader whom one could follow without any anxiety, and these training flights continued for several more days so as to make us practised enough to mount a display over airfields selected by him as being the haunts of those opposed to the adoption of the Typhoon. When I landed from that particular flight, I knew that Paul Richey, by his act of faith, had preserved my own.

"It was not long afterwards that following a splendid party at the home of the Station Commander, Group Captain John Grandy, I was greatly surprised to find the Groupie joining our formation as No.4, 'in the box' — a very uncomfortable position at the back of the formation, which I had never before seen occupied during aerobatics. I was afraid that he might have tagged on in ignorance of the fact that we performed aerobatics in formation. What worried me just as much were the orders which came over the R/T for me, as No.3, to slip in between Nos 2 and 4 when we went into line astern ('Indian File'), for example, without knowing whether the Group Captain had heard the order or was even on the same radio channel as ourselves. All this because Paul wanted to show the other pilots what the Typhoon could do in a performance over their airfields. Happily, none of these pilots was able to see us on our return, drenched in sweat as we were when we landed.

"I noticed that Paul invariably flew on the line of, and directly above, the runway, doing loops, Immelmann turns, and barrel rolls with the ease and effortless proficiency that marked him out as a true professional. And undoubtedly I was rusty in my knowledge of aerobatics for I told Christian how worried I was by the risks involved in changing formation in the course of aerobatics, particularly as the inclusion of a No.4 increased the danger. I must confess that, as No.3, I had my work cut out to avoid colliding with No.2 and No.4. On the other hand, the CO was good in introducing us to novel aerobatic manoeuvres, used after the war by other aerobatic teams, but with the difference that, in our case, the risks were taken to turn out a formidable fighting force without which we would not have succeeded in covering the Normandy landings. Paul was a notable tactician, and had from the start conducted a low level, high speed incursion into enemy airspace, limiting the number of pilots involved to eight or ten.

"At this point, the enemy changed their tactics. The FW190 began to be used as a fighter-bomber to strafe and bomb with impunity towns, ports and coastal convoys in the south of England.The FW190s dived from 20,000 feet, reaching great speeds, too fast to be intercepted in less than 50 kilometers, the width of the English Channel; or sometimes they approached at almost sea-level, thus avoiding detection by radar.

"In June, a FW190 pilot, lost after a combat, landed his aircraft at Pembrey, near Swansea, South Wales. Straight away, Paul flew down from Duxford to inspect this extraordinary aircraft which previously we had only seen in flight over France. Having borrowed a Leica camera from Frank Ziegler, Paul came back with some wonderful pictures of it."

The Typhoon finally became operational in July 1942, sharing Readiness duties although they were not allowed to fly over enemy territory, the Channel being the limit of their early sorties.

However, crunch time for the Typhoon was fast approaching and everyone began to speculate which school of thought would win, those for or against the Typhoon as an operational fighter. Paul wasn't in love with the Typhoon but he could see its potential, knowing from actual experience now that the Typhoon had exceptional qualities at low level, with not only speed but agility, despite its weight. It was only this weight that was precluding the machine from doing what had been intended — a higher altitude day fighter.

Even while Paul was trying to defend the type, one nearly let him down badly. On 24th July he was asked to fly a demonstration flight over Fighter Command HQ at Bentley Priory, and was in his usual machine, R7752 'PR-G' — he always flew aircraft lettered 'G' as his personal machines. He was right over the HQ when, as Paul related:

> "I don't know exactly what happened but the engine back-fired and blew a chunk out of the block, followed by flame and smoke. I was very lucky to get down on Hatfield with the aid of half a gale.
>
> "I did a half circuit, the wind was in the west of Bentley Priory, so I turned left, which one always does in an emergency, I don't know why, looking for an airfield, searching rapidly for something to land on. Then I saw an airfield, which happened to be Hatfield. I pumped everything down and landed. The rest of the Squadron just went home and at Fighter Command, they didn't even bother to find out what the fix was!"

Meantime, the first tentative operations were flown, but only as far as the enemy coast, either sweeps or escorts to Bostons, but always the Spitfires took the bombers over into France while the Typhoon circled off shore or came home.

Paul had a new flight commander at the end of June, replacing de Spirlet, another veteran of the Battle of France and Battle of Britain, Roland Beamont DFC.

The Wing's first operational sortie was organised for the 19th July, but it was then cancelled. Being cancelled, Paul flew up to RAF Coltishall for a visit, but then the operation was on again. For some reason, Coltishall couldn't be contacted and knowing Paul would want to lead his unit, Roland Beamont headed up to Coltishall to get him. At 2.35 pm a Beaufighter landed at Duxford, from which Paul emerged, who then sauntered into the briefing room, was given the general picture of the 'show' and was then driven to dispersal. He was was down as No.3 to Gillam, the rest of the pilots already in their cockpits. Suddenly a Stinson appeared — it was Bee Beamont coming back, but by now he was too late to be part of the operation. The Typhoons took off, but after all this Paul's machine — R7752 — let him down. Developing engine trouble he had no choice but to return to base.

The operation — a low Wing Rodeo to Berck and Hardelot, in support of a Rhubarb sortie by Spitfires, found no enemy aircraft, so it all turned out something of an anti-climax.

The next operation was on Circus 200, flying a patrol between Gravelines and Gris Nez and although some FW190s were seen in the distance, the Typhoon pilots were unable to cross the enemy coast to engage them. This Op was followed by a Rodeo and a Roadstead on 4th and 5th August, Paul leading once again in R7752.

The Wing operated during the Dieppe show, on 19th August, but only really in a supportive way. Gillam led them on the fringes of the main assault in order to counter any enemy aircraft that might be approaching down the Channel, and they were still not allowed over the French coast. Paul led 609.

They did have a brief skirmish with some Germans, 266 Squadron claiming a Dornier destroyed and a FW190 damaged, Gillam damaging another 190. The problem was, however, that the Typhoon looked awfully like 190s, and 266 were attacked by some Spitfires from a Norwegian Squadron. Two pilots of 266 were bounced, shot down and killed.

The Typhoon also looked like a 190 from the ground, so when they began to try and counter the 190's hit-and-run raids, the Typhoons had thin black and white stripes painted on the undersides of their wings to help the AA gunners spot the difference. These stripes were the forerunners to the wider stripes applied to all Allied aircraft during the Normandy invasion in 1944.

Finally the Typhoon was allowed over the French coast. The aeroplane was still being thought of as a fighter, but generally being used as a low level interceptor and 'bomber destroyer' — not that many bombers were found flying around these days, although occasionally they were encountered, but that was in 1943 and by other Typhoon units. Paul led his Squadron on one show over France, and remembered:

"I was leading 609 on a Sweep one day, on our own, sweeping inland over St Omer under 11 Group control. They were getting 'windy' about us because they were reporting 30 plus bandits between us and England. They went on reporting this in a more and more strained way, then someone called and actually said, 'Be careful!' — somebody I knew; I think it was Johnny Walker actually, who had been my flight commander in France in 1940.

"We started diving to come home very fast and they still went on reporting these 30 plus Huns, so I was looking up and ahead where they might be and saw two FW190s diving towards us on our left side. They flattened out to our left and we could have gone after them but it would have meant turning the whole Squadron round with our tails to the other 30 who might be diving down behind these two, so I left them. I've always regretted it. On the other hand I think I was probably right.

"There was another Op to Cherbourg, covering American Fortresses. We were at nought feet so as to be under the enemy radar and pulled up about half way across, into a steep climb to about 20,000 feet over Cherbourg. We turned round and the idea was to stop the Forts being chased back by 190s. 266 Squadron were still down on the water and they stayed down and lost two Typhoons to 190 but we never saw any. The sky is a big place."

Raymond Lallemant also recalls one of the first Typhoon sorties:

"I remember returning from a mission in which ten Typhoons had flown over France at almost ground level. We had all flown well enough to maintain station in line abreast despite the rapid turns executed by the formation leader. I would claim that we demonstrated real facility compared with that required in earlier missions of 36 aircraft.

"When we landed, Paul said to the Wing Commander Flying, 'That is an absolutely ideal formation for those low level missions. Everything was perfect.' But Denys Gillam, who was soaked in traditional ideas about the best way of handling a wing of 36 aircraft, was content merely to give us a faint smile. He had failed to understand what we were up to."

It was about this time that Gillam and Grandy were being pressed to make a decision about the future of the Typhoon. Both men were trying to present a solid defence of the aeroplane, but then Paul got caught on his own by someone in higher authority and speaking honestly he had to say that in his view the present role was wrong and that the Typhoon should not operate in a Wing formation.

Several reports were made, by Gillam, Cocky Dundas, Prosser Hanks, and one by Paul, dated 12 September 1942. Paul's report read:

Paper IV — Typhoon Aircraft — Tactical Policy

INTRODUCTION

The purposes of this paper are:

(a) to describe the use to which the Typhoon (Day) has been and is being put,

(b) to criticise the present policy, and

(c) to suggest certain changes in policy.

DESCRIPTION OF PRESENT POLICY

2. The three Typhoon squadrons under discussion were equipped at Duxford because, amongst other things, it was a quiet sector. Two of them became operational early in May 1942, and the third early in June.

3. As soon as the squadrons became operational they took over

normal sector duties and states, doing 69 Scrambles. In addition, they were used to carry out:

(a) low altitude anti-shipping sweeps along the enemy coastline from Walcheron to Cap Gris Nez (4)*

(b) medium altitude anti-fighter sweeps along the enemy coastline between Ostend and Dieppe, and inland of those places as far as St Omer and Hesdin (19)*

(c) convoy patrols (16)

(d) escorting HSLs (4)

(e) special anti-recce patrols off the Norfolk coast (29)

(f) special anti-fighter-bomber patrols from Manston and Tangmere (number not known)

4. The results of these activities were:

(a) Fighter Roadstead — Nil

(b) Fighter Sweeps — 1 Do217 destroyed — Dieppe Raid
                    1 Do217 probable — Dieppe Raid
                    1 FW190 probable — Dieppe Raid

Our casualties:

                    1 Typhoon missing
                    2 Typhoons destroyed by Spitfires

(c) Convoy patrols — Nil

(d) Escorting HSLs — Nil

(e) Special anti-recce patrols — 2 Ju88s destroyed

(f) Special anti-fighter-bomber patrols — Nil

Our casualties:

                    2 Typhoons destroyed by Spitfires
                    (Wrong use of Typhoons by Group
                    Controller)

5. If the Dieppe Combined Operation, which was not a normal operation, be excepted, it will be seen that the best results were obtained against the enemy recce machines, which are specialised high-speed aircraft. These were easily overtaken and shot down.

CRITICISM OF PRESENT POLICY

6. Apart from the two successes mentioned in para. 5, the results obtained by the Typhoon Wing are on the whole disappointing. It is considered that this is due to the wrong employment of the aircraft.

---

* "Operating as a Wing"

7. The Typhoon is a specialised aircraft primarily designed for intercepting and shooting down low and medium altitude bombers. It was intended to possess certain special qualities for this purpose, and does in fact possess them. These qualities are: high speed below 20,000 feet, a good climb to that height and heavy armament. But certain other qualities have been sacrificed, one of which is manoeuvrability.

8. The present phase of the war, coupled with mental rigidity in certain quarters, has led to the employment of the Typhoon squadrons as a Wing on sweeps. To this type of operation the Typhoon is quite unsuited. It cannot fight the FW190 on the latter's terms, and only has a fair chance of success if it possesses the advantage of height and positioning. This condition has only once been fulfilled (without a kill) and is not likely to be repeated. In addition, it is impossible to keep a whole Wing of three Typhoon squadrons together for long. Visual contact is only maintained with difficulty, and the whole formation is hopelessly unwieldy.

9. The pilots of the three Typhoon squadrons are considerably more experienced than those of the average Spitfire squadron. Some of them carried out a number of sweeps with Spitfires in 1941 when a sweep was a deep penetration into enemy territory, the writer having done 50 of them. It is true to say that many of the Typhoon pilots, especially those with operational experience, feel a very definite sense of inferiority as regards fighting the FW190 on its own terms. This is not unnatural, for the Typhoon was not designed primarily for fighting fighters, whereas the FW190 obviously was. Needless to add that this sense of inferiority and frustration tends to reflect seriously on the morale of the Squadrons.

SUGGESTIONS FOR A CHANGE IN POLICY

10. The following proposals are submitted:

(a) Abandon Wing sweeps, carrying out sweeps at squadron strength in the role, say, of rear support.

(b) Disband the Wing as such, and disperse the squadrons to coastal areas to be used for the role to which they are eminently suited — ie: intercepting low recce and low bombers. The areas that should be covered are the coasts of East Anglia (against low recces), Kent, Sussex, Hampshire, Dorset and S Devon (against FW190s and Me109 bombers). Sectors suggested and distributed of aircraft are: Coltishall Sector — 1 squadron.

Aircraft to be further dispersed in fours at suitable advanced
landing grounds (eg: Friston) if considered desirable, and to maintain advanced readiness states (ie: pilots in cockpits) against
fighter-bombers.

11. In conclusion, it is suggested that there can be no object in
maintaining three squadrons of specialised bomber-interceptors in
a Sector where there is little or nothing to intercept. The obvious
course is to station them in Sectors where there is something to
intercept. The fact that the squadrons already in these latter
Sectors are unable to effect interceptions because their aircraft are
not fast enough would seem to make the argument overwhelming.

P H M Richey
Squadron Leader, Commanding
No.609 (WR) Squadron

Cocky Dundas too had been present at a meeting where Group
Captain Harry Broadhurst, the Group Captain Ops at Fighter
Command, had also decided that the Typhoon wasn't going to be good
at pure fighter operations but Dundas really wanted to see exactly how
the Typhoon could best be used. Finally it was agreed that the
Typhoon's low-level capabilities should be exploited.

Paul's report, which his old boss at HQ, Sholto Douglas could not
have failed to read, helped to finalise things as far as Fighter Command were concerned. Just six days after writing his report, the
Duxford Wing was disbanded. In Paul's papers there is a letter to
Sholto Douglas, dated 28 February 1943, in which Paul noted:

"...the views expressed and action suggested in my paper on
Typhoon Policy were concurred with by your Headquarters, and
by No.11 Group, and have been put into effect with success."

No doubt Denys Gillam was disappointed and perhaps even a little
angry at Paul for helping to 'pull the plug', but it turned out to be
the right decision. Raymond Lallemant remembers:

"Paul Richey wrote such a succinct report, setting out his views on
the operational capacity of the Typhoon. He made clear that these
views were supported by the Commanding Officers of the other two
squadrons. Up to this time, the employment of the Typhoon on
offensive sweeps had yielded no definite results and so was accounted a failure. Paul insisted that the Typhoon's great speed and fire-
power could best be used on defensive tasks over the south of
England, so as to counter the 'tip and run' raids of the FW190s.

"There was a great row, because all the pilots of 266 (Rhodesian) Squadron, threatened to resign their RAF commissions if the Typhoon was withdrawn from operations."

Gillam went off to Staff College, but later returned to the Typhoon when its role and importance had became known and accepted. As history now records the Hawker Typhoon became the backbone of 2nd Tactical Air Force's offensive ground attack operations. Carrying bombs, rockets or just its 20 mm cannons, it helped the invading armies smash through the German defences before and after D-Day, and right up to the final surrender in 1945. As a low level attack aircraft, it was second to none. Gillam ended the war with three DSOs and two DFCs.

Meantime, Paul and 609 left Duxford on 18 September and moved back to Biggin Hill. The Typhoon was finally going to be given the chance of trying to combat the low level hit-and-run raids by Focke Wulf and Messerschmitt fighters, and in the event, they did very well. Later it did need the squadrons to mount standing patrols a mile or so out to sea in order to be 'on the spot' when either 190s or 109s came zooming in. Paul was always against this policy, for he felt it turned the clock back 25 years to the old WW1 tactic of keeping aircraft in the air over the trenches. He also felt it was unhealthy for the Typhoon pilots with their aircraft still prone to shed a tail or have a problem with the Sabre engine. At low level it didn't give them time to bale out.

The Squadron interspersed these sorties with other operations, flying Rodeo, Roadstead and Circus missions, providing escort to 2 Group Bostons or Fighter Command Whirlwinds. Occasionally 190s were spotted on these escorts but never close enough to engage.

However, time was catching up on Paul. He received a direct posting to India, to command, on paper, a Hurricane Wing. Paul told me:

"I went to a cocktail party at HQ Fighter Command and mentioned to Sholto Douglas that I was off. He took me by the arm and said, 'Yes, I know. Come along to my office and we'll discuss it.' Once there he told me Air Ministry had asked him for a young, up-to-date fighter leader to go out to study RAF fighter tactics in the India-Burma Theatre where they were not totally successful (in my view a dead loss!) and revise and re-organise them to meet local conditions. He said he'd chosen me because I had an analytical mind and could write as well as fight. I think he believed too that I could put my finger on the problem areas, as he'd told me

I'd done with the Typhoon problem, although at the moment I should keep that to myself."

So Paul relinquished command of 609 and finally broke ties not only with it, but with the still fresh memories of Michael, and of course with RAF Fighter Command. He recommended that 609 be taken over by Roland Beamont, and so it transpired. Then it was a farewell to England and to Teresa, before departing for the Far East, and the sounds, smells and intrigues of the Orient.

CHAPTER XVI

THE FAR EAST

PAUL and Teresa went up to Blackpool prior to his sailing to India, which was, according to Teresa, where daughter Pauline was conceived. Teresa recalls that it was normal practice for airforce officers who were obviously being posted abroad, to take their wives to Blackpool prior to sailing. Not that Teresa knew where Paul was off to. Strict security forbade telling anyone, in case word got out which might lead to knowledge that a convoy might soon sail.

It was now October 1942. On the 12th Paul had been promoted to acting Wing Commander. He had accepted the task Sholto Douglas had set him, although he had no idea how things might turn out. The war with Japan was less than a year old, and probably all that Paul knew was that the British had been in retreat for much of the first six months, having been surrounded and captured in Singapore, lost Hong Kong, had retreated from Rangoon, then been kicked out of Malaya and southern Burma.

Not that it was the British alone. The Americans had been surprised at Pearl Harbor, pushed out of the Philippines, and lost Guam and Wake. They had started to hit back, by landing at Guadalcanal in the Solomons in August 1942, and at least the British were holding the Burma front below Chittagong on the Bengal coast, while the Australians were fighting to hold Borneo and had so far stopped any threat of invasion of northern Australia around Darwin. Undoubtedly what Paul and many other Europeans and Americans were thinking was how could "these little yellow men from Japan, who all had slope heads and wore thick pebble glasses", have achieved so much in so short a time. He was to find out. Yet this had been the popular feeling when the war with Japan had begun, especially among the Americans.

How could they fly modern aircraft in a war when they could hardly see?! That the Japanese had been doing just that in China for some time, obviously didn't occur to them. That they had successfully knocked out most of the US Fleet at Pearl Harbor was thought more a stab in the back than a successful operation.

It has to be said that Paul too went to the Far East with something of this attitude, for in a radio broadcast soon after he arrived in India, after giving the program announcer a brief resume of his time in and later over France, he was asked if he'd ever been shot down. He replied:

> "Yes, four times. I've been wounded once and baled out three times. However, so far I've been lucky (touch wood), and I don't so much mind being shot down by a human being, even if he is a Hun — but if one of these Japanese monkeys gets me, I'll definitely be annoyed!"

It had been a bit of a bomb-shell when Paul was told of his posting to India, but he then came to see it as a challenge. Perhaps he needed a total change of scene. Paul mentioned to me:

> "At that party when Sholto had told me what he wanted me to do, he had said, 'If you don't want to go I'll stop it.' I thought it unfair to other serving men to take advantage of my friendship with the C-in-C, so like a fool I said, 'What do you think I ought to do, Sir?' He said, 'I think you should get your wing commander's stripe up tomorrow. Our fighters in India are taking a beating and their tactics are all to hell. I think you ought to go.' So I went.
>
> "Of course, Sholto himself was off shortly himself, as C-in-C RAF Middle East. Much later I learnt that he had signalled RAF HQ in Delhi asking for me to be sent to him in Cairo, but unbeknown to me they had replied, 'Wing Commander Richey is doing a very important and valuable job. Trust you will not press for this officer.' Had I known Sholto had asked for me in 1943, I would have risked a court martial to get out of India!
>
> "Not that I got off to a very good start. No sooner had I got to Bombay than I went sick, sinus trouble mostly then appendicitis. No sooner had I got over this and went on sick leave than I went down with jaundice and finally dysentry, which knocked me out till March. So it was not until April 1943 that I arrived at Air Headquarters in Delhi.
>
> "I was immediately sent for by Air Marshal Sir John Baker, SASO India, whom I had known at HQ Fighter Command. His

first words to me were 'Bless you for coming!' then he sent me straight off to report personally to the AOC-in-C, Bengal Command, Air Vice-Marshal T M 'Bill' Williams, at his HQ at Barrackpore, Calcutta.

"I had last seen Williams at the height of the Battle of France. He gave me a great welcome, described the position and gave me carte blanche to go anywhere, see anyone and produce my report and recommendations within a month. Two fighter groups, 221 and 224, plus three fighter wings, 165, 166 and 185, were spread over a vast area, making a month necessary."

Paul became Wing Commander Fighter Ops at HQ Bengal Command in May, despite still suffering from his sinusitis and dysentery. He had no easy task. Although he was there to help, advise and report, he was still regarded as a Fighter Command man sent out to show everyone in India how it should be done. Paul continued:

"During the month Williams had given me I did the job I was sent out to India to do, namely, assessing and overlooking RAF fighter operations on the Burma front and reviewing tactics and strategy. To do this I had to fly around a lot and talk to everyone concerned. Needless to say I ran into a good deal of hostility as a 'new' wing commander, telling the old hands in India how it should be done, and particularly from Air Commodore (later Air Vice-Marshal) Gray, AOC of 224 Group at Chittagong, who, at a conference I requested at his Group HQ, sarcastically suggested I should borrow one of his Hurricanes and show them all how to fight the Japs!"

Paul made a visit to Chittagong on 4th May to investigate a raid which had occured on Dohazari two days earlier. While there, a second attack was made on the town and airfield. Paul reported:

REPORT ON VISIT OF W/CDR RICHEY (OPS II) TO
CHITTAGONG ON 4-5/5/43

INFORMATION

I visited Chittagong on 4/5/43 to investigate the details of the enemy bombing raid on Dohazari on 2/5/43.

2. While I was there two more raids occured, one being a fighter sweep over Ramu on the afternoon of 4/5 and the other a second bombing raid on Dohazari on the morning of 5/5.

3. Owing to shortage of time I was only able to investigate the part played in these raids by the Chittagong fighters and not those at Feni or Ramu.

2/5/43 Raid 1 (Dohazari bombed by 15 Army 97s escorted).

4. 0724 Ramu reported to Group Ops Room plot of 6+ e/a about 60 miles SE of Chittagong. No height. Nothing on Group table.

0729 Ramu reported second plot on raid was 3+ and scrambled their aircraft (18).

0730 Group scrambled 2 sections of 136 Squadron and ordered them to climb south.

0733 Enemy raid still approaching Chittagong, now 3 a/c.

0735 Two sections 136 Squadron off.

0736 Enemy raid was 6+ at 20,000 ft. 1 Flight 146 Sqdn scrambled.

0739 1 Flight 146 Sqdn off.

0741 Enemy raid was 12+, same height. Second flight 146 Sqdn was scrambled.

0742 Enemy raid was at 30,000 ft.

0743 Second flight 146 Sqdn off.

0756 Tally-Ho by 136 Sqdn.

0758 Tally-Ho by 146 Sqdn. Feni Scrambled.

0804 Our fighters attack from above.

0805 Dohazari reported having been bombed.

5. Result of Raid:- 4 Blenheims destroyed on Dohazari aerodrome, 3 damaged. 1 lorry destroyed. Slight injuries to personnel. 50 yards of strip u/s. 1 fighter missing. 1 e/a destroyed.

6. It will be seen that:—

(a) The raid was plotted below its true strength until it was approaching Chittagong (a common fault in the RDF reporting in 224 Group is the over-estimation of small raids and the under-estimation of large ones).

(b) The Group Controller delayed 6 minutes after Ramu's warning (until the plot appeared on his table) before scrambling his fighters and then only sent off two sections.

(c) He delayed a further 6 mins (until the plot became 6+ at 20,000 ft) before sending off any more fighters and then he only sent 1 section.

(d) He delayed a further 5 mins before sending off any more fighters.

(e) 17 mins after this, he Scrambled Feni.

7. It is suggested that the Controller should have sent off at least one squadron and if possible two squadrons immediately the warning of a 6+ plot came from Ramu. The result of his not doing so was that the fighters were not able to intercept until the raiders had bombed and were diving for home.

8. Feni should not have been Scrambled but kept as a reserve against a follow-up.

9. The main reason our fighters did not shoot down more, apart from the above reasons, was the efficiency of the enemy escort, but I would like to discuss this point verbally.

[Paul had probably been told by now that the Japanese fighters were light and highly manoeuvrable, and that it was no use dog-fighting them like the RAF in Europe could dog-fight the 109s. In a turning battle the Japanese pilot could out-turn the Hurricane every time. The 'dive and zoom' tactics were now being adopted by the Burma squadrons. Ed.]

4/5/43 No.2 Raid (Ramu swept by 20 Army 01s).

10. 1524 False plot (due to bad W/T) over sea SW of Ramu. No number or height. 136 Squadron Scrambled.

1532 Same raid re-appeared in different place (SE of Ramu) 6+ e/a.

1544 136 and 146 Squadrons off. 67 Squadron Scrambled.

1548 67 Squadron off.

11. Ramu had meantime Scrambed without referring to Group because the tie line was u/s.

12. It will be seen that the Controller again delayed, this time 11 mins before Scrambling 136 and 146 Squadrons after receiving the first plot (which, though false, was a plot). 3 minutes of this 11 mins delay was due to the breakdown of (a) the R/T and (b) the tie line to the aerodrome.

13. Ramu intercepted from above, but I have not been able to investigate the reasons for them not shooting any down. I would again like to discuss this point verbally.

14. Chittagong did not intercept, probably because they were too high.

5/5/43 No.3 Raid (Bombing of Dohazari by 24 Army 97s).

15. 0728 Ramu warned Group of a 12+ plot about 50 miles east of Chittagong.

0730 Group got a blank plot near the same place. 136 Squadron Scrambled plus 2 sections of 146 Squadron.

0738 136 Sqdn and 4 a/c 146 Sqdn off. 67 Sqdn Scrambled.

0745 67 Sqdn off.

16. It will be seen that the Group Controller again delayed before Scrambling the first aircraft after receiving Ramu's warning, though this time for only two minutes. 67 Sqdn however, were

not Scrambled until 7 mins after the warning, because of the 224 instruction that no a/c on AASO stand-by were to be used for interceptions without ref to Air Staff.

17. No interception was made by Chittagong because our fighters climbed NW to gain height and rendezvous. They then got too far behind the raid, which dived S and then E. I would also like to discuss this point verbally.

GENERAL

18. From the above records and the brief preliminary survey I have been able to make, it would seem that a combination of faults is leading to our lack of success against the enemy raids. These I tentatively suggest are:

(a) Faults in RDF reporting, probably due to the inexperience of the operators.

(b) Delays and mistakes on the part of the Group Controller.

(c) Wrong tactics on the part of the fighter leaders, probably originally caused by past deficiencies in the warning system.

19. There is also no doubt that the Hurricane is not up to the job.

20. I would suggest that I go to Chittagong, preferably with a Hurricane at my disposal, and spend a week or so there thoroughly investigating the whole position. I could then present a detailed and comprehensive report on my return, for what action is considered necessary.

P H M Richey

W/Cdr Ops II

6th May 1943

Never one for mincing words, one can easily see that people could be upset by some of the things said or suggested in this report and maybe it was his suggestion in the final paragraph which led Air Commodore Gray to make his remark about Paul having a Hurricane and showing everyone how it should be done!

Nevertheless, we must credit Paul for knowing something of his job, not only having been a fighter pilot, but also a fighter controller. However, it has to be admitted that conditions in Burma were a lot different to those he had been used to in England. For one thing the hills and mountains inland from the Bengal coast always made the radar picture difficult to interpret.

There was obviously some reaction from Delhi concerning his report for Paul wrote a Loose Minute dated 10th May covering points raised. I haven't been able to find reference to Williams' letter, but from the contents of Paul's Minute, he was still on the attack.

LOOSE MINUTE

Ref Enc. 10A and AOC's letter DO/TMW/1.

2. It is agreed that the wording of the SASO India's letter is unfortunate.

3. It is considered, however, that the Air Staff has played ostrich for long enough in this matter of the respective points of the Hurricane and the 01. If everyone, from the pilots to the AOC-in-C is agreed that Japanese fighters have our fighters at a disadvantage in certain circumstances let it be admitted and let steps be taken to avoid those circumstances. No useful purpose can be served by telling the pilots they have the best aircraft in the world, because they know they have not and will merely regard the Air Staff as a bunch of nit-wits.

4. Rather let this be our line:- The Japanese fighters have good and bad points. Our own fighters have good and bad points. A comparison of the Japanese Army 01 and the British Hurricane makes it obvious from the start that in a certain type of fighting the Japs should come off best. On the other hand, in another kind of fighting we should come off best. This is borne our by experience: the Japs can dog-fight better than we can; however, they are lightly armed and need to get in good long bursts against our heavily armoured aircraft before they can shoot them down. Their manoeuvrability enables them to do this if we try and dog-fight them. On the other hand, one short accurate burst from a Hurricane usually causes the disintegration of an 01 — and the Hurricane is faster. All this being so, the obvious thing to do is to work out tactics to give ourselves the maximum advantage. We won't dog-fight. We will only attack from above, diving and firing a short burst before climbing again. If we are caught out and are below the Japs or at their level we will immediately take steps to reverse this situation by diving away and climbing up again before attacking. We will defeat the Japs by cleverness.

5. It is suggested that talk along these lines would encourage our pilots as well as help them, for they will see that their problems are understood by the Air Staff and not, as they appear to think at the moment, merely ignored.

6. It is recommended that our Squadron Commanders and Wing Leaders be told to make a study of the tactics employed by the German fighters against our offensive sweeps over France. The German has often proved himself a more intelligent, if less tenacious fighter than ourselves. Our bulldog tactics have proved successful against the Germans. Against the Japanese we shall

not assert our superiority until we use our heads a bit more.

7. I request that I may draft a memorandum for distribution to the pilots outlining what it is considered should be the general lines of our tactics. The injuctions contained in SASO India's letter may be sound enough, but they are stated in such a way that pilots' morale may very well be undermined. I think I could put the case more optimistically and constructively.

8. Para 3 of DO/TMW/1 is supported.

P H M Richey

10.5.43   W/Cdr Ops II

As it was to prove, the tactic which defeated the Japanese fighters, not only adopted by the British and Commonwealth forces in Burma, but by the Americans in the Pacific, was to change completely from the historic turning dog-fight in favour of a high speed dive and zoom tactic. In the early months of the Japanese war, the British and American fighter pilots, trained for so long in the turning air fight, were simply shot out of the sky by the more nimble and light Japanese fighters such as the Army 01 (Nakajima Ki-43) and the Navy Zero (Mitsubishi A6M). Not so from now on.

For the British it was even more of a culture shock, for many of the squadron and flight commanders who were sent out to Singapore and Burma when the war in the east erupted, were experienced fighter pilots against the Germans over Europe, and had been brought up to fight the Me109 in a turning fight, where the Spitfire and Hurricane could generally turn better than the Messerschmitt. Using this successful tactic against the Japanese fighters was simply suicide.

In this Loose Minute we see Paul again hitting from the shoulder, especially in Paragraph 3, with terms such as "ostrich" and "nit-wits". As he did throughout his career, he was battling valiantly for the fighter pilots in the front line but winning no friends back in Delhi or Calcutta.

More of the same was to follow, once Paul had written his report and presumably a Tactical Memoradum as referred to in his last paragraph above. We know that the Memorandum was circulated because Paul had a letter from an old journalist friend from France 1940 — Charles Gardner who, when war came, became a BBC War Correspondent. He went to France as such in 1939 and from his time there, wrote a book entitled *AASF* (Advanced Air Striking Force), which was published by the Huchinson Company in 1940. In 1943 Gardner was at HQ 222 Group, Ceylon, and wrote to Paul on 23rd June 1943.

Dear Paul,

Your AHQ Bengal Tactical Memorandum No.1 has just come through and has been promptly whisked off to all our squadrons. The 'gen' you give is exactly the sort of stuff we have been wanting to get hold of, and will be invaluable to our fighter boys. Any other TM's on similar lines which you can produce will be assured of a very warm welcome here.

I heard from Wilfred Russell that you were in these parts, and I hoped we might bump into each other again, if only to lament the lost days of Paris. I am stuck at this Group here during my Ops rest from Catalinas and am, at the moment, stooging on Training and Tactics.

Belated congratulations on your book; it is still the best one the war has produced; on your gong (or is it gongs) and on your promotion. Salaams.

Charles Gardner.

Meantime, Bill Williams called Paul into see him; as Paul related to me, the conversation was as follows:

"One of the things I had said in my report I submitted to Williams was: 'Of course there is no doubt the Hurricane is not up to the job and we must have Spitfires.' Bill Williams called me into his office, smilingly congratulated me on the report, then took out a pair of scissors and said, 'There's just one thing I can't let through.' He then proceeded to cut out the sentence about Hurricanes and Spitfires, and destroyed it, saying, 'That's true, and both you and I know it, but we must never let the boys [the pilots] suspect it — it would destroy morale.' As if they didn't know it!

"I later discovered that the real reason for this curious action was that a year previously the C-in-C India, Sir Richard Pierce, had refused Spitfires on the grounds that the Hurricane was better for the job. Probably because of its sturdier undercarriage when used on jungle airstrips. Also, presumably, this decision must have been made on Williams' recommendation! However, by 1943, I had learned my way about the service and so had already, as was my wont (just like my Typhoon report in 1942), sent copy of my Bengal Report to my friend Group Captain John Hawtrey, in charge of Fighter Ops at HQ RAF India, at Delhi.

"Pretty quickly after my Report hit Delhi, Bill Williams sent for me again. I thought, 'Here it comes, he's found out about my back-door methods!' But he greeted me with a big smile and said, 'Paul, we're getting Spits! How would you like to take command of the first Wing? I'm giving them to No.165 at Comilla.'

"Unfortunately, when Lord Mountbatten took over as Supremo later in the year, all plans were chucked into the melting pot and turned upside down and reversed several times. By that time I was no longer fit medically, so, sadly, it never happened."

Meantime, Williams wrote to the AOC 221 Group, on 30th September 1943 concerning Paul's Draft Tactical Memoradum, following a letter from that AOC — Air Commodore H Rowley, about it. Probably Paul had been wrong to write about Sweeps over France, escorting Blenheims and Bostons etc, in an effort to force home points about tactics. Other Commands never like comparisons with other fronts or Commands. Rowley had thought the draft good but:

> "The general hints and points for fighter pilots again are really excellent as are also the hints for bomber leaders. It is obvious however, that when discussing the bomber leader, Wing Commander Richey has been influenced by operations at home where mainly Bostons were used...
>
> "... To sum up, my general impression of this paper is that although it is written by a Wing Commander of great experience of Fighter Command at home, he has not quite appreciated our problems for the forthcoming fine weather..." [End of the Monsoon period. Ed.]

Even if Rowley was right, it was equally obvious that he had begun to lose Paul's overall train of thought, due to making these comparisons. Paul wasn't a fan of Rowley anyway, as he confided to his friend Johnny Hawtrey. Williams had written back to Rowley:

> 1. With reference to your letter 221G/S.54/Air dated 28th August 1943, I agree generally with your remarks that the memorandum on the above subject produced by Wing Commander Richey contains a number of valuable hints and tips. The tactical staff at this HQ and Air Headquarters, India, are in general agreement with your remarks but not with several of the tactical points made by Wing Commander Richey. It is also noted that a large proportion of the data produced in the memorandum has already appeared in Tactical Memorandum issued by Air HQ, India, but in a more concise form.
>
> 2. In general, while the memorandum makes useful and instructive reading, it does not quite meet the bill as a tactical memorandum applicable to this Command. A copy has been supplied to Air HQ, INDIA who are making necessary extracts and in due

course will issue a suitable tactical memorandum covering all the points raised by Wing Commander Richey.

T M Williams
Air Vice-Marshal
Air Officer Commanding
BENGAL COMMAND, RAF.

However, as far as Paul was concerned, he had helped, by whatever means, to get Spitfires to the fighter pilots in India/Burma and they started to arrive in October 1943. Due to their arrival in time for the next offensive in the Arakan in early 1944, they were able to blind the Japanese, by being finally able to intercept their high-flying Dinah photo reconnaissance aircraft, and gain air superiority over the Arakan, thus supporting the British and Indian armies to remove the Japanese from that part of Burma. They were also able to help defend the beseiged Imphal Valley in 1944, which in turn helped stop the Japanese getting into India via Imphal and Kohima.

But Paul was still not making any friends 'on high'. Indeed, his report had made some more scathing references to people and positions which must surely lead to his downfall. Having spoken to many Burma fighter pilots over the years, especially in connection with three books I wrote covering this period of the air war over the Arakan and at Imphal (*Hurricanes over the Arakan, Spitfires over the Arakan* and *The Air Battle of Imphal* all published between 1985 and 1989), I know for a fact that many of the things Paul was fighting for and writing about were in line with the ordinary squadron pilot's needs and requirements: and in many ways he was reflecting the view the front-line pilots had of those in high places in far away Delhi. Not that everyone in these HQ units were either uncaring or unthinking, but some of the decisions made, especially as it affected the squadron pilots and ground crews, made them wonder who was running the war in Burma, and how.

Some of the things mentioned in another of Paul's reports, written in 1944 for Air Ministry in London, I note here, to show how easily it was for him to 'rock the boat'. Under various sub-sections, he noted:

"The Staffs through which command is exercised are large and numerous. They attract to themselves some of the better operational, administrative and organising brains, but owing to the cumbrous administrative machinery they find themselves largely impotent.

"Judged by results, it would seem that the High Command at Delhi, some 1,200 miles from the front, is too far away, and that a fair proportion of the staffs of the higher formations would be more profitably employed in the smaller formations and units nearer the front line which have been debilitated by these gargantuan and vampire-like organisations.

"Past disasters, offensives that have misfired, and many sudden and radical changes of plan have all contributed to the RAF junior ranks' loss of confidence in their own commanders and in the Army as a whole."

Or —

"The Air Command in India has forfeited the confidence of the pilots because it has in the past deliberately shut its eyes to the inferiority of the Hurricane as an inteceptor fighter, eg: whilst in the post of W/C Fighter Operations at Bengal Command in May 1943, I wrote a minute (a copy of which is still in my possession) to the AOC. 'There is no doubt that the Hurricane is not up to the job (of fighting Jap fighters)'. The AOC, in deleting this passage from my minute in front of me, said, 'I know that is true, but we must not admit it. Once we admit it, all is lost.' This attitude is not unique, and though possibly necessary and possibly having the best motives, I still consider it criminally irresponsible."

And —

"Visits by Staff Officers, and especially Commanders, to forward stations and units are very rare. When they do occur, their object appears to be sight-seeing and nothing results beyond a shrinkage in the unit's slender stocks of refreshments."

Also:

"There are two classes of officer that exist in large and equally undesirable quantities in India:-

(i) The old deadbeat who is ignorant, inefficient, out-of-date and out of sympathy with the young element in the service, who knows he would not last five minutes elsewhere.

(ii) The deadbeat, young or old, who has been sent to India because he is not wanted elsewhere. These deadbeats were first in India and have dug themselves in. They constitute a deadweight which the newer, younger, more up-to-date and more energetic arrivals find impossible to move in any direction and unwise to try to disturb. A 'new broom' is urgently needed to clean them out."

These were the really pointed comments which undoubtedly some took exception to, either because they genuinely thought them unfair, or because, although they would never admit it, they were unashamedly true. That they were half hidden within 22 pages of items, which covered every aspect of life in wartime India/Burma, made them no less noticeable to those who read them. Paul had covered things like airfields, native labour, monsoons, flying kit, personal kit, supply systems, local beers, mail, newspapers, refrigerators, food, electric fans, accommodation, medical problems, entertainment, leave, sport and a host of other subjects. Perhaps he might have achieved more by leaving out the above sniping paragraphs but that was not Paul's way. If he saw a problem he spoke about it. After all, he would have felt that to get the pilots and groundcrew better food or equipment was just as important as getting them proper leadership and a sympathetic understanding from the 'powers that be'.

Then again, although he had lived and fought in Europe in no less deadly an air space than over Burma, his and his brother airmen in England at least could enjoy reasonable food, accommodation and equipment. For years the men in Burma had to contend with poor food, bad or indifferent accommodation, often no better than bamboo bashas or even holes in the ground in the Imphal Valley, not to mention things such as insects, snakes, heat, insanitary conditions, little leave, long tours of duty, maleria, dysentry, prickly heat, dengue fever — the list was endless.

It didn't help his case with the powers in Delhi that he sent a copy of this report to Air Vice-Marshal D Harries CB AFC, Director General of Personal Services in England, although that was after he had returned home from India. In July 1944, Paul had a letter from Harries thanking him for the report and saying he'd showed it to the Air Member for Personnel.

Harries also noted the Air Member saying that: "... it contained valuable material on which to work and that it should be circulated after one or two excisions had been made..." One wonders which excisions were made and if they had anything to do with the above few paragraphs.

But Paul's over-riding fulfillment was that he had achieved something in India even if he had stepped on a few corns. He told me:

"My Tactical Memorandum, with my recommendation for Spitfires turned the tactical situation of our fighters in India/ Burma from a series of defeats into a series of victories. So at least I did what I had been sent out to do. My Report on the RAF in

India made for Air Ministry, at their request, upon my return to the UK in 1944, was circulated to all members of the Air Council — a rare event — and caused more radical changes out east, including the rolling of some distinguished heads."

Throughout his time in India and Burma, Paul constantly wrote home to his wife and parents. Sometimes it was not possible to be too regular in this regard, but whenever time permitted he would drop a line home, using those blue Air Mail Letter Cards — in reality a flimsy 10″ x 8″ single sheet page that would then be folded into four, stuck down by the Censor, to be posted as a 5″ x 4″ item. Any number of his letters to his parents survive and some extracts from them give a remarkable picture of his life in the Far East, with subjects ranging from his job, to pay, to conditions, to weather and to life in general. Some of these extracts I record here. To spare some blushes, the 'censored' items are mine, not the RAF Censor of the time:

5 March 1943. "Darling Folks, . . . I'm afraid I haven't been over-industrious with my letter writing, chiefly because I have felt like lying down and dying with this ruddy jaundice. However, its nearly gone now and I feel much restored to life, if not to strength and fitness, having got very thin and weak. Sometimes I feel a tinge of conscience but at most times I'm damned if I care, having done a fair bit and not having asked to come out here — and having, moreover, done something about going back to the war, for I've written to Sholto. So now I just make the best of it."

21 April 1943. ". . . I expect you have all heard that poor Christian was killed in action on 1st April. It isn't clear yet how, but I am going to find out when I get down to Air HQ, Bengal, where I shall be for a bit. I had a reply from S [Sholto] in the form of a very nice and friendly letter. I've given Teresa some extracts which are more personal than official. I can't give you the rest because it is more official than personal . . ."

9 May 1943. ". . . Christian appears to have been killed by a wound almost identical with my own. Curious. I'm damned sorry about it — he was a hell of a good chap and very fond of me for some reason."

3 June 1943. "Darling Mum and Dad, I've had a lot of expense out here (mostly) through buying kit which I had to have — shirts,

boots, bedding, vests, socks, bush-jackets, shorts and slacks, monsoon-cape etc. All this, added to the reorganisation of the pay system out here which suddenly stopped pay for two months, made me temporarily very short. My bearer cost me quite a bit in medical expenses in Bombay and I eventually discharged him when I found he had syphilis! ... My pay was knocked down to S/Ldr for Feb, Mar & Apr and has only been back to W/Cdr for May. My pay as S/Ldr was, with allowances, supposed to be 1305 Rupees; 400 to Teresa, 154 Income Tax, 50 to lodging, and I got 701 — about £50. Now, I'm supposed to get 1485 Rupees. Income Tax in this [censored] place Bengal is higher — 228 Rupees and I finish up with 782 Rupees a month. An example of the type of swindle to which we are subjected by the Indian Government for the priviledge of keeping the Japs out of their bloody country is this: I am granted, on paper, 75 Rupees a month lodging allowance; my accommodation however, by a most curious coincidence, costs me just 75 Rupees, whether I live in a palace or, as at present, in a ruddy bamboo basha; so I don't get the 75 Rupees; I do, however, pay Income Tax on it to this swindling [censored] of [censored] called the Bengal Government. .... While at Air HQ, Bengal, I spent most of my time touring the forward areas between Cox's Bazaar, South of Chittagong, and Imphal, up in Assam. The Chin Hills are vicious razor-backs of rock, with dense jungle in which many air crews have descended but from which none have returned. The natives vary in their attitude, all being savage and some head-hunters. ... I have (now) left Air HQ Bengal and have just taken over a Fighter Wing and the Station commandership of Comilla. Everything is rather primitive here and it is all new and mostly not ready. ... Apparently Sholto asked for me the other day. He asked Garrod, our new Deputy AOC-in-C, saying he had made a mistake in sending me here. But Garrod wouldn't let me go. I haven't met him yet. Personally I am fatalistic as ever about it. I would, naturally, like to join S and go to the Middle East, but there is work to be done here and someone has to do it — preferably chaps who know their stuff from experience, of whom there are all too few out here."

21 June 1943. "Darling Dad, ... I was only a few days in Delhi and not particularly sorry. It is cluttered up with the worst type of old dug-outs who don't know their arse from their elbow, on the one hand, and on the other the even less tolerable young careerers who also don't know A from E and who are solely interested in

accumulating rank and dodging bullets. God, Sir, I don't know what the services are coming to! I'm now on the Staff of Bengal Command. This is largely the doing of S [Sholto], who is still taking a great interest in me, apparently. It's jolly decent of him and I'm very glad I wrote to him. This bloody place Bengal has a lousy climate as I expect you know. It's not so much the heat — it's about 100 degres now — as the humidity. ...You will see that our army is progressing in the usual direction in Burma, in spite of RAF support, etc. Either the Japs are too good or the [censored] can't fight, or both.

21 June 1943. "Darling Folks, ... I'm already getting 'Bengal Memory', to add to my prickly heat, 'Bengal foot-rot' and dyspepsia!... Life is pretty expensive out here, added to which Income Tax has been knocked up by this [censored] Government; (that's all right but why should we fight and pay?) I now pay £17 monthly."

22 June 1943. "Darling Folks, This country's Pongo-ridden, Pongo-minded, and stuffed full of them. A pity. If they'd handed the country over to the Air Force, as they did Iraq, we'd have got it organised and well in hand years ago. ... I am now settled in at my Station, which I command in addition to my Fighter Wing. I'm afraid I get very little time for flying, and anyway, the Monsoon is on now. The weather was very unpleasant a few days ago, not very hot (105 degrees or so) but very steamy, exhausting and uncomfortable, what with prickly-heat and so on. There ain't no amenities of civilization, the local town being almost entirely native. Drink is scarce and most of it bad. ... The country is pleasant but monotonous — its all the same for thousands of square miles at a time. I think the climate is the worst part, after all, it's one of the worst in the world and was avoided until recently except by a few jute-wallahs who were lured by gold... I'm afraid my new book is long neglected — after a day sweating in the office and all over the enormous camp area, one doesn't feel like sitting down and sweating more — one can't do it.The raid you saw by FW190s on Brighton must have been very exciting. Those are the gentlemen I got the Typhoons moved for. I'm so glad you had Teresa and the children to stay. I'm sure they must have enjoyed it. I'm naturally longing to get back and see them and all of you — like several other hundreds of thousands of chaps overseas. ... Delhi was interesting in a way, but rather out of touch with reality. Calcutta dirty, hot and full of Pongos.

Paul's Mother later wrote up several of Paul's notes in August 1943, which expands on some of the things he was doing:

"On 20th June went to Chittagong for a Conference; on 25th to to Calcutta for another, on top of which I was given 48 hours leave to do some shopping. Then the weather got bad and I didn't get back here till 1st July and only then by flying in extremely bad weather at 100 ft, in heavy rain for 100 miles. Next day I had a temperature of 100 degrees...Then just as I was about to expire, a signal came detailing me to go to Simla to lecture to two courses of Senior Army Officers. I set off for Delhi (I had Dengue Fever and a painful antrim infection, foot rot, bad prickly heat and a bad tummy.) The journey to Delhi was by air and the plane went to 15,000 ft and nearly burst my antrim infection and ear drum.

"Delhi is hotter than Calcutta but slightly drier. My friend John Hawtrey made all arrangements and I spent a comfortable night in the C-in-C's house, where he lives. Pierse was very pleasant to me and is a nice chap.

"Next day we went by train to Kalka which is at the bottom of the hill. This took all night. My companion was Paddy Bandon — the Earl of Bandon, commonly known as 'the abandoned Earl' — who is Group Captain Ops at Delhi. I knew him before — a very good chap and very amusing. From Kalka we went up into the hills by car. It took about four hours to do the 50 miles or so up to Simla. As we wound up through the hills, away from the stinking hot plains, it got gradually cooler and soon we came to pines instead of ruddy palm trees. Simla is 7,000 ft up and delightfully cool.

"At Simla John and I went for many walks — mostly in cloud and rain — the weather having got bad the second week, but it was nice fresh cold rain.

"We danced at the Cecil Hotel and at the Club. In general we had a marvellous rest. On my way down, at the end of the magic fortnight, I again stayed with the C-in-C — this time for two nights. Delhi itself is in two sections — Old Delhi, native, chaotic, but rather attractive, and New Delhi — a great flat dispersed place, laid out in an ordered pattern of bungalows and gardens, and dominated by the huge Lutyens' creations of red stone, black columns and white domes and cupolas."

9 August 1943. "My Darling Folks, A long gap, I'm afraid. This has been due to a series of absences on duty of various kinds at

several different places, some of which were a long way off —
Chittagong, Calcutta, Delhi and Simla being the main ones. The
duties were usually conferences of one kind or another and the
visit to Simla was not leave but a lecture to senior army officers,
plus some RAF ones, on Fighter Operations. This latter was quite
interesting and the trip to the hills just about saved my life. It had
been damned hot and sticky down here and I had prickly-heat and
various other ailments on various parts of my anatomy due to
sweating, plus a very painful infection. In addition, I got dengue
(a very unpleasant, if non-dangerous, fever, passed on by mosquitoes). At the time I had a lot of urgent work to do and couldn't
go to bed, so felt pretty bloody. On the way to and from Simla I
stayed with our C-in-C, Sir Richard Pierce. I saw a lot of Jack
Baldwin (Air Marshal), who was Deputy AOC-in-C and is now
'seconded for Special Duties'. In Delhi I had the odd meal or
drink or swim with [Sir Guy] Garrod (Air Marshal), the new
Deputy AOC-in-C, who was, until recently on the Air Council,
and [Sir John] Baker (AVM) the new SASO, whose conferences
I used to attend at Air Ministry when I was at Fighter Command.
Garrod and Baker are two very good and able men."

10 August 1943. ... I have come across less bugs of late. Also my
blood is used to the mosquitoes and they don't worry me now.
The other insects I don't mind — one gets used to anything — but
sometimes they are annoying when they come in plagues and fill
the rooms at night.... I often have the strange feeling that I have
seen everything before and know it all well. I had it in France and
I have it out here. It's all exactly as I expected it. ... I also
sometimes feel I am not living my life, but following some sort of
destiny, merely filling in the pattern of a pre-arranged design. I
have a secret feeling that I am going somewhere. ... A Station
Commander's life is one of continual interruptions and badgerings
and rushings about. The AOC and GOC are just about to land
and I must meet them. — Interval — They've gone, having had
lunch in my Mess, which they profess to have enjoyed. Bill
Williams (AVM) the AOC Bengal, is a good chap. I last saw him
at Pontavert, in France, during the Blitz, just after my second
bale-out. He was then a Wg Cdr, of course."

23 October 1943. "My darling Mum and Dad, I'm sorry for not
having written for such a hell of a time. As you may know, I've
been on leave in Kashmir, where there was no way of sending

service letters. ...India is expensive at the best of times but now it is fantastic. There is no proper Government control and the whole place is a racket. A tube of toothpaste, for instance, costs 6-8 Rupees — 10 shillings! It's criminal, of course. And one has to keep oneself. Kit wears out much quicker, due to harder wear and frequent washing. I had to borrow 1,000 Rupees from John Hawtrey on my way through Delhi from Kashmir. This is £75. Add 40 Rupees for something else, total £78. Will you pay him this as soon as he arrives, which will be about the middle of November. Meanwhile, I am saving. My pay has just been increased by £15 per month and I am due some allowances, about £22.10.0. My pay, minus allotments of £36, will now be £71.10.0 per month. I am shortly going off into the jungle where expenses will, of course, be nil. ...These (censored) Indians have stated officially that India will not bear the cost of any offensive by SE Asia Command; and we may all go over to Imperial rates of pay, which means about as much money but more Income Tax. Lord Louis [Mountbatten] visited my Station the other day. We had a parade and he went round every rank, talking to about every other man and meeting every officer. He gave a short, cheerful, straight talk and made a very favourable impression on us all. I sat beside him in my car during a fairly protracted tour of the place — it covers a very large area. He said, 'I'm glad I'm seeing the Air Force first, because after all, they are doing the fighting. The army is not doing any fighting at all.' He said the last sentence with a contempt, perhaps unintentional, perhaps not — with which I fully sympathised. ...This country, for all its nasty bits, is getting to me. It definitely has a lure, a subtle attraction that gets under your skin. The open air, the sun, the great mountains and rivers and forests and plains, the wide open spaces... The very vastness of the country, so depressing and bloody at first, I now find attractive."

28 October 1943. "My Darling Mother, This is to wish you very very many happy returns of the day. I think you're an amazing woman. I would also like to tell you once more how grateful I am to you for everything you have done for me. I owe everything I have to you, and you are still and always will be my greatest friend. I shall try not to let you down."

Paul mentioned the Monsoon in his letters. For those who have never experienced one, writing of them is no substitute. However, Paul did write to his parents in November 1943, painting a vivid picture of what it was like:

"One evening I sat out in my jeep on one of my landing-strips, watching an enormous pile of thunder-clouds that had been building up over the hills all day, to 30,000 ft or more and now overhung our tiny camp and threatened to topple over onto it. From the bottom of this mountainous mass of cloud I could see it pouring in a solid black sheet that was stabbed almost continuously with lightning-flashes. The noise of the thunder and the torrential down-pour must have been terrific and I hoped the Japs crouching in their fox-holes were enjoying it. I could also imagine our men cursing it. All I could hear was an occasional shaking rumble. And yet the top of this gigantic cloud curled over in a great sweep, right over the top of me, rising in a churning tumult from its thick black base to its feathery white crest like some tremendous comber that was about to crash down on us in a thundering annihilation. But it never did. It never even rained on us. It remained poised above us as if held back by God to spare us: impotently seething, but not daring to move. And as the sun set amid whispy golden clouds to the west, this powerful thursting cloud-wave, became slowly frozen into a mountain of stone, its peaks and turrets and bastions, being lit up with the most fantastic lights and lines and colours I have ever seen.

"It was both wonderful and beautiful. Every time one looked to the west at the blaze of light there, and then back to the cloud-mountain, it had changed its colours. And then one looked to the west again and the lights there had changed. One could see the colours and shades changing as one looked. One had scarcely time to see the glory of one combination of lines than one's breath was taken away by another that replaced it. Across it all, always from the south, like handfulls of bright beads thrown across the sky, flew flocks of green parrots. I have never seen anything like it. I think it is the most wonderful sight I have ever seen. No words could possibly describe it adequately."

CHAPTER XVII

HOME AGAIN

IN his letters, Paul mentioned Christian Ortmans, and his death on 1st April 1943. When Paul had received notification of his posting to the Far East, Christian, who had been his No.2 in 609 Squadron during his time as Commanding Officer, had formally requested permission to go too. Once Paul realised he was serious about the move, he put in the request but the Belgian authorities in England felt the posting inappropriate. There was no precedent for it, there being no other Belgian fighter pilots in Burma, and there were few enough in England as it was. Paul made an appeal on behalf of his Belgian friend and finally it was agreed that he could go.

It is not certain what Christian or Paul thought his erstwhile No.2 would do in India, Paul knowing that initially he would be working on some sort of staff job in order to be able to report to Sholto Douglas. However, once in India, and Paul having fallen ill, Christian must have been at something of a loose end.

He was posted to a Vengeance Squadron but when Paul heard of this, he managed to get him sent to 615 Hurricane Squadron, and in doing so Ortmans became the only Belgian fighter pilot to see action against the Japanese in Burma. It was to be a brief and far from happy posting.

On 11 March 1943, Christian due to his overall experience, was leading a six-man patrol over the Arakan jungle into the Donbaik area. There had recently been a note in Routine Orders that it was suspected that the Japanese had managed to get one or two Hurricanes, captured in the retreat through Malaya and Burma, airworthy and might well be using them over the front. As often happens in these circumstances, rumour becomes false fact but in the meantime, it influences people's thinking. It was only a short time after this announcement, that Christian found himself in the position of wondering if he was about to face a captured Hurricane.

In the air at the same moment, was Flying Officer Ray Prince from 135 Squadron, an experienced Burma pilot, who had taken off from Hove, on the Bengal coast, north of Maungdaw. He was only on an air-test, but it is assumed he spotted the six Hurricanes of 615. Exactly what was in Prince's mind is unclear. He either decided to make a mock attack on them as a bit of fun, or perhaps, as one of his squadron pals suggested, thought he would liven things up as the six may have been swanning along without any apparent cause for concern, and Ray may have thought a little lesson would not go amiss.

In the event, Christian saw the Hurricane of to one side, suddenly turn in ahead of his patrol, coming in for a head-on pass from 450 yards. He watched it as it approached, began to take evasive action, and waggled his wings violently to show the approaching Hurricane pilot they were friendly aircraft. But Ray Prince kept on coming, and Christian was obviously thinking, was this one of those captured Hurricanes? The 615 pilots saw the wing guns begin to sparkle and immediately Christian returned fire and was dead on target. One cannot imagine that Prince had failed to recognise 615 as Allied planes, for one thing the Japanese were not using any aircraft at that time which did not have radial engines. It seems difficult to comprehend too that he had begun to fire. Whatever had been in his mind ended suddenly for him. Christian's fire shot down the Hurricane which crashed into the jungle and burst into flames.

Christian was devastated of course, but what had happened could not be altered. Just a few weeks later, on 1st April 1943 — the 25th Anniversary of the Royal Air Force — Christian led 615 on a Scramble to intercept a Japanese raid by 27 bombers escorted by fighters. Once in the air the enemy raid seemed to start a turn for home, but 615 were kept up. All that was really happening was that part of the force had broken away to head for Chittagong. Ortmans was then ordered to engage the original bunch and upon spotting them, led his pilots down but in the subsequent fight, Ortmans was shot down and killed by a Japanese fighter, to crash at Fazilpur, south of Feni, claimed by a pilot of the 64th Japanese Sentai.

Paul was unable, of course, to write to Christian's family in occupied Belgium, but in early 1945 when he was in Brussels, it was possible for him to meet them and talk of Christian, and Vicki, who was still a prisoner of the Germans. A couple of days later he wrote to Mr and Mrs Ortmans about their son who had died in Burma.

27th February 1945

I was very glad to have the opportunity of seeing you the other day, and am only sorry that the circumstances under which we met could not have been happier.

I promised to let you have the details covering Christian's period of service with me and all I know of his death.

I should start by telling you that, when I was a Flight Commander in No.609 Squadron in 1941, I made your other son, Vicki, fly as my No.2. I don't know what he thought of this arrangement — not much probably — but I had a very high regard for him and his flying and we at any rate finished the summer's fighting together without serious mishap. I was then promoted to Squadron Leader and sent to another Squadron. Vicki subsequently went "missing".

In May 1942 I returned to No.609 Squadron to command. Christian had joined the Squadron since I left in 1941. Naturally I took an interest in him and I soon found that he was in a depressed condition and did not want to stay in the Squadron. He was worried about Vicki and had differences with some of the other Belgians. However, I also found he was a very good pilot and, although inexperienced, had great possibilities. Because I liked him, because he was a good pilot, because he needed help and encouragement and because he was Vicki's brother and I wanted to look after him, I asked him if he would like to fly with me as my permanent No.2. He said Yes.

During the spring of 1942 the Squadron was converted from Spitfires to the new Typhoons, being one of the three squadrons which formed the new Typhoon Wing. We were based at Duxford, near Cambridge. Because of the somewhat special nature of our work we did a lot of flying during the summer of 1942 but had few combats with the enemy. At the end of the summer, however, having completed the first stage of the operational development of the new aircraft, we moved down to our old 1941 base of Biggin Hill to undertake more active operations against the enemy.

During the six months that we flew and worked and played together, a strong bond of friendship was created between Christian and myself. I think Christian became happy with the Squadron and I was certainly very pleased with him and very glad to have such a good No.2. His flying and behaviour all round were excellent. When I was promoted to Wing Commander in October 1942, therefore, and posted to India, I was very sorry at the prospect of leaving Christian and flattered when he came to me of his own accord and asked to come with me. However, I told him that I did not think he would find much interest in fighting far away from his own country, and advised him against it. I also told him it was very doubtful if I could arrange it. When he insisted several times, I told him to consider it carefully for twenty-four hours. He remained firm in his request after this period and so I made arrangements (with a good deal of difficulty) to take him. The Belgian authorities only let him go as a special favour to me. I was naturally very glad to have him.

We had a long but very good, journey by sea to India. First we spent a week together with my wife in Blackpool, waiting for our ship. The ship was a 27,000 ton luxury liner, and life was pleasant after we left the cold rain of the North Atlantic. We called at Bahia, in Brazil, where it was very hot but where we had an amusing few days ashore. Our next call was at Durban, in South Africa, which was again hot, but very gay and attractive. A week before Christmas, after two months at sea, we reached Bombay. Here we spent a very pleasant week together, awaiting further orders and having a good time swimming and dancing, and so on. We spent Christmas with some Scottish residents of Bombay out at their bungalow at a famous beach called Juhu, which is very attractive with its sand and palm-trees. And then, most unfortunately, I got appendicitis and had to be operated on, and Christian was posted on to a squadron near Madras.

I did not know about Christian's posting until I received a letter from him saying he was for some reason in a dive-bomber squadron and did not like it. I thereupon wrote to a friend at Delhi and had him transferred to a fighter squadron in the Arakan, on the Burma front, South of Chittagong, which is what he wanted — the CO was a friend of mine. The intention was that when I became well again and went over to Burma I would get him sent to my Wing.

Unfortunately my appendicitis was followed by acute jaundice and I was delayed nearly four months altogether in Bombay. Meanwhile, Christian and I exchanged letters. He seemed to be getting on well and interested in the new conditions, but I think he was hoping I would be over soon; so was I. A week before I left Bombay I received word that Christian had been killed on 1st April 1943.

When I eventually reached Bengal I naturally made all possible inquiries with a view to ascertaining the exact circumstances of

Christian's death. This was difficult, because a number of people with direct knowledge of the case had been either killed or posted elsewhere subsequently, and the great distances and lack of communication increased the difficulties. But, as far as I could make out, these are the facts.

On the afternoon of 1st April 1943, the Japs attacked the airfield at Feni, in Eastern Bengal and where Christian's Wing was stationed. The Jap raid consisted of the usual twenty-odd bombers in close formation at 25,000 feet escorted by fighters. The raid was intercepted by Christian's Wing [sic] near Feni and attacked, a number of bombers being shot down for the loss of some of our fighters. Most of the Japs' bombs fell in the village of Feni and not on the target, which was the airfield.

Because of his position in his Squadron formation on this flight, Christian and his No.2, a Sergeant Pilot, attacked last. The last to attack an escorted formation are usually in the most dangerous position, as the escort naturally selects the rear aircraft to attack. Christian's No.2 saw Christian attack a bomber but both he and Christian were immediately attacked from behind by Jap fighters. In chasing his Jap off, the No.2 temporarily lost Christian, and before he could rejoin him he saw a Jap fighter on Christian's tail. He saw Christian's Hurricane dive vertically and Christian bale out just before the aircraft caught fire. He saw Christian's parachute open and his aircraft diving towards the ground. The No.2 than had his attention taken up by the Japs, who engaged him again.

An RAF Officer and some airmen of a radio reporting unit a few miles from Feni saw a man in a parachute coming down from a high altitude. One of the men noticed that the man seemed to be coming down fast. Some Indians also saw this and saw a Hurricane crash in flames in a big water-tank in their village. One of the Indians reported seeing a Jap shooting at the man in the parachute. The parachutist came down a mile from the RAF Officer. When the RAF Officer reached the parachutist he found him surrounded by Indian soldiers. His parachute, which was damaged, had been detached and lay a short distance away, and he was dead.

The Senior RAF Medical Officer at Feni, who had come out to India in the same ship as Christian, was so upset by his death that he did not examine him too closely. The other RAF Medical Officer examined him but did not carry out a post-mortem because of the pressure of work caused by the killing of 70 villagers and the severe injuries of 200, caused by the bombing of Feni. He reported that Christian had evidently been killed by a bullet which had cleanly entered the right side of the neck in an upwards direction towards the brain.

Christian's No.2 was killed in another action shortly after this one. The RAF Officer who found Christian on the ground was posted and could not be interviewed. The Indian Regiment to which the soldiers belonged had gone to the jungle front. I interviewed both the Doctor, and also Christian's CO — Squadron Leader Holland. Squadron Leader Holland, whom I knew well, told me Christian was most popular in his squadron, No.615, and he personally thought a great deal of him and he offered him a Flight Commandership, which he had refused.

From the details available, it is evident that (a) Christian's aircraft was damaged by a Jap fighter, (b) he was possibly wounded as well, (c) he baled out, (d) he was possibly wounded whilst baling out and his parachute damaged, (e) he was possibly attacked and wounded on the way down by a Jap fighter, and his parachute damaged. At any rate, the cause of death was certainly the bullet which penetrated his brain, and according to the Doctors, death must have occured within a matter of seconds and been quite painless. Christian was buried with full military honours in the Military Cemetery at Feni.

I need not tell you how grieved I was at this tragedy, especially as I felt myself in India more than ever responsible for him, my loyal partner and friend. I can only imagine what the loss of your fine son means to you, his parents, and to Vicki. Yet you have the eternal and inviolate consolation that he was and is in every sense Christian. He died for us and for Freedom, and is now for ever with God.

Madame Ortmans replied to Paul's letter, which was, as ever, frank in its detail, from their Brussels home, on 6 June, barely a month after the war had ended.

Dear Sir,
It is with intense emotion that my husband and I thank you for the precious pages you have sent us. You have gone to great trouble and shown such sensitivity in giving us the details of the last known events in the life of our beloved son, Christian, and we hope you will know just how deeply you have touched us in writing them.

Each line, each word you have written, has become a priceless treasure to our irredeemiably shattered hearts.

Thank you for all the sensibility you show in speaking of Christian's death, and for the care you take in trying to make our suffering less unbearable, and we remain deeply impressed by the affection our son had for you, and that you reciprocate it.

I hope that your presence in Belgium will soon coincide with that of our dear Vicki, close to us, and that we would be thus able to have the very great pleasure to have you join us for lunch one day.

The great friendship based on admiration that Vicki had for you, added to the devotion of his dear brother for you, has spontaneously engendered in us too the deepest and most affectionate understanding for you, which makes us wish to see you again as often as circumstances allow.

Please accept this expression of all our sympathetic understanding, deeply moved.

Vicki Ortmans did indeed return home, only to die in an air crash after the war.

However busy Paul was in gathering information and writing reports and tactical memoranda while in India, he still had some social activity. Needless to say it involved a woman or two. He was ever the 'Adonis', looking even more handsome, and now bronzed by the tropical sun.

Group Captain Frank Carey DFC & 2 bars DFM, in early 1944 Chief of the Air Fighting Training Unit at Armarda Road, near Calcutta, met him once at one of the swimming clubs in Calcutta itself. Frank Carey had known Paul before the war when he had been with 43 Squadron at Tangmere, when Paul had joined 1 Squadron on the same base.

Carey was sitting down in the sun by himself, with the usual hubbub about him when he suddenly noticed the noise and chatter had died away. Opening his eyes to see if there was a reason, he spotted Paul, in swimming trunks and with a towel round his neck, strolling through the array of tables and deckchairs. All the women had spotted this vision and almost as one had stopped to look. Whether he was totally aware of it himself can only be speculated, he didn't seem to show it but spotting Frank Carey, and, pleased to see someone he knew, Paul walked over, sat down and they had quite a chat.

Frank knew something about one of Paul's ladies in question, almost everyone did, for she was the wife of an army officer, who lived in Calcutta. The husband too lived and worked in the city and must have known not only of Paul but of others, for she apparently was quite friendly with a number of men. Unfortunately one of the others was none other than the C-in-C of the 3rd Tactical Air Force, South East Asian Command — Air Marshal Sir John Baldwin KBE CB DSO. Paul ran into trouble now, for the lady had made a date with Paul when Sir John apparently telephoned her to say he was in town and could they meet. She had to decline, she told the Air Marshal, as she had already promised to go out with Paul Richey. That must have put Paul in bad odour with Sir John.

By this time, Paul had been given command, not of the first Spitfire Wing as promised by Bill Williams, but No. 165 Wing at Comilla, in 224 Group, which still had Hurricanes. The Wing consisted of 79, 146 and 258 Squadrons, and later 11 Squadron. The Group Commander was still Air Commodore Alec Gray MC! Paul was continuing to suffer with his sinusitis and dysentery and also had a touch of dengue fever in July 1943. It was, of course, the time of the Monsoon, so operations had all but ceased in the Arakan, the Wing having been moved back to Calcutta. At least it gave time for Paul to try and shake off his sickness problems before the next offensive began. But he did not improve and in November he had to see an ear, nose and throat specialist. Alec Gray then arranged for his replacement. This turned out to be Wing Commander T A F Elsdon DFC, a former Battle of Britain pilot, who had brought 136 Squadron out from England at the end of 1941, and who had personally seen brief action over Rangoon before the retreat. Jimmy Elsdon recalls:

"I 'assumed' command of 165 Wing and I use the word in inverted commas as it is used in both a military sense and a presumptive sense. The incident may provide a unique anecdote and, incidentally, perhaps support any theory about the arrogance of local Commanders in the Far East at the time.

"In October 1943, after I had commanded 169 Wing at Agartala for some nine months, the AOC of No.224 Group, Alec Gray, said he would like me to move down to Feni to form a new Fighter/ Ground Attack Wing, designated No.185 Wing, although no squadrons had yet been selected for it. However, I could start getting the Wing Headquarters organised as staff were posted in.

"The following month (still before there were any squadrons in 185 Wing) Alec Gray asked me if I would take over Paul Richey's No.165 Wing in the Arakan temporarily, as operations were expected to start there very soon and Paul was in Calcutta and still unfit for flying duties. It was not known for how long I would be needed, but Paul Richey was around and about in Calcutta by then so the AOC did not expect it would be long. Moreover, 165 Wing was scheduled to be requipped with Spitfires in the near future.

"In one of those rare moments of inspiration I asked the AOC if he would allow me to keep 165 Wing (instead of forming a new 185 Wing) if Paul did not return within a specific and reasonable time. He thought this was a reasonable request under all the circumstances and I believe we agreed on a fortnight, with a decision date of 10th December, but I asked him if he would send a formal notification to HQ 165 Wing, confirming the attachment and potential command date. This he did.

"A day or two after the appointment date, Paul Richey turned up at Ramu to re-assume command of the Wing. I don't think I was very popular when I told my story and produced the signal from my pocket confirming my appointment a day or so earlier. Paul accepted the situation and asked if he could visit the Officer's Mess for some refreshment before collecting his personal effects etc, and returning to civilisation in Calcutta. When he returned, he thanked me, accepted a lift down to the airstrip with all his kit to rejoin the aircraft that had brought him into Ramu about an hour earlier. I understood the pilot to say he was setting off for Chittagong, so I assumed Paul was reporting to the AOC before returning to Calcutta.

"Later that day, when I returned to the Mess, the steward said that Wing Commander Richey had asked for one of the (very precious) bottles of Johnnie Walker Black Label whisky. When the Mess steward asked Paul whether he would sign for it or pay cash, Paul apparently replied, 'Neither — Wing Commander Elsdon owes me a bottle of whisky,' — which I probably did!"

Paul continued his story to me:

"The RAF had operated thoughout the 1943 Monsoon just to show it could — an idiotic decision taken by Air Chief Marshal Sir Richard Pierse, AOC-in-C India, from his air conditioned house in Delhi. The Japanese airforce went to rest and recuperate in dry and pleasant Indonesia. Then Air Marshal Sir John Baldwin, ex-AOC No.1 Bomber Group in England, who had been poodle-faking in Delhi for a year without a job, was given Bengal Command by his friend Pierce, when it was renamed 3rd TAF and up-graded, while poor old Bill Williams was shoved out.

"On 11 December 1943 I took over 189 Wing at Palel in the Imphal Valley — four squadrons of bomber-Hurricanes. My new AOC was Victor Rowley, whom I liked but thought had reached his career limit. In charge of fighters in the Valley was Group Captain Seton Broughall, a Canadian and like Rowley, RAF since WW1 — a great man. The only Spitfires I ever saw were the Mark VIIIs of No.1 Indian Squadron, which were on one of my strips for a period."

No.189 Wing was officially formed in December, and Paul's adjutant was Flying Officer J W McCombie, while his Squadron Leader Flying was Flight Lieutenant D S Edwards, who had also seen active service in UK. Paul was responsible for 28, 34 and 42 Squadrons as well as No.1 IAF Squadron. During January 1944, Paul underwent more medical treatment, and Wing Commander P K Devitt was brought in to take over the Wing — which had just moved to Silchar, taking over from Paul's deputy, Squadron Leader C P N Newman DFC, OC 34 Squadron. Paul continued:

"In February 1944 my sinusitis became hopeless and I was invalided to the UK. Then Victor Rowley was sacked by Baldwin for standing up to him (in spite of an appeal to Mountbatten, who wouldn't 'interfere' with the RAF). Broughall was also sacked by Baldwin for refusing to order No.5 Squadron to fly their Mohawks after the wings came off two of them. He got an Adverse Report by grounding that Squadron pending investigation, then Delhi ordered them to fly, which they did, only to lose another aircraft from the same cause. Broughall then disobeyed orders and grounded the Squadron permanently. Baldwin, of course, was behind his sacking too. Seton told me all this when we travelled on the same ship together on the trip home. After I got back to England, I received an Adverse Report from Gray, countersigned by Baldwin, no doubt because I had crossed swords with Baldwin over a lady. Lovely fellow Baldwin.

"The 'official' reason used for my adverse report was because I was late back from leave. It was a 3,000-mile journey and I'd been held up by my transport, although I knew nothing of this until I had returned to England.

"Back in the UK in March 1944, before being hospitalised for chronic sinusitis and amoebic dysentry, Air Ministry asked me for a report on the RAF in India which I actually wrote whilst in hospital. This became a fair-sized work, pulling no punches, and was favourably received to the point of being circularised to all

FIGHTER PILOT'S SUMMER

the Air Council — a very rare procedure. I was not displeased to see some heads roll, notably two of my former antagonists, because I believed the war could be better prosecuted without them."

Then came the shock of the Adverse Report, by which time Paul had taken up a post with SHAEF — Supreme Headquarters Allied Expeditionary Force. Paul had been offered a Group Captain's rank in the SHAEF Mission to Belgium, as A3 (Operations) in Brussels in November but finished up a Wing Commander because of Baldwin's Adverse Report. Paul then managed to get himself into the War Room at HQ 2nd TAF in March 1945, with the hopeful view of returning to operational flying, but the war came to an end before he could achieve his aim.

Meanwhile, ever the fighter, he responded to his Adverse Report with a letter to Sir Roderick Hill, the C-in-C of ADGB (Air Defence Great Britain), the old Fighter Command at Bentley Priory. This was in October, when Paul was stationed at the Officers Advanced Training School at the RAF College, Cranwell. It read:

CONFIDENTIAL 6th October, 1944

ADVERSE CONFIDENTIAL REPORT RECEIVED FROM
HEADQUARTERS, THIRD TACTICAL AIR FORCE

Sir,

I have the honour to inform you that on 19th September 1944, I was sent for by the Officer Commanding, Air Defence of Great Britain (Unit) and required to sign a Form 1369 containing adverse comments on me.

2. I exercised my right to send in a letter to accompany the report, but have since realised that this letter suffered from being too hastily composed. Having had time to think further over the relevant facts, I wish to bring them to your notice.

3. The adverse comments were signed by Air Commodore A. Gray, AOC No.224 Group and under whom I served for six months, and by Air Marshal Sir John Baldwin, AOC Third Tactical Air Force, and under whom I served for about two-and-a-half months when I was in No.221 Group. Both these officers complain that I had a lot of leave and did not take sufficient interest in my work.

4. The full details of my tour of duty in India are tabulated and appended, but I would like to invite your attention to the following points:

(i) I was posted to India after three operational tours that included the Battle of France, in which I was seriously wounded, and most of the offensive fighter sweeps of 1941 and 1942.

(ii) Whilst in transit, I developed acute sinusitis and appendicitis. I had my appendix removed on arrival in Bombay, but subsequently developed jaundice, which carries with it acute depression.

(iii) When I was passed fit for duty four months after arrival in India, I still had acute sinusitis and had also developed dysentry. I did not, however, report sick again.

(iv) As a result of the above circumstances, I was in very poor health when I eventually took up my appointment in Bengal in the hot weather. Amongst other things, I subsequently got dengue fever, with the usual acute depression that accompanies it. Because of my work, however, I did not go sick.

(v) Later on, as I was still suffering from acute sinusitis and dysentry, I took the opportunity of a slack period during the Monsoon to take leave and go to the hills to try and get fit for the forthcoming dry-weather operations. I returned, from a journey of over 3,000 miles, one day late, primarily because of a breakdown in part of my transport arrangements.

(vi) I was asked for an explanation of my lateness by Air Commodore Gray. Apart from this I was given no hint that my work or conduct were unsatisfactory.

(vii) Later, as I was still suffering from acute sinusitis, I asked the AOC whether I could go to the nearest Ear, Nose and Throat Specialist, who was in Calcutta, for treatment for a month during which my Wing was to be deprived of pilots and aircraft. I stressed the point that I did not want to lose my Wing and would not go if it entailed doing that. Air Commodore Gray was non-committal, but said I could go if I went sick. This I did.

(viii) On the third of my weekly visits to keep in touch with my Wing during the treatment, I found I had been supplanted in my command without my knowledge. I shortly afterwards requested and was granted an interview with the AOC. I was then told by him personally that there was 'absolutely no question of an adverse report' but that, as I was sick, he had had to replace me.

(ix) I was immediately given command of another Wing, this time in No.221 Group, under Air Commodore Rowley. Air Marshal Sir John Baldwin had just taken over 3rd TAF.

(x) Three weeks later I had to ask permission to attend the ENT Specialist again, though not officially going sick, and after a series of tests and examinations was given a medical classification of A4hBh and invalided home with chronic sinusitis, amoebic dysentery being discovered after my arrival in the United Kingdom.

(xi) Air Commodore Gray's adverse report on me was dated February 1944, ie: almost three months after I had left his Group.

(xii) Of the two-and-a-half months I served under Air Marshal Baldwin I was fit and on duty for about three weeks. I never saw him except once or twice socially, and he never visited my station.

(xiii) I had strong differences of opinion with Air Commodore Gray over certain Service matters, and with Air Marshal Sir John Baldwin over certain purely private matters, which may possibly have influenced their judgement of me.

5. I now realise that I should have gone sick long before I did, and that my work may very well have suffered as a result of my illness. My motives for hanging on and trying to cure myself, however, were based only on my determination to do my share in fighting the war. As it turned out, I not only became seriously ill, but suffered a serious setback in my career.

6. I submit with very great respect that:—

(i) Air Commodore Gray's comments on my Form 1369 are inconsistent with his personal assurance in para. 4, sub para (viii) above, which was given when I left his Group in December 1943, and that, since they are dated February 1944, they are the result of an afterthought.

(ii) If my work was unsatisfactory, I should have been warned, instead of being given another command of equal rank.

(iii) The two-and-a-half months I served under Air Marshal Baldwin did not give him sufficient knowledge of me to report accurately, especially in view of my illnesses and various medical examinations.

7. I therefore have the honour to request that you will forward my remarks to Air Ministry with a recommendation that representation may be made to have the comments on my Form 1369 varied.

I have the honour to be,

Sir,

your obedient Servant

Whether anything happened about this letter is now unknown but one must assume very little did. One doesn't usually win against senior officers, one being a Knight of the Realm, and however unjustly Paul may have felt he was treated, the adverse report remained. As he

pointed out to me, in the case of Sir John and the lady in Calcutta —
and everyone knew about it, at least in India — Paul was forbidden
to make mention specifically of it in his defence, only able to refer to
a 'private matter'. What also upset Paul as he told me, was that they
had waited for him to leave India before they put in the report, so,
presumably, he could not confront them personally about it.

We have a couple of examples of letters Paul wrote to his parents in
early 1945. Paul was now 28 years old, still young in age, but his youth
had past now; he had been robbed of his early manhood by war, as had
thousands of other young men. But now we encounter the mature
Paul, with time at long last to see life about him as it really was. In
his second letter too, there is the poignant reflection when at last he
sees the human face of his enemies.

18 January 1945

Darling Mother & Father, ...I had a nice Christmas with the de
Selys in the country. I've given Teresa all the details.[1] They are
really extremely kind to me and it is awfully nice living with them.
...“I'm afraid my life nowadays has little connection with the war
and I am also afraid that I do not regret this fact. For the first time
I am willing to admit I have done my whack of fighting. For the
first time, also, in five years, I have time to really look at the world
we live in, to do more than just glance in passing at its beauties
and its ugliness, to look seriously at specimens of architecture and
paintings, to read a book of poetry or a political thesis. I feel no
twinge of conscience — or hardly any — because there are now
plenty of young boys to get on with the war and finish it.

“I am also conscious that the time has come for those of us who
are left to take up our new responsibilities of reconstructing the
world. I feel that my recent and present easy times are not a waste
as far as I am concerned, and that they are helping me to find
myself again and become a civilized human being. You know how
I have always hated fighting, even from boyhood; yet because I
was good at it, I have always had to do it...”

---

[1] Jean de Selys (Flight Lieutenant Baron J M P de Selys Longchamps DFC), flew
with 609 Squadron but was killed with another squadron in 1943. He had been
Godfather to Paul's daughter the previous year.

9 April 1945

My Darling Parents, ...I have just been to see Cologne. It is
utterly devastated. We drove in, in our jeep, past miles of badly
damaged houses. As we neared the centre of the city the devastation increased. The smaller streets were choked with rubble; the
main ones, which had been fine avenues and boulevards, were
now lined with gaunt facades, the houses behind them having
crashed to the ground. Great areas were completely flattened,
others filled with mountains of masonry...

"Down by the cathedral we were stopped by two Yank sentries:
the Huns had the road under observation from one of the towers
of the Hohenzollern Bridge across the Rhine; as we stood there
talking, half a dozen bullets plopped into the debris round the
corner. Across the street lay a dead Panther tank with a sign hung
on it — 'Boobie-trapped'; not so dead apparently. ...We asked
permission to look in the cathedral. We had to cross the under-
fire area to reach it, which we did in a fittingly British saunter...

"[The German people near our HQ]... keep to themselves,
avoid one's eyes, give one an uncomfortable feeling as one passes
them; but if asked or told to do anything they are pathetically
ready and eager and fairly scurry around. They look arrogant and
hostile — or is it that one has thought of them so for so long?
Anyway, they are in fact docile, servile, cowed, miserable in spirit
if not materially. In these circumstances those perhaps two
qualities of compassion and mercy that I inherit from you, Mother,
are something of a burden to me: I find the whole spectacle of
Europe today deeply sad. Worst of all, our post-war policy seems
to be as far removed from the Christian way of thinking as war
itself. 'Vengeance is mine, saith the Lord. I will repay.' The
irresponsible and indiscriminate desire for revenge among my
companions and compatriots is appalling. I am certain the world
cannot survive on this basis of revenge. Of course, time will soothe
us and calm us down. But I fear lest the harm may be done first,
in the first two years or so, as happened last time when we starved
Germany after the Armistice. We shall see."

EPILOGUE

THE primary purpose of this book has been my attempt to tell the story of Paul Richey's war, continuing where his famous *Fighter Pilot* ended. Paul would have made a far better job of it than I but as he never got around to writing it, this has to be better than nothing.

He was a very complex character, very much his own man, and although he could make friends easily and was much admired, equally he made enemies by his forthright approach to the problems he confronted. He did not suffer fools gladly — and showed it. But in that he is not alone.

I make no attempt here to write about his post-war life other than a brief thumb-nail sketch. Paul remained in the RAF for a year, having moved to Germany in April 1945 with the 2nd Tactical Air Force, from Brussels, where he had been Wing Commander Operations in the War Room of the Headquarters. The devastation he saw, the liberation of the concentration camps, the tragedy of the aftermath of that terrible war, affected him profoundly.

When he was making the decision to leave the Service, no less a figure than the legendary Air Marshal Sir Basil Embry KBE CB DSO (and 3 bars!) DFC AFC (later Air Chief Marshal GCB) — who was the first to recognise the worth of any genuine fighting man and leader — tried to persuade Paul to stay in. So much for the Adverse Report.

In May 1949 he was awarded his last wartime decoration, becoming an Officer of the Order of the Crown of Belgium, in recognition of his work with Belgian fighter pilots while with 609 Squadron and for his work with the SHAEF Mission to Belgium. The Adverse Report didn't affect that either.

After leaving the service, Paul joined the Anglo-Iranian Oil

Company (British Petroleum) and became European Area Manager for Aviation Products, recruited by Max Aitken (Group Captain DSO DFC, later Sir Max, son of Lord Beaverbrook), as Air Correspondent to *The Daily Express* newspaper, a post at which he excelled and became both prominent and controversial.

The lure of flying and the desire to contribute saw him joining the Auxiliary Air Force in 1948, as a member of No. 601 (County of London) Squadron, being senior flight commander and second-in-command, under Max Aiken, at RAF Hendon flying Spitfire XVIs. When 601 converted to jet De Havilland Vampires at North Weald in October 1949, Paul became Commanding Officer, until 1952, also flying Meteors; he returned to full-time service briefly during the Korean War crisis.

He was a man of many and diverse interests. He travelled widely and his love of adventure and physical challenge found outlets in mountaineering, ocean racing and deep sea diving. In the latter sport he was invited to dive with members of Jacques Cousteau's celebrated French underwater team.

On the domestic scene (throughout the war and for some years after) his life went through a period of great turbulence. His marriage to Teresa produced four childen, Ann in 1941, Pauline in 1943, while Paul was in India, Peter in 1945 and Simon in 1946. Unhappily this marriage ended in divorce, like so many other war marriages. His second marriage, to Mary Tylor, also ended in divorce within five years, but not before a daughter, Emma, was born to them in 1958.

In peace as in war, it was not long before Paul was once again in the headlines on the Continent and in England. This time for an heroic life-saving escapade which won him the Royal Humane Society's Bronze Medal for Saving Life from Drowning. On 7th April 1959, Paul and a young lady friend, Sally Butler, were lunching with friends at a villa near the Italian fishing village of Portofino, on the west Italian coast, not far from Sorrento. Paul, Sally and a solicitor friend climbed half-way down the cliffs after lunch, and as Sally was standing on a shelf of rock, Paul was taking photographs of her, the cliffs, and the sea, which was running high and magnificently wild. The feared and respected Sirrocco (the strong regional wind, like the Mistral in the south of France) was blowing a gale.

While Paul was framing the photograph in his view-finder, the scene was suddenly blacked-out as a freak wave driven by the Sirrocco, swelled up and ran along the coast, rising the 30 feet or so to where Sally stood, snatching her off the rock and sweeping her into the sea, where she was suckled deep into the wave's undertow. Paul's response was typical — instinctive, immediate and regardless. As the wave receded he dived, fully clad, straight into the sea after her. There was not the slightest hesitation, despite the fact that he had quite a bit of money in his pocket, an expensive wristwatch on and the camera still about his neck. The other man with them had been mercifully spared by clinging to an iron stanchion on the rockface.

Sally's disappearance had been so quick and dramatic that he did not believe she would or could survive. And watching Paul dive in after her, the friend did not think there was any hope that he would even find her, let alone save her life. But although Paul knew himself that his chances of rescuing Sally were remote, probably impossible, it still did not stop him trying.

He, too, was sucked down very deep in the undertow and after fighting his way to the surface where the spume was all but solid in the high wind, searching and shouting, he suddenly heard her calling his name quite close. Desperately groping about he found her. He got hold of her shirt and knotted it to give him a good grip, did his best to reassure her and assessed their situation.

There was no way of him bringing her back to shore. The heavy seas were pounding the cliffs and the rocks were impassable; there was no choice but to take her further out to sea. Knowing that part of the coastline well, he reckoned that he would be unable to get her round the headland into Portofino harbour — although he could have possibly made it on his own — so unless there was a rescue party from the shore, they were finished.

Sally was very brave, but after a while quite naturally went into a panic and Paul had to knock her unconscious. Meantime, the solicitor friend had scrambled up the rocks and sounded the alarm, and the drama was being witnessed from the clifftops. The news spread quickly that a man and a woman were in the sea and the Commandante of the port of Portofino went into action. He called for volunteers to launch the lifeboat, but then decided it was too dangerous in such weather. But the village fishermen over-ruled him and so he agreed that the Portofino lifeboat, *Onda II*, commanded by Capitano Attilio Cupido, should make an attempt at rescue. And the Commandante, Francesco Cavallaro, insisted on going out with them.

They nearly didn't make it out of port, fouling their rope, but recovered and set off. Although organised and on their way as fast as was humanly possible, it was to be a full hour more before they would reach Paul and Sally. While all this was happening in the port, Paul could just make out specks on the cliffs that he thought (rightly) could be people, and therefore determined to survive and support Sally as long as he could, knowing that a rescue of some kind must be in train.

When the *Onda II* almost ran them down in the water and violently choppy seas it was the greatest sight he'd ever seen in his life. For the sailors it was an amazing incident. They almost ran down a man holding a woman as high above the spume as he could to help her breathe, by a knotted shirt — the only clothing left on either of them. The sailors dragged them aboard and Paul immediately, to their astonishment, started working frantically over the blackened and seriously endangered body of Sally, applying artificial respiration. He did not stop until she gave a cough, at which the sailors cheered, and took over from the exhausted Paul. She would survive.

It was a jubilant crew of volunteer seamen who returned safely to the port with the man and the women they had rescued, against the odds, from the sea. Paul returned to Portofino with gifts for the seamen — and he had special fisherman's knives made and engraved for each one of the men who had saved their lives.

After his second wife left him, Paul met Diana in 1961, in London. Australian, Diana had perhaps as strong a personality as Paul's. Here she recalls one of her first impressions of the man she would marry eight years later.

"Soon after I met Paul, in 1961, he invited me to a luncheon at his home in Belgravia. I was working in television at the time and at first refused, because we rarely took lunch breaks. But he was so determined and so insistent that it was important that I should accept. A last minute flap at work caused me to be late. Sergeant Smith, Paul's formidable butler-valet, opened the front door to me. Ex-Life Guards, (said to be the only man who could dress them correctly on full ceremonial occasions), severe and straight as a poker, he clearly enjoyed being awe-inspiring — and he was. I was already regretting my acceptance.

"As Sergeant Smith took my coat, I heard Paul calling from the top of the staircase: 'Diana, I'm on my way. Sorry I wasn't at the door to meet you...' Then he appeared on the first floor landing, carrying a fragile old lady in his arms, and smiling. He came smoothly down the stairs into the hall and leant forward formally to kiss my cheek, his Mother cradled in his arms between us. Welcome to my schloss,' he said.

"Sergeant Smith led us into the dining room where Paul gently eased his venerable Mama into a mahogany carver chair at the foot of the table. 'Comfortable?' he asked, kissing her hand. Then he showed me to my chair on his right at the head of the table, pushing it in for me with a theatrically gallant bow, then proceeded to introduce me to my fellow guests: an Indian Maharajah, a broadcasting baron, an industrialist and his glamorous wife, a limpidly beautiful Indian Princess, a Reuters correspondent. An elegantly served delicious meal followed. It was a very happy occasion in stimulating and agreeable company, but my enduring memory of that day was of what, in retrospect, seemed almost a vision that he appeared above me on the staircase landing. A beautiful Adonis of a man, impeccably dressed, with an aura about him that crackled with strength, and with humour, carrying his mother in his arms. As Paul carried Mrs Richey slowly and smoothly down the stairs, I could see that although one of her hands shook uncontrollably (she had suffered a stroke) she was entirely relaxed, looking serene and dignified, the Imperial Roman cast of her features blending with her maiden name of Titus.

"Carrying her so effortlessly, Paul made me think of an oak tree holding his Mother secure in his branches. I was to think of Paul as an oak tree many times during the 28 years we shared together, for there were to be many occasions when he would have to carry me too. And I was to find that the heart of this oak was of a rare purity; generous to a fault and capable of a range of kindnesses and unselfishness such as I would not have believed could be an integral part of this man's nature, so expertly disguised beneath the flamoyant playboy veneer with a reputation to match."

Diana and Paul were married in February 1969 and lived in England, then in France, in the region of the Cher, first in a broken-down moated Chateau, then in a 17th-century gamekeeper's lodge with their own wild pond, hundreds of wild duck, resident herons and their rescued swan 'Samovar'.

Here Paul did the major part of his work for the history he was preparing on Anglo-French relations, culminating in the Air Battle of France, May-June 1940. He had been researching it for many years and regarded it as the central work of his life. Unfortunately he did not live to complete it.

During the time, a great French friend, the dramatist, novelist, journalist and broadcaster, Marcel Haedrich, spontaneously wrote a 'Document' feature on Paul's *Fighter Pilot*, a book that he particularly admired.

The French are meticulous in the enquiry they automatically set in train for the military section of their Ordre National de la Legion d'Honneur. It is called an 'etude' (study) and it is painstaking and comprehensive. The Minister asked for an 'etude' on Paul Richey, the English writer living modestly in the Cher, with his Australian wife and their animals.

The final report was sent to the Minister 'magnifique' — and with Claude Cheysson, another Minister, seconding the nomination, the award was made. The British authorities however, felt that this was an award concerning events of war too far in the past, and refused permission for Paul to be able to accept it. But the French also wished the award to represent Paul's contribution to Anglo-French relations over more recent years, and for his writings. Finally he was made a Chevalier of the Legion d'Honneur for 'Faits de Guerre' and for his 'Ecritures'.

Everything to do with this honour bestowed on him by the French at such a time in his life, and their refusal to allow it to be deflected, gave Paul a mixture of pleasure and pride that he expressed with sincerity and emotion at the reception, in London, given by his Excellency the Ambassador for France, M. 'Bobbie', de Margerie, for the presentation of the 'Croix'.

Paul and Diana returned to live in England in 1982, Paul continuing further research and work on his history. This was abruptly inter-rupted when he found himself fighting his last battle in trying to stop a book and television series adapted from it, that he believed not only infringed the copyright of *his* book, but denigrated and ridiculed all pilots engaged in action during the first year of World War II. However, his death, on 23rd February, 1989, at the age of 72, brought that fight to a dramatic end, although Diana continues to fight on in his name.

At the time of his death, the tenth edition of *Fighter Pilot* was in preparation, to be published by Leo Cooper. Paul had checked it and agreed the text, Diana wrote a posthumous Editor's Note.

Whatever the edition, Paul's book has always stood as a fine testa-ment not only to him but to those many other young men who helped in the struggle for freedom and liberty, sitting in the cockpit of a fighter aeroplane, and proud to be, or remembered as, a wartime Royal Air Force fighter pilot.

APPENDIX A

HONOURS, AWARDS AND CITATIONS

Wing Commander Paul Richey's citations:

London Gazette 5th November 1940
DISTINGUISHED FLYING CROSS — Flying Officer P H M Richey,
No.1 Squadron

> "On 29 March, 1940, near Metz, this officer shot down one Messerschmitt 109. Since 10th May, he has destroyed six enemy aircraft, has landed by parachute twice, and was finally shot down and wounded.
>
> "In all these engagements he displayed courage of the highest order when faced with overwhelming odds."

London Gazette 8th August, 1941
BAR to DISTINGUISHED FLYING CROSS — Flight Lieutenant P H M Richey
DFC No.609 Squadron

> "This officer has displayed great skill and coolness throughout numerous operational missions in which he has participated and has destroyed at least nine enemy aircraft and damaged a further seven. As a flight commander he has invariably displayed a high sense of responsibility for the safety of his fellow pilots."

London, 11 November 1941 — Squadron Leader P H M Richey DFC
CROIX DE GUERRE BELGE WITH PALME Gazetted 25 November 1941

> "Pour la bravoure et le sang-froid dont il a fait preuve en conduisant un peleton de pilotes de chase belges au cours de nombreuses operations offensives au-dessus du Continent.
>
> "Cet officier a remporte neuf victoires confirmees et sept victoires probables."

London, 15 February, 1943 — Squadron Leader P H M Richey DFC
French CROIX DE GUERRE WITH PALME

> "Pilote d'un courage et d'une audace exceptionels qui apres avoir participe brillamment aux operations de la campagnes en France, au cours de laquelle il a

ete tres grievement blesse, a repris sa place en escadrille en 1941. A depuis lors effectue de tres nombreuses operations offensives au-dessus des territoires occupes, comme Flight Commander puis comme Squadron Leader, donnant ainsi le plus bel exemple personnel et la plus grande emulation aux pilotes Francais qui faisaient partie de l'Unite qu'il commandait.

"Type parfait du Fighter Pilot de la Royal Air Force Britannique."

ORDER OF THE CROWN OF BELGIUM. — 6 May 1949.
CHEVALIER DE LA LEGION D'HONNEUR, 31 December 1982
FELLOW OF THE ROYAL GEOGRAPHICAL SOCIETY (FRGS) — 2 June 1947
FELLOW OF THE ROYAL SOCIETY OF ARTS (FRSA) — 9 January 1956

Citations to various members of No.609 Squadron AAF, in 1941

Squadron Leader M L Robinson DFC RAF (37300)
DISTINGUISHED SERVICE ORDER — *London Gazette* 5 August 1941

"This officer has commanded the Squadron since October 1940. He has acted as leader in recent offensive operations over occupied territory and on numerous occasions, has led his Wing with determination, skill and courage. The success obtained reflects the greatest credit on the leadership and devotion to duty of this officer. He has destroyed at least 14 enemy aircraft and damaged others."

Flight Lieutenant J D Bisdee RAFVR (76575)
DISTINGUISHED FLYING CROSS — *London Gazette* 11 July 1941

"This officer has led his Flight and section with great skill and determination. He has participated in a large number of operational flights against the enemy and has destroyed at least six of their aircraft besides damaging many others. He has set a fine example."

Flying Officer A K Ogilvie (42872)
DISTINGUISHED FLYING CROSS — *London Gazette* 11 July 1941

"This officer has displayed great keenness and determination in his efforts to seek and destroy the enemy. He has shot down at least five hostile aircraft."

Sergeant J A Hughes-Rees RAFVR (745790)
DISTINGUISHED FLYING MEDAL — *London Gazette* 8 August 1941

"This airman has completed a large number of operational sorties against the enemy and has destroyed at least four of their aircraft. In every engagement he has shown courage and enterprise."

Sergeant A G Palmer RAFVR (741982)
DISTINGUISHED FLYING MEDAL — *London Gazette* 8 August 1941

"This airman has taken part in 88 operational sorties. He has at all times shown tenacity and great devotion to duty and has destroyed one of the enemy's aircraft."

Sergeant T C Rigler (904492)
DISTINGUISHED FLYING MEDAL — *London Gazette* 16 September 1941

"This airman has carried out 82 sorties since March 1941. He has displayed out-standing keenness to destroy the enemy in combat and to harrass him on the ground. Sergeant Rigler has destroyed at least seven hostile aircraft (three were destroyed in one sweep) and has damaged a further two."

APPENDIX B

OPS FLOWN BY PAUL RICHLEY IN 1941-42

Paul Richey's Operations 1941

11 April	Escort to 75 Wing Blenheim to Dunkirk
	Diverted to intercept Dornier 17, ran out of petrol and made 'dead-stick' landing at base
15 April	Sweep, Hardelot-Gravelines
20 April	Patrol
29 April	Roadstead between Gravelines-Dunkirk
4 May	Patrol Dungeness and Channel. Saw some 109s, did not engage
6 May	Sweep off French coast
7 May	Convoy Patrol. Engagement with 109s, no result
8 May	Air Sea Rescue patrol. Squadron engaged 109s
10 May	Patrol Dungeness
11 May	Patrol Dungeness
16 May	Wing Sweep, Channel
„	Patrol Dover. Engaged with 109s
21 May	Circus No 10 to Bethune. 109s engaged
4 June	Roadstead off Boulogne
„	Air Sea Rescue search off Dover. 109s sighted
9 June	Convoy Patrol
11 June	Roadstead off Dunkirk
17 June	Circus No 17 to Bethune. 109s sighted
18 June	Rear Support Sweep, Gravelines-North Foreland
23 June	Circus No 19 to Bethune. Spitfire W3240 hit in header tank off Le Touquet by Me109
„	Circus No 20 to Mardyck. Target Support
24 June	Circus No 21 to Comines. 109s engaged
25 June	Circus No 22 to Hazebrouck. High Cover
„	Circus No 23 to St Omer/Longuenesse. Target Support
26 June	Circus No 24 to Comines. Target Support
27 June	Roadstead off Calais

,,	Circus No 25 to Fives/Lille. Escort Cover. Landed at Manston
	Spitfire W3240 1 ME109F DAMAGED
28 June	Circus No 26 to Comines. Dog-fight with Me109
29 June	Wing Sweep
30 June	Circus No 27 to Pont-a-Vendin, Lens 1 ME109E DESTROYED
	Spitfire W3240. Target Support ½ ME109E PROBABLE
1 July	Wing Sweep, Gravelines-Etapes
2 July	Circus No 29 to Lille. Escort Cover
,,	Roadstead off Le Touquet
3 July	Circus No 30 to Hazebrouck. Target Support
,,	Circus No 31 to Hazebrouck. Target Support
4 July	Circus No 32 to Bethune. Close Escort 2 ME109Fs DAMAGED
	Spitfire W3240. Landed at Manston
5 July	Circus No 33 to Lille. Target Support. Landed at Manston
6 July	Roadstead to Gravelines
,,	Circus No 35 to Lille. Close Escort. Landed at Hawkinge
7 July	Circus No 37 to Albert. Escort Cover
,,	Circus No 38 to Bethune. Out of petrol mid-Channel, crash-landed at Hawkinge in Spitfire W3313
8 July	Circus No 39 to Lens. Escort Cover. Landed at Hawkinge with broken piston ring and little oil. Spitfire W3240
,,	Circus No 40. Withdrawal Support
9 July	Circus No 41 to Mazingarbe. Extra High Cover
10 July	Circus No 42 to Chocques. Target Support. 1 ME109F DAMAGED
	Landed at Detling. Spitfire W3240
11 July	Circus No 44.
	Diversionary Sweep to Cassel area. 1 ME109F PROBABLE
	Spitfire W3240 2 ME109Fs DAMAGED
12 July	Circus No 47. Diversionary Sweep
20 July	Circus No 52 to Hazebrouck
,,	Scramble over Horsham
,,	Sweep to Le Touquet
21 July	Circus No 54 to Lille. Escort Cover
,,	Circus No 55 to Mazingarbe. Target Support
23 July	Circus No 60 to Mazingarbe. Escort Cover. 1 ME109E DESTROYED
	Spitfire W3187
24 July	Roadstead off Fecamp. Engaged with Me109
4 August	Weather and Shipping Recce
5 August	Wing Sweep
6 August	Wing Sweep
,,	ASR Lysander Escort. Landed at Manston
7 August	Circus No 67 to St Omer. Escort Cover. Spitfire W3240. Crash-landed at Manston after combat with Me109
12 August	Circus No 70 to Gosnay. Escort Cover. Attacked by 109s
,,	Circus No 71 to Le Trait

Operations flown as CO of 609 Squadron, 1942

30 July	Circus 200. Gravelines-Gris Nez; FW 109s seen. Typhoon R7752
4 August	Rodeo

5 August	Roadstead
19 August	Dieppe operation — returned with engine trouble
„	Dieppe operation — patrol
„	Dieppe operation — patrol
20 August	Circus 206. Furnes-Gris Nez
23 August	Patrol
27 August	Patrol — anti-FW190
„	Circus 209 to Abbeville. FW190s seen but not engaged
2 September	Rodeo to Le Touquet
3 September	Rodeo, support to Whirlwinds attacking Lille
6 September	Circus 215 — rear support to Abbeville. FW190s seen
16 September	Roadstead. Cover Bostons returning from Holland
23 September	Patrol — anti-FW190
26 September	Interception patrol after a Ju88 — ret'd with door problem
30 September	Patrol — anti-FW190
1 October	Patrol — anti-FW190
„	Patrol — anti-FW190
2 October	Circus 221. Rear support for Bostons to Le Harve
11 October	Rodeo. Two FW190s seen
12 October	Patrol — anti-FW190

APPENDIX C

COMBAT SUCCESSES OF PAUL RICHEY AND M L ROBINSON

Paul Richey's Combat Successes in WWII

Date	E/A	Remarks	Place	Aircraft	
1940					
29 March	Messerschmitt 109E	Destroyed	Saarburg	Hurricane	N2382
10 May	Dornier 17z	Destroyed[1]	Longwy	„	L1679
11 May	Dornier 17z	Probable	Mezieres	„	L1679
„	Messerschmitt 110	Destroyed	Brunehamel	„	L1685
„	Messerschmitt 110	„	„	„	„
15 May	Messerschmitt 110	Destroyed	Vouziers	„	?
„	Messerschmitt 110	Destroyed	„	„	?
19 May	Heinkel 111	Destroyed	Chateau-Thierry	„	P2805
„	Heinkel 111	Destroyed	„	„	„
„	Heinkel 111	Destroyed	„	„	„
1941					
27 June	Messerschmitt 109F	Damaged		Spitfire	W3240
30 June	Messerschmitt 109E	Destroyed	St Omer	„	„
„	Messerschmitt 109E	Probable[2]	Nieppe	„	„
4 July	Messerschmitt 109F	Damaged	Dunkirk	„	„
„	Messerschmitt 109F	Damaged	„	„	„
10 July	Messerschmitt 109F	Damaged	St Omer	„	„
11 July	Messerschmitt 109F	Probable	Cassel	„	„
„	Messerschmitt 109F	Damaged	Dunkirk	„	„
„	Messerschmitt 109F	Damaged	„	„	„
23 July	Messerschmitt 109E	Destroyed	St Omer	„	W3187

[1] Shared with F/Lt P R Walker and FO M H Brown
[2] Shared with PO R Malengreau
Total 10⅓ destroyed, 2½ probables, 6 damaged

Combat Successes of WC M L Robinson DSO DFC in WWII

Date	Destroyed	Probable	Damaged	Unit	Aircraft	Op
1940						
31 Aug	Me109E	Me109E	Me109E	601 Sqdn	UF−S	Patrol
4 Sep		Me110		„ „		„
6 Sep	Me109E			„ „		„
25 Sep		Me110		„ „	UF−S	„
30 Sep	Me109E			238 Sqdn	R4099 'S'	„
„	Me110			„ „	„	„
„	Me110			„ „	„	„
7 Oct	Me110			609 Sqdn	L1096	„
„	Me110			„ „	„	„
1941						
7 May			Me109E	„ „	P7881	Escort
8 May	Me109E			„ „	„	ASR
„	Me109E			„ „	„	„
4 Jun			Me109F	„ „	P7881	ASR
30 Jun			Me109E	„ „	W3238	C27
3 Jul	Me109F		Me109F	„ „	„	C30
„	Me109F			„ „	„	C31
4 Jul			Me109F	„ „	„	C32
8 Jul			Me109F	„ „	„	C39
10 Jul	Me109F			„ „	„	C42
11 Jul	Me109F			„ „	„	C44
12 Jul	Me109F			„ „	„	C47
14 Jul	Me109F			„ „	W3240	C48
19 Jul			Me109F	„ „	W3184	C51
24 Jul	Me109F		Me109F	„ „	W3187	C61
7 Aug		Me109F		B/Hill Wg	ML−R	C67
24 Aug	Me109F			„ „	W3413	C
27 Aug	Me109F			„ „	ML−R	C85

Total: 18 destroyed, four probables and nine damaged

APPENDIX D

609 SQUADRON'S CLAIMS AND LOSSES, APRIL–AUGUST 1941

Date	Pilot	Destroyed	Probable	Damaged
7 May	SL M L Robinson			Me109
8 May	SL M L Robinson	2 Me109s		
,,	FL J Curchin	Me109		
,,	FL J Curchin	Me109		
	Sgt J A Hughes-Rees			
,,	Sgt T C Rigler	2 Me109s		
,,	Sgt A G Palmer		Me109	
,,	Sgt R T D Mercer		Me109	
9 May	PO S J Hill			Me109
16 May	PO A K Ogilvie	Me109		
,,	PO S J Hill	Me109		
,,	PO V Ortmans			Me109
21 May	Sgt J A Hughes-Rees			Me109
,,	FO FL J D Bisdee	Me109		
	PO V Ortmans			
3 Jun	PO Y G Du Monceau			Me109
4 Jun	SL M L Robinson			Me109
	Sgt T C Rigler			
,,	Sgt T C Rigler	Me109		
,,	PO V Ortmans	Me109		
11 Jun	FL J D Bisdee			Me109
17 Jun	FL J D Bisdee	Me109		
,,	FO A K Ogilvie	Me109		
,,	PO F X E de Spirlet	Me109		
18 Jun	PO S J Hill		Me109	
21 Jun	FO A K Ogilvie	Me109		
,,	Sgt R Boyd	Me109		
,,	PO V Ortmans			Me109

Date	Name			
22 Jun	FL J D Bisdee	Me109		
,,	Sgt T C Rigler	3 Me109s		
,,	PO J Offenberg			Me109
24 Jun	FL J D Bisdee		Me109	
,,	Sgt T C Rigler		Me109	Me109
,,	Sgt R Boyd		Me109	
27 Jun	FL P H M Richey			Me109
30 Jun	FL P H M Richey	Me109		
,,	PO V Ortmans	Me109		
,,	Sgt J A Hughes-Rees	Me109		
,,	FL P H M Richey / PO R F G Malengreau		Me109	
,,	SL M L Robinson			Me109
3 Jul	SL M L Robinson	2 Me109s		
,,	PO Y G Du Monceau			Me109
4 Jul	FL P H M Richey			2 Me109s
,,	SL M L Robinson			Me109
7 Jun	PO J Offenberg	Me109		
8 Jul	Sgt J A Hughes-Rees	Me109	Me109	
,,	SL M L Robinson			Me109
9 Jul	FL J D Bisdee	Me109		
10 Jul	SL M L Robinson	Me109		
,,	FL P H M Richey			Me109
11 Jul	SL M L Robinson	Me109		
,,	GC P R Barwell	Me109		
,,	PO E G A Seghers	Me109		
,,	Sgt R Boyd	Me109		Me109
,,	FL P H M Richey		Me109	2 Me109s
,,	PO Y G Du Monceau		Me109	
,,	Sgt K W Bramble			Me109
12 Jul	SL M L Robinson	Me109		
14 Jul	SL M L Robinson	Me109		
,,	FO R F G Malengreau		Me109	
19 Jul	SL M L Robinson			Me109
21 Jul	Sgt J E Van Shaick			2 Me109s
23 Jul	FL P H M Richey	Me109		
,,	Sgt A G Palmer			Me109
24 Jul	Sgt T C Rigler	Me109		
,,	SL M L Robinson		Me109	Me109
7 Aug	PO M Choron		Me109	
,,	Sgt T C Rigler			Me109
,,	Sgt P Nash			Me109
9 Aug	PO M Choron		Me109	
16 Aug	FO B de Hemptinne	Me109		
,,	Sgt P Nash			Me109
18 Aug	PO Y G Du Monceau	Me109		
,,	PO V Ortmans	Me109		
19 Aug	FO B de Hemptinne			Me109
,,	PO V Ortmans			Me109

19 Aug	Sgt E W Pollard			Me109
,,	PO Y G Du Monceau			Me109
21 Aug	Sgt J E Van Shaick		Me109	
27 Aug	PO M Choron	Me109		
29 Aug	PO F X E de Spirlet	Me109		
,,	PO V Ortmans			Me109
,,	Sgt A G Palmer			

Losses

Date	Pilot	A/C	Location	Remarks
29 Apr	F/Sgt G C Bennett	P7669	Channel	KIA
9 May	Sgt R T D Mercer	P7305	St Margaret's Bay	KIA
21 May	PO R C C de Grunne	P7521	Channel	KIA
4 Jun	FL J Curchin DFC	P8204	Channel	KIA
11 Jun	Sgt G A Chestnut	P8654	Ramsgate	KIA
18 Jun	PO S J Hill	W3211	W of Dover	KIA
22 Jun	PO F X E de Spirlet		Off Calais, baled out	Rescued
4 Jul	FO A K Ogilvie DFC	W3207	France	POW
6 Jul	PO R Malengreau	W3179	Deal, force landing	Safe
7 Jul	Sgt G Evans	W3115	Channel, baled out	Injured
,,	FL P H M Richey DFC	W3313	Manston, force landing	Safe
8 Jul	Sgt J A Hughes-Rees	W3239	S Goodwins, ditched	Rescued
21 Jul	Sgt K W Bramble	W3307	Channel	KIA
,,	Sgt J E Van Shaick	W3372	Channel, shot up	Safe
31 Jul	Sgt R Boyd	W3187	Channel, damaged	Safe
7 Aug	Sgt R Boyd	W3187	Channel, baled out	Safe
,,	FL P H M Richey DFC	W3240	Manston, force landing	Safe
9 Aug	PO A Nitelet	W3240	Campagne	Evaded
16 Aug	PO D L Cropper	W8745	Cap Gris Nez	KIA
19 Aug	PO V Ortmans	W3241	Channel, baled out	Rescued
21 Aug	Sgt E W Pollard	W3651	Gravelines	KIA

APPENDIX E

TRANSCRIPT OF RADIO BROADCAST
BY PAUL RICHEY, INDIA, 1944

Script of a Radio Broadcast written by Paul Richey and made by him during his time in India. Of necessity it is a trifle nationalistic, in an effort to keep morale high among the RAF and Indian squadrons in the Arakan and Central Burma front, but one feels certain that Paul put it over with his usual authority helping to achieve the overall aim — winning a victory at last over the Japanese in Burma.

"Well, I've just come back from the eastern front where I commanded a fighter wing. Conditions there are difficult to picture unless you've actually been there. The aerodrome from which we were operating was nothing like a normal aerodrome. It consisted of a number of strips cut out of the jungle and paddy which were dispersed over a wide area. The squadrons lived under palm clumps in carefully concealed camps constructed of bamboos.

"The country's very attractive — one might almost say romantic. It's mainly paddy fields interspersed with areas of solid jungle, and small hills, some of which are topped with Buddist temples and pagodas. Not far away to the west is the blue tropical sea that one reads about; and to the east a series of razor-backed hills that stretch away into the heart of Burma. These hills aren't very nice to fly over because a forced landing there would inevitably mean a more or less serious crash and would certainly involve, under the very best circumstances, a long and arduous trek home which might last many weeks.

"All the same, quite a number of pilots have walked back and they haven't found the jungle as frightening as they'd supposed. Many of the tales about snakes and wild animals have been grossly exaggerated. In fact, all the time I've been on the eastern front, living an open air life in the jungle, I've seen less snakes than in London Zoo. One does come across wild animals from time to time — tiger, elephant and panther — but as a rule they're far more frightened of you than you are of them. The main difficulty in the jungle is to keep your lines of direction and keep yourself supplied with food, but the common sense of the average pilot is well up to any problem that the jungle can set him.

"The other big problem that faces the pilot on this eastern front is the weather. During the monsoon period this can be extremely bad. Most people picture the monsoon as a solid sheet of water during which no flying can possibly take place. This is not by any means the case. There are periods of extremely heavy rain, but these are broken by fair spells. Most of the rain comes from enormous masses of cumulus cloud with their base at 200 feet and rising to well over 40,000 feet. This may sound extraordinary even to weather experts, but reports brought home by pilots leave no doubt that these clouds do go up to well over seven miles in one solid mass and often stretching over a front of one hundred miles. Flying in these clouds is inclined to be unpleasant because of the violent air currents. And sometimes it can be very dangerous too.

"During the past monsoon the Royal Air Force out on this eastern front demonstrated its ability to continue effective operations by flying throughout the whole period, and we were thus able to harry the enemy all the time. The Japanese on the other hand withdrew practically the whole of their air force in Burma during the monsoon and so this harrying process was carried out almost unopposed which was very convenient for us.

"This withdrawal of the Japanese air force, though they may have had reasons that made it necessary, appears to be merely a demonstration of peculiar Japanese mentality. In 1942, when the Japanese air force was unopposed it built up a reputation of excellence that we since found to be based on exaggerated reports largely from uninformed civilian sources. Now any air force in the world can demonstrate its excellence if it's unopposed, and the forces that we were able to spare to oppose them in 1942 were very meagre. But since those days victories elsewhere have enabled us to strengthen the all-important air arm out here and the Japanese have had one or two rude shocks.

"Before we actually challenged the Japanese air arm we knew we were superior in training and tactics, but there were stories about the Japanese Navy Zero and Army 01 fighters that made us wonder whether they didn't have superior equipment to our own.

"Now aircraft design is all a matter of compromise, and you can only bring out one quality at the expense of another. For instance, if you want more power you've got to have a heavier engine and you make your aeroplane heavier — thus possibly reducing your manoeuvrability and rate of climb.

"I think the average fighter pilot would ask for the following qualities in designing a fighter: speed, manoeuvrability and rate of climb. If he's superior to his adversary in all these respects he should win his fight, but the trouble is (as I've said) that you can't have everything.

"Now the Japanese fighters possess a very high degree of manoeuvrability. They're undoubtedly beautiful aircraft to fly. However, they've achieved this manoeuvrability at the expense of other qualities. One of them is speed, another is strength and the third is armament. They're very lightly constructed. The engine is comparatively small and they carry no armour plating for protection. That's why when you hit a Japanese fighter you almost invariably get him.

"Our own Spitfires on the other hand, although they may not be as manoeuvrable as the Japanese Zero, are superior in speed, rate of climb, strength and fire power, and our better training and tactics enables us to assert our all round superiority against the Japanese pilots.

"The most recent examples of our superiority happened a few weeks ago when

I was in the Arakan. A squadron of our fighters intercepted a large formation of Japanese bombers escorted by 01 fighters. In the ensuing fight they shot down in flames about half as many again as their own number, and damaged several more that possibly never got back to their base — and all for no loss to ourselves. The Spitfires repeated this performance on two succeeding days on much the same lines with the result that the Japanese didn't again attempt to do what they were trying to do: bomb supply lines of the Army just before its present offensive in the Arakan.

"Talking of the Army, Indian Air Force squadrons have rendered them invaluable service in very skilful low-level reconnaissance, and strafing in close support.

"It isn't for me to assess the effect of the part played by the air on the subsequent army battle that is still making successful progress. But it's a generally recognised fact that air superiority is indispensable to successful land or sea operations. It's four years now since Hitler, being fully aware of this fact, sent his air armadas against Britain. That great Royal Air Force victory was the turning point of the war. Since then the United Nations' unbroken air strength has grown to undreamt of proportions, and Germany is now staggering under fantastic blows from the air which are the prelude to her invasion, defeat and elimination from the war.

"When that's been accomplished Japan has been promised that the full weight of this enormous air power will be swung out to the east. Already the air forces out here in India are pressing her and building up experience that will be used later on. But until the hour of victory comes and the bogus Japanese Empire has been crushed into the dust, British, American and Indian pilots, fighting side by side, will continue to attack, harry and destroy the Japanese."

There is no date of this Broadcast but from his words, it was obviously written in early 1944. The second Arakan campaign was underway, which was victorious, made so in no small measure by the introduction of the Spitfire, made possible, in part, by Paul's insistence that they should be made available in India/Burma. Once the Spitfire began to arrive in a handful of RAF front-line squadrons in SEAC, they immediately had the effect of blinding the enemy by being able for the first time to intercept and destroy their high-flying reconnaissance aeroplanes. They then wrested complete air superiority over the Japanese air force, which assisted the British and Indian forces on the ground, by air support and supply.

The Spitfire successes mentioned by Paul in his narrative, occured in December 1943 and January 1944. 615 Squadron gained a victory over a raid on Chittagong on 26 December, while 136 Squadron gained a resounding victory over a large raiding force off the Arakan coast on the 31st. Then on 15 January 1944, 136 and 607 Squadrons claimed no fewer than 16 Japanese fighters destroyed with 23 more probably destroyed or damaged for the loss of one Spitfire, one pilot and two other Spitfires damaged in crash landings.

It was the beginning of the end for the Japanese in the Arakan, and following the successful defence of Imphal and Kohima in March to June 1944, the Japanese began to crumble in Central Burma too. There were other factors too, of course, but a major contribution was, as before, the arrival of the Spitfire to the Burma front.

APPENDIX F

ADOLF GLUNZ ON RAF TACTICS

I put the same questions I'd put to Adolf Galland to another successful German fighter pilot, Adolf Gluntz. His reply came too late to be included in Chapter Eight so his comments are added here.

'Addi' Gluntz had joined the 4th Staffel of II/JG52 in November 1940 and his first operational sorties were flown over England that winter and the following spring. He claimed his first two victories over Kent in May 1941 but then had gone off to Russia in June where he brought his score to five. But he was soon to return to the Western Front as he told me:

> "Nearly all the squadrons were transferred to the East shortly before the start of the war against Russia. Only JG2 and JG26 remained at the Channel Coast. As a consequence, the numerical superiority of the British fighter planes was so great that the air battles took place less often over southern England and more and more over Northern France, Holland and Belgium.
>
> "Our numerical inferiority initially led to a major increase in our losses and made it necessary to strengthen the Western squadrons. As a result, there was a search for people with experience in the West to be transferred back from Russia to the Channel. Because of this, I was transferred from JG52 to JG26, and I remained there until the end of the war.
>
> "Naturally we preferred it when we could engage the RAF on our side of the Channel. An inevitable consequence of a forced landing or parachute jump over England was imprisonment. We also had many total losses when attempting to return across the Channel in damaged aircraft.
>
> "I myself once received a hit in the radiator of my Me109 in an air-fight over Dover. By frequently turning the ignition on and off, thus using very little fuel, I managed to delay the complete overheating of my engine and reached St Omer in a long gliding flight. Luckily my altitude over Dover was about 8,000 metres (12,000 ft), and I was not attacked by any Spitfires, otherwise I would certainly not have made it back over the Channel.
>
> "We didn't have any major attacks by bombers until about the beginning of 1942. The Abwehr were prepared for fighter planes, especially Spitfires. The massed bomber attacks started about the middle of 1942. Until then there were only combats involving fighter planes which took place not over one area but over the entire Channel.
>
> "The necessity of dealing primarily with bombers only arose with the arrival of the large fleets of US bombers. At the same time there was a return to pure fights with fighters forming a protective escort, which made it difficult for us to reach the bombers. The escorting fighter planes therefore posed a severe threat to us, especially since they were considerably superior numerically to us."

Addi Glunz ended the war with over 70 victories and had received the Knight's Cross with Oak Leaves, and the German Cross in Gold. The fact that he claimed 35 RAF Spitfires and 21 American four-engined bombers amongst his kills, gives him a unique position amongst the fighter pilots in the West.

INDEX